THE POEMS *of* JOHN HENRY NEWMAN

afterwards CARDINAL

LONDON
JOHN LANE
The Bodley Head
NEW YORK
JOHN LANE COMPANY

JOHN HENRY
NEWMAN

IN HOMAGE

TO THE COMPOSER WHO

HAS WEDDED NEWMAN'S NOBLEST POEM

TO EQUALLY NOBLE MUSIC

THIS EDITION OF NEWMAN'S POEMS

IS DEDICATED TO

SIR EDWARD ELGAR

INTRODUCTION

"I AM not a poet," wrote Newman in 1879. The passage occurs in his reply to a letter asking him to explain exactly what he meant in his poem " Lead, kindly Light " by the expression "angel faces," and, in full, it runs, " I think it was Keble who when asked [a similar question] answered that poets were not bound to be critics, or to give a sense to what they had written ; and although I am not like him, a poet, at least I may plead that I am not bound to *remember* my own meaning, whatever it was, at the end of almost fifty years." What exactly Newman meant by his disclaimer, it is somewhat difficult to decide. The implication may have been that he had long since abandoned claims which he at one time was inclined to prefer. Or it may have been that he felt his work as a poet had been merged in work of such infinitely greater moment to himself, that his experiments in verse might be relegated to a position so subordinate, in comparison with his work in other directions, as to be properly esteemed merely a recreation. Yet that he was a poet, and a poet of no mean order, few students of nineteenth-century literature would deny. Although his productive period in the strict sense was of short duration, and many of the volumes in which his verse was contained were merely compilations from and rearrangements of earlier writings, he was responsible from 1821 to 1868 for eight separate volumes of verse, and the retouching and repolishing to which he subjected his poems can perhaps only be paralleled in the case of Tennyson.

A guess may be hazarded as to how far Newman deliberately resisted his natural impulse to express himself in verse, for his was not a case of—

"Rafael made a century of sonnets.
* * * *
Dante once prepared to paint an angel."

The popular imagination has in later years come to think almost exclusively of Newman as a prince of the Church. His name instantly evokes a mental picture of a scholarly recluse, whose native dignity can yet support undaunted the purple splendours of the Sacred College, so that to turn afresh to his verses is to experience something of the amazement of a child who suddenly discovers hitherto unsuspected powers in a senior whose abilities he has long supposed incapable of yielding a fresh surprise. But with

INTRODUCTION

Newman verse-writing was never a *tour de force*.

To speculate about the probable achievement of a man great in one walk of life had he pursued another, which at one time seems to have allured him very persistently, is perhaps idle, if fascinating. In Newman's case it is at any rate pardonable, for the evidences he has left us of his poetical equipment are such as would have justified his contemporaries in anticipating his eventual arrival at the highest rank. Poetry has, however, always been an exacting mistress, and the work done by a poet in other directions usually eclipses, or is eclipsed by, his poetry. Of the thousands who know "L'Allegro," "Il Penseroso," and "Lycidas," how many know "Areopagitica"? What proportion of the readers of "Alastor" and "The Sensitive Plant" is acquainted with Shelley, the pamphleteer? Of the innumerable aspirants to culture who hang their walls with photographs of "The Girlhood of Mary Virgin" or "Dante's Dream," how many know even the names of "The House of Life" and "The White Ship"? And is not Mr. Swinburne the critic altogether overlooked in Mr. Swinburne the poet?

The first of Newman's poetical works that has been preserved to us dates from 1818, and consists of a poem in two cantos, entitled "St. Bartholomew's Eve," written at Oxford in collaboration with his friend, J. W. Bowden. This poem in its completed state was published in 1821, and is of the utmost rarity. When in 1868 Newman published his "Verses on Various Occasions," he preserved from it the twenty-two lines beginning "There is in stillness oft a magic power," but except for a small edition issued by his brother, Francis William Newman, through Mr. Gill, of Weston-super-Mare, in 1899, the complete poem has been hitherto inaccessible. Professor Newman's reprint differs in innumerable minute points from the original edition which has been followed here, a copy in the British Museum, formerly the property of the Rev. Dr. Bloxam, having been consulted, in which Newman himself had pencilled in the margins the initials of himself and Bowden against those portions assignable to each contributor. The poem is much of the kind that the average undergraduate produces for the Newdigate, and its interest is mainly confined to its authorship. One can imagine Newman's amusement in after years when he recalled such expressions as the "dark-stoled fathers," or the "crosiered priest," or the description of the monks as "piously false or credulously good." The fragment which he preserved was not allowed to remain unpolished. Many slight modifications were made, not all felicitous. For instance, in the line " No mortal measure swells that silent sound," the word

INTRODUCTION

"silent" was changed to "mystic," as though his feeling had been against the retention of the paradox. Of course his original inspiration was the better, and, curiously enough, it was a thought which we find recurring at intervals in other passages of his verse. One thinks instantly of "Heard melodies are sweet, but those unheard are sweeter." One little point is worthy of note. The general knowledge of America was in those days so slight that Niagára was written for Niagara, just as Heber wrote Céylon for Ceylon. To distinguish the work of the two contributors, Bowden's portions have here been printed in italics.

Eleven years passed before Newman again adventured on the publication of poetry, and then appeared a little volume to which, despite the personal character of the larger part of the contents and the comparative youth of the author, the suggestive title "Memorials of the Past" was given. From one of the poems in this volume, addressed to a sister, the meaning of the title may probably be deduced. In so entitling it the author was definitely putting behind him the temptation to expend, in the making of verse, time which he considered might be more profitably devoted to other employments. The passage runs—

"Ill 'seems it the devoted hand
That has touched the plough, to trifle now
With the toys of verse again."

Already it would seem that the "stern daughter of the voice of God" had arrested the feet from a path that appeared to the young poet to be merely a path of dalliance. Toys should no more distract. So the harp was hung up, and not again tuned until, during the memorable Mediterranean trip, in the company of Hurrell Froude, the idea of the "Lyra Apostolica" was conceived. For the service of his great cause he could sing anew, and the songs themselves are evidence that while he had been musing the fire had kindled.

In the "Apologia" we find the account of the inception in the following words: "It was at Rome that we began the 'Lyra Apostolica.' The motto shows the feeling of both Froude and myself at the time. We borrowed from M. Bunsen a Homer, and Froude chose the words in which Achilles, on returning to the battle, says, 'You shall know the difference now that I am back again.'" Why it was decided that the sword of the Lord should take the form of verse, after Newman's recent summarizing of it as a "toy," is not easily accounted for. Probably it was Hurrell Froude's doing. He does not seem himself to have been gifted with particular facility as a verse-writer, but his must have been a singularly discriminating intellect, and he no doubt discerned that for Newman's hands no keener weapon could be forged. The sections of the "Lyra Apostolica"

INTRODUCTION xiii

began to appear in the *British Magazine*, under the editorship of Hugh James Rose, in June, 1833, and of the grand total Newman provided almost three times as many poems as the next considerable contributor, John Keble. Isaac Williams, Hurrell Froude, and J. W. Bowden wrote barely more than half a dozen each, and Robert Isaac Wilberforce but one. When the poems came to be reprinted Froude was dead, and it was decided, in order that his poems might be designated his beyond possibility of future doubt, to mark the authorship of each poem by a letter of the Greek alphabet. The letter allotted to Newman was Delta, a circumstance which was recalled thirty years later, when, republishing two of his early poems from the 1832 volume in *The Month*, in 1865, he adopted the signature " Daleth." In the poems of Newman, at least, as reprinted in the volume, changes were in places made from the *British Magazine* versions, but the text followed in the present reprint is that of the book and not of the magazine, the only instance in which it has been deemed advisable to depart from the rule of using the earliest printed version.

After the appearance of " Lyra Apostolica " seventeen years passed before Newman again published a volume of poems, and it almost seemed as though he had completely abandoned his muse. A possible explanation of this long silence is to be found in the autobiography of Isaac Williams. He says—

"When Newman published the 'Lyra Apostolica,' he got Samuel Wilberforce—now the Bishop of Oxford—to review it, as one who would do it in a popular manner. Newman was then much annoyed with the reflections of the review on himself, and this was the cause, I consider, of his never writing a verse afterwards. [Williams, though his autobiography was not published until many years later, wrote in 1851.] Indeed, I have heard Miss Keble observe that it appeared to have stopped in Newman what Providence seemed to have designed as a natural vent to ardent and strong feelings; whereas, had it not met with that untimely discouragement, he would probably have continued to write poetry, as he had then begun, to the profit of himself and us all. For, she said, *her* brother would never have written verses were it not for the encouragement he met with in his own family." Wilberforce's strictness amounted to a charge of involved construction, and obscurity of language, a charge which a man of Newman's critical powers would acknowledge as in a measure just, and it is more than doubtful whether the conjectures of Williams and Miss Keble had any foundation beyond the momentary pique to which Newman had given expression when the review first appeared. Far more probable

INTRODUCTION

is it that the weapon, having served its purpose, was again laid aside, not to be unsheathed until need arose; that Newman's aim was to be a serviceable soldier rather than to display his skill as a swordsman.

The translations from the Roman breviary, and from St. Gregory Nazianzen, which appeared respectively in Tract 75 and in "The Church of the Fathers," were of course made about the same time as the "Lyra Apostolica."

In 1853, at Dublin, eight years after his submission to the Holy See, Newman issued his "Verses on Religious Subjects," in the prefatory note to which he says, "The following compositions are selected from a larger number, and have, nearly all of them, already been put into print. They are brought together by the writer in the present form, in the hope that they may be acceptable and useful to his immediate friends, penitents, and people." The volume contains a number of the poems from "Lyra Apostolica," the breviary translations with considerable additions, and, most noteworthy of all, a group of poems which he entitles "Songs," mainly in honour of the Blessed Virgin, and of the founder of the oratorians, St. Philip Neri, these being his principal output in verse subsequent to the transfer of his allegiance to Rome. It is impossible to allow to the majority of these poems anything like the magic of those of his more youthful days, though they have a lightness of touch, and what one might almost call a sparkle, foreign to his verse after the early domestic poems. To display their merits, however, it is only necessary to compare the poems on St. Philip with those on the same subject by F. W. Faber, when it will be at once observed that if they do not move with the stateliness of the older poems, they are at least far removed from the over-sentimentality of the Catholic hymns then most popular, and unburdened by the saccharine vocabulary then too freely indulged in.

The copy of this 1853 volume, which has been employed for the purposes of the present edition, has exceptional interest from its having formerly been the property of John Keble, whose autograph it contains.

In 1860 a small volume, entitled "Verses for Penitents," was privately printed. It has proved impossible to obtain a sight of this opusculum, but, according to Mr. W. S. Lilly, it contained nothing which did not reappear in "Verses on Various Occasions."

In 1866 Newman's last and greatest poem appeared. In "The Dream of Gerontius" it would seem as though there had been gathered up all the forces that had for so many years been restrained, and the poet, when he is already approaching rapidly his three score and ten years, shows us, in a sudden blaze of almost intolerable light, the high and awful thoughts that devout meditation and self-suppression have stored up in a mind compounded of reverence and imagination, for which poetic expression was the only natural outlet. The copyright of "The Dream of Gerontius" being still unexpired, it is not possible to include it in the present edition, although, apart from that poem, the present is a more complete edition of Newman's verse than any hitherto published, including, as it does, over thirty poems not contained elsewhere. Amongst these are the three long Eclogues, experiments in a form little exploited in England, and not again employed by any writer of distinction until during the last few years Mr. Davidson produced his "Fleet St. Eclogues."

In 1868 Newman published his "Verses on Various Occasions," for which on December 21, 1867, he wrote a dedicatory letter to his friend, Edward Badeley. In this letter he states that it would never have occurred to him to bring together effusions which he has ever considered ephemeral had he not found from publications of the day, what he never suspected before, that there were critics, strangers to him, who think well both of some of his compositions and of his power of composing. He goes on to say that, being in despair of discovering any standard by which to discriminate between one poetical attempt and another, he is thrown upon his own judgment, which is disposed either to preserve all or to put all aside. Yet in the end his 1868 volume was a selection merely, and so anxiously did its author watch its reception that within a brief space after its appearance a privately printed addendum appeared, of twenty pages, which later on was incorporated in the published volume. Slight modifications and additions occurred in succeeding editions up to the last issued in the lifetime of the author.

It is worthy of notice here that although the 1832 volume had its dedication signed with initials, like that of 1868, and none of the intervening volumes was, in the generally accepted sense, anonymous, not one of them bore Newman's name upon its title-page.

No attempt at serious criticism of Newman's poems is here made. It has been thought that a cheap reprint of them would place them in the hands of many to whom they are unknown, and, in the course of compilation, so little presented itself that seemed inappropriate to the series for which the volume was designed that it was decided to make it as complete as possible, and, by the chronological arrangement, representative also of Newman's poetic development. All changes indicating developments of opinion have been regarded as unimportant on the

INTRODUCTION

strength of a note of the poet's own, in which he expresses his determination finally, after some vacillation, not to attempt to reconcile opinions which he no longer held with opinions adopted later, by the modification, from a doctrinal standpoint, of poems already given to the public. As remarked on the half-title of the poems from "Callista," the song of Juba is here printed as indicative of a possible development of Newman's muse in a secular direction had he permitted it free play.

The poem on page 257, from Tract 75, is included, despite the fact that Newman never himself acknowledged it, for this reason. The whole of the poems in the tract, with two exceptions, are translations of ancient office hymns, the one in question being a translation of *Invicte Martyr unicum*. The two exceptions are two excerpts from poems in "The Christian Year." But as Newman acknowledged the authorship of all the other translations, and this particular poem was followed by one for the same feast, which he afterwards reprinted, it was concluded that he merely rejected it through some personal fastidiousness. It is a much finer poem than Caswall's translation of the same Latin original, in "Lyra Catholica."

The portrait which forms the frontispiece is reproduced by kind permission of H. E. Wilberforce, Esq., from the original drawing made by George Richmond, R.A., in 1844. In

INTRODUCTION

nearly all previous reproductions the details of the costume, which was what Newman wore as an Anglican, have been modified by the engraver. So far as is known the only reproduction of the portrait as Richmond drew it, previous to the one here presented, appeared in Miss Anne Mozley's "Letters and Correspondence of Cardinal Newman."

FREDERIC CHAPMAN.

ST. BARTHOLOMEW'S EVE
[1821]

JOHN HENRY NEWMAN

AND

JOHN WILLIAM BOWDEN

St. Bartholomew's Eve ; / A Tale / of / the Sixteenth Century. / In Two Cantos. /

Oxford : / Printed and Published by Munday and Slatter, Herald Office, / High-Street : sold by G. and W. B. Whittaker, / Ave-Maria-Lane, London. / 1821. /

The two cantos appear to have been issued separately ; and Professor F. W. Newman assigned the first canto to 1818, and the second to 1820. Probably in 1821 what stock remained of the separate issues was published with a new title-page, worded as above.

In the copy from which this reprint is made Newman has initialled in the margins the portions contributed by himself and Bowden respectively. For the sake of clearness, Bowden's parts are here printed in italics.

ST. BARTHOLOMEW'S EVE

CANTO I

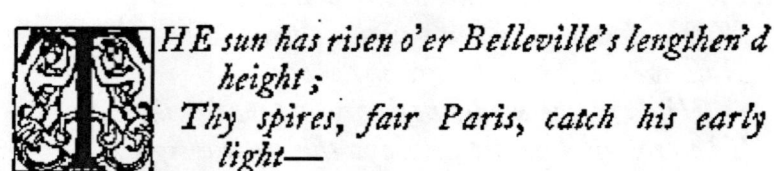

THE sun has risen o'er Belleville's lengthen'd
    height;
    Thy spires, fair Paris, catch his early
    light—
Mid Seine's blue waves his beams reflected play,
And Earth reviving greets the new-born day.—

  Fast by the northern shore of that fair stream,
Deck'd with new glories by the orient beam,
Their height reliev'd against the brightening skies,
The princely Louvre's palace piles arise;
Seat of the royal Charles,* whose powerful sway
Extended Gallia's vine-clad hills obey,
From Britain's seas and Belgium's fruitful plain,
To Rhone's broad current, and the inland main.
  Lo! where the river parts his silver tides
And round yon isle in circling eddies glides,
In solemn grandeur soaring from the plain,
Stand the vast turrets of the Virgin's fane;
Majestic work, which ages toil'd to raise,
The matchless monument of elder days.

---

    * Charles the Ninth.

—Hark! the slow summons from its echoing tower
With sullen peal proclaims the matin hour;
Now through each massive aisle and long arcade
The dark-stol'd fathers move in dull parade;
Count the slow bead; or kiss the sacred wood,
Piously false, or credulously good.
Its sacred notes the full-ton'd organ pours,
Till the rapt soul on bolder pinions soars;—
Soft strains ascending from the swelling choir
Float on the gale, and breathe seraphic fire;
While clouds of incense curling toward the sky
Roll over head, a fragrant canopy.
—High in the midst before yon taper'd shrine
The crosier'd priest displays the mystic sign;
With reverent awe adoring myriads see,
Bow the meek head, and drop the humbled knee.
 Amid that group, with heart full fraught with woe,
Where some for worship bow'd and some for show,
Fair Florence knelt; Oh! little might he guess
Who view'd that sylph-like form of loveliness,
Who mark'd that blue eye fix'd as tho' in prayer,
That thought of earth had dimm'd the lustre there!
For such she was, as fancy loves to paint
Some cloister'd vot'ress, or sequester'd saint,
Gazing on night's pale queen, with raptur'd eye,
And thoughts that mount toward their native sky.
No purer form th' enamour'd artist chose
When Grecian Venus from his chisel rose;
No purer form, in angel robes of light,
Seems to descend to suff'ring martyr's sight,

JOHN HENRY NEWMAN

*With Heav'n's own joys, to chase his pains away
And greet his entrance to the realms of day.*

*Now all is hush'd—no more the organ's sound
Thro' the arch'd nave re-echoing rolls around.
The crowds disperse—but still that fair one knelt,
As tho' she still on things celestial dwelt.
Alike unheeded by her vacant eye
The incense fail'd; the pageant flitted by;
Still as some form of monumental stone,
She saw not, mark'd not, there she knelt alone.
Then as awaken'd from a wildering dream
She seem'd to muse o'er some uncertain theme,
Gaz'd for a moment round, while short surprise
With beauteous wildness lit her azure eyes;
Then slowly sought her ag'd instructor's cell,
The secret sorrows of her heart to tell.*

'Mid the recesses of that pillar'd wall
Stood reverent Clement's dark confessional.
Here Rapine's son with superstition pale
Oft thro' the grated lattice told his tale;
Here blood-stain'd Murder faulter'd, tho' secure
Of absolution from a faith impure.—

Mistaken worship! can the outward tear
Make clean the breast devoid of godly fear?
Shall pomp and splendour holy love supply,
The grateful heart, the meek submissive eye?
Mistaken worship! where the priestly plan
In servile bondage rules degraded man,

Proclaims on high in proud, imperious tone
Devotion springs from ignorance alone ;
And dares prefer to sorrow for the past
The scourge of penance or the groans of fast !
—Where every crime a price appointed brings
To sooth the churchman's pride, the sinner's stings,
Where righteous grief and penitence are made
An holy market and a pious trade !

The Father view'd Count Albert's child advance,
And scann'd her mien with scrutinizing glance;
" Daughter," he said—and as he spoke he tried
T' unbend the stiffness of his cloister'd pride—
" Daughter, all hail ! The grief those sighs disclose,
" Say, from what cause unknown its torrent flows;
" Whate'er it be, declare at once thy grief,
" When thine to ask, 'tis mine to grant relief."—

The maid was speechless—for his tone represt
The dawning hope that warm'd her fluttering breast ;
In seeming mockery of her birth and name
The coldness of his condescension came.
There was a time, she thought, no voice austere
Fell chill and comfortless on Florence' ear ;
When kind prevention spar'd the suppliant's part,
And bound with kind surprise the grateful heart.
—Slowly she sunk and, prostrate at his feet,
Seem'd his compassion breathless to entreat :

" Sure to a heart like thine," the Sire rejoined,
" Corroding guilt can never entrance find—
" Sin stains the cheek with red—some latent woe
" That paler hue and wilder aspect show.
" And who so well can claim a right to share
" Joy in thy joy and sorrow in thy care?
" But speak, my child "—The maid with frantic eye
Gaz'd on his furrow'd face imploringly—
Tears chok'd her voice—she clung with wild affright,
And feebly breath'd the words—" To-night, to-night!"

The Monk was vers'd his feelings to controul
And hide the subtle workings of his soul;
But when those words with fever'd accents came,
Dark deadly fury fill'd his eye with flame;
His pale and quivering lips refus'd to speak,
And ebbing life-blood left his wither'd cheek.
At length with vain endeavour to conceal
The consciousness he seem'd asham'd to feel—
" To-night? What mean thy words?"

" Oh! Father, well,
" Too well, thou know'st the secret I would tell;
" But yesternight a strange and fearful chance
" Disclos'd the woes that wait on fated France—
" Told how to-night the good, the great, the brave
" Are doomed by royal mandate to the grave;

"How streams of blood thro' Paris' streets must
    flow,
"And civil discord wave her torch of woe.—
"Priests should have softer breasts—how many a
    sire
"Must see his offspring, pierc'd with wounds, expire!
"How many a wife in solitude must mourn
"And hope in vain a husband's glad return!
"How many an orphan miss a father's care,
"In life's first entrance sentenc'd to despair!"

"To aid the virtuous and sustain the weak,
"Is what high Heaven inspires our souls to seek;"—
Replied the priest—"The laws of God demand
"The pitying heart, the charitable hand.
"Our foes may injure us and be forgiven,
"Vengeance awaits the enemies of Heaven.
"What! when apostates, glorying in the name,
"Trample each law that God or man can frame,
"With impious mirth our mystic rites deride,
"And scorn the image of the crucified!
"When o'er their heads the hand of wrath impends,
"When the red thunderbolt in air descends,
"Wilt thou for these with tears of pity sue,
"Defrauding Justice of the vengeance due?
"Unworthy daughter of a noble race,
"Shame to thy faith, thy name's, thy Sire's disgrace!
"Hence to thy chamber! For each pitying thought
"By fervent prayer forgiveness must be sought,
"Sighs, heartfelt sighs, and penitence must pay,
"And tears must wash each sinful word away!"

"*Yet one—e'en tho' the deed of blood be done—*
"*Is it too much to spare the life of* one?
"*Oh! let him live—but live—and he shall fly*
"*To barbarous climes 'neath some remoter sky—*
"*What tho' he bless these tearful eyes no more,*
"*Yet shall he ever shun his native shore*
"*But* must *he fly?—Oh! Father, did'st thou ne'er*
"*Feel the keen pangs that hearts united tear?—*
"*Oh! he was once to better prospects born,*
"*His King to serve, his country to adorn—*
"*Sage in the senate, dreaded in the field,*
"*In peace her ornament, in war her shield!—*
"*Yes, Julian*"—

"*Julian!*" *stern the Monk exclaim'd,*
"*Whom have those lips, rash girl, in madness nam'd!*
"*Julian, Montauban's son? Is this thy plea?*
"*Thy faith's,* thy country's direst enemy?*
"*No more!—in silence wait th' approaching deed,*
"*Thy hopes are vain—the renegade must bleed!—*
"*'Mid the dark morn, when from St. Germain's tower*
"*The thrice repeated bell declares the hour,*
"*Each Christian champion knows th' appointed sign,*
"*And owns the summons to the work divine.*
"*No mercy then our impious foes may know.*
"*'Tis Justice calls, Religion strikes the blow.*
"*For, as of old, in Egypt's palmy clime,*
"*In just atonement of a monarch's crime,*

---

* "Faith" in original edition; corrected to "faith's" by F. W. N.

" Unseen and shrouded in the dark'ning blast,
" Thro' Memphis' streets thy angel, Vengeance, past;
" Yet once again, a suffering Church to aid,
" And heal the wounds by proud apostates made,
" All-righteous Heaven inspires our daring plan;
" But delegates the work of wrath to man!
" Woke from their dream of fancied joy and ease,
" Their minds what horror, what despair will seize,
" When the deep tolling of the midnight bell
" Sounds to their ears, their last, their funeral knell,
" When flickering torches scare the lowering shade,
" And Christ's true soldiers wave the glittering
 blade!
—" Hence! if to mortal man thou dar'st reveal
" The deed my words have warn'd thee to conceal,
" No more expect in earthly ills to share
" The fostering grace of Heaven's paternal care;
" For as the Saint on Malta's rugged strand
" Shook the loath'd reptile from his sacred hand,
" The church forsakes thee, casts thee off with shame,
" And lasting infamy attends thy name.
" Sever'd from all by virtuous spirits priz'd,
" Barr'd from all rites, unpitied and despis'd,
" Long may'st thou live, to wait in fear thy doom,
" No hope on earth, no prospect in the tomb!"—

 He ceas'd, and rose—the maid with quiver-
  ing thrill
Before his fancied presence trembled still,—
And, breathless knelt, as if in dread to hear
That fearful curse return upon her ear—

In silent agony she shrunk to feel
How fierce his soul, how bigotted his zeal—
For he had been to her from early youth
From vice her guardian and her guide to truth;
Her memory told her that he once was kind,
Ere the Monk's cowl had chang'd his gentler mind;
But now of late his holy call had thrown
A haughty coldness o'er him not his own.
Yet still she paid him reverence, tho' no more
She told her bosom secrets as before.
True he was stern, but they who knew him best,
Said fast and penance steel'd that holy breast;
She knew him harsh t' avenge Heaven's injur'd laws,
But deem'd superior sanctity the cause;
She knew him oft mysterious, wild, and strange,
But hop'd that heav'nly converse wrought the change.—

With brow of gloom that half his mind pourtray'd—
The musing Clement sought his convent's shade;
Cursing the chance which told—what none should hear—
The dark, dread secret to a woman's ear.
What should he do?—Say, did some fiend inspire
The thought which thro' his bosom shot like fire?—
'Twas but a moment—no, it could not be—
She who had smil'd on him from infancy,

She who had found, when friendless and alone,
In him a father, in his faith her own.—
—It could not be—but Julian—he might bleed—
And Heaven itself would sanctify the deed!
" Yes! he shall fall! ere from his noon-tide height
" The Sun declining seeks the shades of night,
" Fit act of prologue to th' impending blow;
" This day, this hour, Montauban's blood must
    flow!"

Fill'd with these thoughts, amid the cloister's gloom,
He sought th' assembled votaries of Rome—

'Midst the pale towers in which his years
    were spent,
Which once receiv'd him young and innocent,
When first the venerable paths he trod,
Shunning the world for converse with his God,
—Ere zeal misguided and ambition blind
Had marr'd the youthful promise of his mind,—
A lonely chapel rose; the voice of prayer,
Or anthem-peal no longer sounded there;
Yet, tho' forsaken, still might stranger deem
That place well suited to celestial theme.

'Twixt tapering mullions there the noon-tide ray
Thro' darken'd panes diffus'd a softer day;
From time-worn walls each pillar seem'd to start,
In rich luxuriance of Gothic art;
While crumbling shafts with flowery chaplets crown'd
In mournful grandeur strew'd the hallow'd ground.

In this lone spot secure, to mortal ear
Save Rome's true sons their dire debates might hear,
The leaguers met, to chide the tardy Sun
And wish the work of massacre begun.—
Different in temper, bigotry had join'd
The haughty spirit and the crafty mind;
There were who wish'd to sanctify the sword
By the proud title, "Champions of the Lord";
And those whom hopes of plunder urg'd to rear
The gainful fury of the sacred spear.

—But now the portal's opening sound was heard,
And Clement's form beneath its arch appeared;
All rose with one accord; the saintly man
Cast one keen glance around and thus began:
" *Warriors of God; foredoom'd by Heaven's decree*
" *To right its violated majesty;*
" *Well pleas'd I see your martial spirits pine*
" *For full completion of the wrath divine;*
" *Nor pine in vain; the white-rob'd queen of night*
" *O'er the dread scene shall shed her fav'ring light;*
" *Yet but few hours, the wish'd-for signal tolls—*
" *A peal of terror to apostate souls—*
" *Yet but few hours, the long, long gathering cloud,*
" *With wrath o'ercharg'd, in thunder speaks aloud.*
" *Then on, true servants of your Saviour's will,*
" *His cause to aid, his mandates to fulfil;*
" *To drown in blood their faith, their pow'r, their name,*
" *To whelm Heaven's outcasts in eternal flame;*

"And gain for ever, by one glorious deed,
"The praise of those in God's own cause who
    bleed.
"No tears this night your fury must assuage;
"The cries of youth, the impotence of age
"Alike in vain must sue; the hoary brow,
"The smile of infancy avails not now.
"One sweeping vengeance, deaf to every plea
"That sways the children of mortality,
"Our cause demands; one great, one final blow,
"Approv'd by powers above, and fear'd by fiends
    below!

"Yet, ere the Sun shall gild the western skies,
"Must our primitial offering arise;—
"Some luckless chance, I know not what, betray'd
"Last night our secret to a babbling maid;
"And, lest some fate unseen discover all,
"This hour must Julian of Montauban fall!"—

 He ceas'd; when swift, by maddening zeal in-
    spir'd,
With hope of blood and hasten'd vengeance fir'd,
Bertrand, a soul to every ill inclin'd,
Of all that murderous crew the fiercest mind,
With transport cried—"To me alone be given
"The envied task to aid the will of Heaven—
"Be mine the deed; by one avenging blow,
"To lay this hour our first, great victim low.
"Farewell!—yet ere I part attend my vow;
"If Heaven shall crown its votary's project now,

"My sword, yet reeking with the clotted gore
"Of him who soon shall injure us no more,
"With pious awe before yon hallow'd shrine,
"A grateful record of the aid divine,
"This hand shall consecrate; there long to rest
"And Bertrand's zeal to latest times attest—
"Farewell!" he said, and sheath'd the gleaming
    brand,
And clench'd with fierce resolve his iron hand;
Then strode in haste, as tho' one moment's stay
Were Heaven's imperious call to disobey;
As though each breath the fated Julian drew
With seven-fold fury fir'd his hate anew.

With looks of wonder, not unmix'd with awe,
The silent band his steps departing saw.
Now they behold them thro' the portal's gloom,
His visage shaded by the sable plume;
Now thro' the fretted cloisters, deep and dread,
The vaulted roof returns his heavy tread.
Faint and more faint the lessening echoes thrill,
Then, lost in distance, cease—and all is still.—

"Now sainted brethren, till the fated hour,"
Exclaimed the priest, " we meet again no more.
"Yet ere we part, with hearts from passion free,
"Before yon altar meekly bow the knee.
"To him who ever makes his Church his care,
"To him whose cause ye serve address your pray'r;
"His saving grace implore, your deeds to bless,
"And shield the vent'rous sons of righteousness."

Then low before the shrine in concert bow'd
The fierce, the wild, the crafty and the proud.
Infatuate men ! shall He who reigns above,
Father of all, the God of peace and love,
Shall he be honour'd by the murderer's blade ?
Shall he accept the prayers in vengeance made ?
And thou, misguided Ruler of the land,
Weak to comply, or cruel to command,
Hop'st thou in peace to pass a length of days,
Happy in virtue's love, and wisdom's praise ?—
Lo ! tho' success thy scheme of blood may gain,
Remorse and suff'ring follow in its train,
The sleepless couch, the day of wild affright,
And spectres flitting thro' the shades of night.

    Meanwhile exhausted, feeble, trembling, slow,
With terror pallid, stupefied with woe,
The maid in secret mourn'd her hapless fate,
Her Julian's peril and the churchman's hate.
Her shrinking spirit knew not how to bear
The rankling dart of slow-consuming care ;
On her, a father's hope and only child,
Prosperity's warm beams had ever smil'd ;
Prop of his age, his solace, and his pride,
For her he liv'd, nor reck'd the world beside ;
But he alas ! was dead ; the burning tear
Was scarcely dried she dropp'd upon his bier,
And Albert's dying accents had consign'd
To Clement's care the maid he left behind.

—She kneels in pray'r, and views with glist'n-
  ing eyes
The emblem of th' atoning sacrifice,
Her fluttering bosom holy soothings calm,
And o'er her wounds distil celestial balm.
  " Angelic guardians, natives of the sky,
" Who, seeming distant, hover ever nigh,
" To aid the virtuous, cheer the sad, delight,—
" Too blest to feel our woes, too good to slight,
" With holy anger for what crime of France
" Relax ye thus your wonted vigilance?
" And thou, blest Saint and Martyr to the
    faith,
" Scorn'd in thy life, victorious in thy death,
" Let not the carping world in mockery say
" This deed of massacre disgrac'd thy day.
" Forbid it, Heav'n!—Oh God! my heart is
    faint—
" Shall true religion mourn so foul a taint?—
" Shall persecution doom her foes to bleed?
" In God's own vineyard, Oh! how rank a
    weed!"

  Thus while the powers of prayer her tears
    controul
To send for Julian struck her calmer soul—
She knew not why — or how she might
    prevent
The sad conclusion, if for him she sent;
It was a wild and desperate hope, which though
It promis'd nothing cheer'd her depth of woe—

Perhaps she wish'd to take one last farewell,
One last sad parting ere that fire-bolt fell—
Perhaps she hop'd her arms might guard his breast,
Or she, at least, might sink with him to rest.
    Swift went the bearer of the maid's desires,
And now fear chills, now hope her bosom fires;
In vain he speeds, in vain attempts to earn
His lady's favour by his quick return;
His swiftest course is slowness to her eye,
He seems to loiter when he hopes to fly.
Once more his foot resounds—she hears his tread
With beating heart and cheek of livelier red;
She starts! no Julian's eye, with passion bright,
In silence eloquent, transports her sight.
Fear chains her tongue—the cause she dreads to hear
When these glad words surprise her anxious ear:—
" Few hours have past since Julian rais'd his shield,
" And pois'd his lance, and hurried to the field;
" A sudden mandate came, which ill could spare
" Time for adieus or any softer care.
" Exploits of valour now his thoughts employ,
" He glows with chivalry and martial joy,
" Clasps thy white scarf across his ardent breast,
" And wears thy colour in his towering crest!"

End of the First Canto

CANTO II

ILL-FATED France! still reckless of repose,
Say, must again thy festering wounds unclose?
When white-rob'd Peace descending hastes to shed
Her choicest blessings on thy war-worn head;
Shall all those blessings be bestow'd in vain,
And must the Seraph seek her skies again?
Yes! all in vain through many a ling'ring year
Thy children's fall hath claim'd thy pitying tear;
In vain thy bravest strew'd Moncontour's shore,
And Jarnac's plain was dyed with Condé's gore:
Again by interest led, or fir'd by zeal,
Lo! fell Ambition grasps his crimson'd steel,
Insatiate Murder mounts his blood-stain'd car,
To crown with perfidy the woes of war!—
Land of the chivalrous and mighty dead!
Was it for this thy crested warriors bled?
Was it for this, when Yemen's locust horde
O'er thy rich plains and winding valleys pour'd,
Triumphant victor o'er unnumber'd foes,
To avenge thy wrongs Austrasian Charles arose?
Was it for this, on Gihon's sedgy side,
Thy sainted Louis dar'd the Moslem's pride?
O'er Barca's deserts spread thy sceptre's fame,
And wav'd 'neath Afric's skies thy oriflamme?

—*In vain victorious o'er invading power,
Mid thy clear sky no foreign tempests lower;
In vain the fav'ring heav'ns their frowns assuage,
If thine own sons will bid the whirlwind rage!*

*But are there none, ere yet the blow descend,
In mercy's cause their generous aid to lend?
Can superstitious awe the valiant bind,
And zeal attune to blood the gentle mind?
Alas! in vain is bleeding pity's prayer—
All, all are steel'd—e'en Florence bids despair—
Silence her faith, and tears her feelings show,
She mourns, but thinks not to avert the blow;
And, as in Eastern tales, the enchanter's skill
Bows the bright spirit to his tyrant will,
So fancied crimes her timorous bosom fright,
And each kind thought ideal duties blight.—*

*Sweet is the hour, when o'er th' ethereal plain
The star of eve extends her tranquil reign—
When all the sweets the rival blossoms lend,
In one soft mellow'd soothing fragrance blend;
When now no more the rudeness of the breeze
Shakes their green honours from the quiv'ring trees,
But 'twixt the leaves in whispers loves to play,
And sighs in sorrow for the close of day.—
There is in stillness oft a magic power
To calm the breast when struggling passions
      lower;
Touch'd by its influence, in the soul arise
Diviner feelings, kindred with the skies.*

Through this the Arab's kindling thoughts
    expand,
When circling skies on all sides kiss the
    sand;
For this the hermit seeks the silent grove
To court th' inspiring glow of heavenly love.
—It is not solely in the freedom given,
T' abstract our thoughts and fix the soul on
    heaven;
There is a spirit singing aye in air,
That lifts us high above each mortal care;
No mortal measure swells that silent sound,
No mortal minstrel breathes such tones
    around;—
—The angels' hymn—the melting harmony
That guides the rolling bodies through the sky—
And hence perchance the tales of saints who
    view'd
And heard angelic choirs in solitude.
By most unheard, because the busy din,
Of Pleasure's courts the heedless many win;
Alas! for man; he knows not of the bliss,
The heav'n, attending such a life as this!

   And Florence gazes on that heavenly sight,
The silent beauty of approaching night;
Amid her garden's shade her form reclin'd,
Her tresses curling to the wanton wind—
Where she in happier time, had rear'd each flow'r
That glows in spring or scents th' autumnal hour;
Train'd up the sides the thickening branches grew,
Shade after shade, scarce pervious to the view;

*Above, the lattice clust'ring roses bound
And clematis had wreath'd its circlets round.*

*Pensive she sits—and views the orb of day
Mid clouds of radiance bend his western way—
On spire and turret rests his golden beam,
And glows in ripples on the redden'd stream;
Alas! when next that lord of light shall rise,
In glory bursting from the orient skies,
Far different cause that lucid flood shall stain
Chok'd with the ghastly corpses of the slain;
One sheet of blood those sanguin'd waves shall glide,
And roll pollution to the ocean's tide!*

*There as she rests, her wand'ring thoughts employ
The wild vicissitudes of grief and joy;
The thankful meaning of that heavenward eye
Betrays the thought—Montauban shall not die—
That quiv'ring lip and deep-drawn sigh disclose
How numerous still, how resolute his foes!*

*" All-pitying heaven, and is it thy decree,
" Canst thou this scene of blood approving see?
" Shall man in arms against his brother rise
" And dare to plead commission from the skies?
" It cannot be!"—" Who then," she heard exclaim
A low deep voice, whose accents shook her frame—
" Who then disputes in sacrilegious tone
" The right of heaven to vindicate its own?"—
With dark'ning brow, that told of deeds of blood,
His fix'd eye glaring on her Clement stood—*

So in the land where Niagara's roar
Wakes the lone echoes of Ontario's shore,
The venom'd monarch of the forest eyes
The trembling prey, his helpless sacrifice,

" Lost, hapless girl"—he cried, "thy tender youth
" In vain I nurtur'd in the paths of truth—
" Too long, in rev'rence to thy father's shade,
" My pitying soul thy rightful doom delay'd—
" But it must be—ere yet yon planet pale,
" Now rising beauteous from her cloudy veil,
" Her beam renews, in dark sequester'd cell
" A solitary vestal shalt thou dwell,
" Or mid the choir the chant united raise
" And tune thy wayward lips to notes of praise!"

She spoke not, for she read in that fix'd eye
No ling'ring love, no beaming clemency—
Prone at his feet she fell, his knees she press'd,
And bade her silent anguish speak the rest—
" And for thy Julian," fury in his eyes
The sire rejoin'd, " despair! this night he dies!
" No thought of him shall e'er again controul,
" Or wean from virtue's purer joys thy soul;
" Despis'd, unfriended, hopeless, unforgiven,
" He dies—so perish all the foes of heaven!"—

—" Hold! all good pow'rs will shield my husband's
    life;
" Yes! start not, tyrant! Florence is—his wife!—
" Our fates are join'd, and let not priestly pride
" Annul the bonds which God hath ratified!

" *My plighted vow is register'd on high,*
" *With him to prosper, or with him to die!*" —

Mark ye the glimm'rings yonder chamber's light
Flings o'er the bosom of the silent night?
Doth sleep no more the eyes of Florence seal,
Shed balm around and ev'ry suff'ring heal?
Oh! while the span of one short day flits by,
How many cares may cloud life's sun-bright sky!—
Or is it hope, in airy falsehoods dress'd,
Plays o'er her bosom and dissuades from rest?
The soothing hope, that treachery points her dart
With vain despatch against Montauban's heart?
That soft glad thought her sinking bosom cheers,
And calms the ling'ring conflict of her fears.—
 Whose voice is that, so low, the breezes bear
Through the still midnight of the startled air?
Whose form is that the taper's rays illume,
So dimly shadow'd from encircling gloom?
The glitt'ring morion and the sheathed blade,
Signs of the warrior, gleam amid the shade.—
He mounts—and now, as if by custom taught,
The winding corridor his steps have sought—
And Florence knows—see! see! the quick-drawn breath,
The cold cheek sick'ning with the hues of death—

The starting eye—the feeble tott'ring frame—
The faint wild shriek with which she sounds
    his name—
"Julian!"—"My wife, my dearest, then again
"I see thee, love! and have not pray'd in vain!
"Oh! kind, blest mandate! cares of diff'rent
    kind
"I thought must wean all softness from my
    mind—
"The tented field, the ranks with armour
    bright,
"The distant skirmish, and the closing fight—
"Kind mandate! yes, my Florence! didst
    thou mourn
"My hasty flight, and sigh for my return?
"The army's sudden call allow'd no stay—
"The need was urgent, fatal were delay;
"But now, beyond all hope, the royal word
"Allows short respite to my thirsty sword.
"Florence! that eye so wild?"—

                        "Fly, Julian, fly!
"Delay not, ask not—for a foe is nigh!—
"Hark! heardst thou not that sound, that
    moaning sound,
"Which fell so heavily and deadly round?
"He comes! alas, that blade in murder dyed!
"Craft veils his steps, and power hath arm'd
    his side!
"Fir'd with abhorrence, yet enslaved with awe,
"I shrink from dwelling on the scenes I saw:

"I dare not tell!—but fly—'tis I entreat—
"Thy wife, thy lov'd one, prostrate at thy
    feet!"

"Florence!"—he could not more—the
    eventful whole
In that short moment flash'd upon his soul—
The army's call—the leader's urgent need—
His flight o'ertaken by the warrior's steed—
The signet to return—the pretext fair—
The wily kindness of the stranger's air—
The brook—the beetling rocks—the torrent's
    roar—
The narrow plank that cross'd from shore to
    shore—
Th' uplifted dagger, threat'ning treacherous
    death—
The mortal struggle o'er the gulf beneath—
The bandit's corpse, which, hurrying down the
    flood,
Ting'd the blue curling of the waves with
    blood—
His fears for Florence, which the traitor,
    fir'd
With mad incautious fury, had inspir'd—
And then his transport, when he saw her
    here,
Burst on his sight and chas'd away each fear—
Sad wither'd hopes! and dreams of fancied
    rest!
And false assurance of a flattering breast!"

But Florence, she the while, with trembling
    eye,
Survey'd the keenness of his agony.
The phrensy of her soul was o'er, the flow
Of tears had lull'd th' intenseness of her
    woe—
" Oh ! knew'st thou, Julian, half this bosom's
    strife,
" Clement hath conquer'd, and . . . thy life
    . . . thy life . . .
" 'Twas no kind mandate—'twas thy death
    decreed—
" Nor thou alone, but all thy sect must bleed—
" Too much I've said—each moment on its
    wings
" More certain death and nearer ruin brings !
" While yet escape is granted—fly, oh, fly !
" The very air doth breathe of treachery !
—" Thou wilt not—and thy Florence sues in
    vain—
" Too weak to act—too sensitive of pain ! "—

    " Daughter of Albert," said the youth, " for
        thee
" Have heav'n and man for ever destin'd
    me—
" And must I fly ? and leave thee here alone,
" No friends to aid—midst enemies unknown—
" To crouch before a bigot's despot sway,
" To waste in tears the long, slow, burden'd
    day,

"Thy free soul chain'd, compell'd to frame each thought,
" By the drear rules a Monk's stern tongue hath taught;
" To shrink from sinful mem'ry's busy powers,
" And find a prison in thine own proud towers?—
" Think on that hour, when to his fate resign'd,
" Our trembling hands thy dying father join'd—
" 'Twas twilight—we alone—' My friend,' he said,
" ' To thee I leave this helpless orphan maid '—
" And shall a priest, whom holy vestments shield,
" Cancel the bond a father's lips have seal'd?
" No! fly with me, mid fav'ring shades—the while
—" Thy father's ghost upon our flight will smile!"

 Swift thro' the garden's shade, with falt'ring tread,
His trembling bride the anxious Julian led;
'Mid fleeting clouds the vestal lamp of night,
Shed o'er their pallid forms a fitful light;
Now, wrapt in darkest shades, their flight conceal'd,
Then in her fullest blaze their forms reveal'd.
He might have thought, who gaz'd on Florence then,
No feeble daughter of the sons of men,
But wand'ring spirit of the night was there—
If wand'ring spirit own a form so fair!—

'Tis silence all—no undulating sound
Disturbs the deep repose which reigns around,
Save where, with graceful bend, those aspen trees
Sigh to the murmurs of the southern breeze;
Save where, reflecting yon pure planet's rays,
In silver show'rs the rippling fountain plays.
No thought of scenes like these, alas! had power
O'er the sad victims of that trying hour!
In vain for them yon lucid orb on high
Pour'd her full tide of glory from the sky;
In vain for them shone heav'n's high vault serene,
And mildest zephyrs fann'd the silver scene—
—They marked them not—but shrank at ev'ry sound
Of their light footsteps on the echoing ground.

There is a calm which fav'ring skies dispense,
Hush'd as the sleep of infant innocence—
When nought disturbs that wild, that nameless thrill,
The heart's mute language, when all else is still—
When not a night-breath mars creation's rest,
And nature's peace reflected warms the breast.—
Far other stillness o'er that tranquil plain
In treach'rous beauty held her midnight reign—
Soon low'ring tempests shall those skies deform,
—'Tis but the calm that heralds in the storm!—
And the storm comes—what awful sound of fear
Peals its deep thunders on the startled ear!
—The hour—the fated hour—yon echoing bell
In notes discordant strikes a people's knell!

The die is cast—no hope of mercy now
Th' assembled murd'rers' eager swords allow—
No chance hath flight—and what can force avail?
Shall one the banded multitudes assail?—

Soon as she heard the dreaded signal made
Her onward step the breathless Florence stayed—
No feature mov'd—fix'd grew that ampler eye,
As if it strained to gaze on vacancy—
No flutt'ring tremor told her heart opprest—
No half-heav'd sigh reliev'd her suff'ring breast—
Pale, cold, and tearless, stood the conscious fair,
The pow'rless, nerveless, statue of despair!

But hark! the volleys, thund'ring from afar,
And nearer horrors of a midnight war;
The clash of arms, th' uplifted threat'ning hand;
The victim shrinking from the murd'rer's brand;—
The lurid waving of the torch's glow
Denotes the acting of that scene of woe.—
" Florence," the youth exclaim'd, " for thee I fear,
Oh my vain folly which has led thee here!"—

He said—when issuing from the tangled shade
The sudden glare a murd'rous hand bewray'd.
But who their leader? o'er whose locks of white
The varying torches cast a deeper light—
'Tis he—'tis Clement—dripping now with gore,
'Mid their bright blades the cross profan'd he bore—
Ill-minded man! too well thy wiles succeed,
Thy toils are laid—the helpless prey must bleed—

Feast with thy victim's blood thy longing eyes,
And glut thee with the murd'rous sacrifice!

Fir'd at the sight, upon his ready blade
Th' impetuous youth his hand in vengeance laid;
Deign'd not to wait until the nearer foe
In clos'd attack anticipate his blow—
But with one glance towards her he lov'd in vain,
Sprung like the lion on the hunter train.
—Now sword meets sword with equal fury driven,
The targe is broke—the crested helm is riv'n—
The willing dagger leaves its idle sheath—
The whizzing carbine wings the bolt of death.
But though alone against a host the might
Of Julian's arm maintains th' unequal fight.

Now prone on earth his first opponent lies,
In death a second seals his swimming eyes—
The right prevails—and now the ruffian band
Shun the rous'd fury of his vengeful hand;
No more to trust the chance of fight presume,
But seek the friendly covert of the gloom—
Heedless what course they took, the victor's eye
Turn'd towards his Florence' form instinctively—
He saw her not—perchance the flitting light
Mock'd the imperfect wand'ring of his sight—
"Florence!" he call'd—perchance the clamour round,
With louder din his whisper'd accents drown'd

There, where a ball had pierc'd her, Florence lay
On earth's chill lap—her soul had past away!—

O'er her pale cheek the moonbeam sought to dwell;
From her cold temple trickling life-drops fell;
A lily blighted by the tempests' power,
She lay, a drooping melancholy flow'r.

   But where is Julian?—groan, nor tear, nor sigh,
Told the full pressure of his agony—
That fix'd, but mute despair—that more than grief—
That burden'd heart, too full to seek relief,
Denied him utt'rance—Lo! once more around
The rallying murd'rers press the nearer ground,
And Clement leads them—more than mortal ire
Lit in that glance the warrior's eye of fire,
For one last blow he pois'd his thirsty sword,
In one last effort all his fury pour'd—
The steel descends: the miscreant shrinks in vain,
His heaving limbs bestrew the gory plain—
One phrensied look of rage and hate he cast,
His lips essay'd to speak—and all was past.—

   In closer combat round their sinking foe,
With ceaseless rage the thick'ning bandits glow;
Hemm'd in by numbers, vain the practis'd might,
Which oft had turn'd the current of the fight—
Each ready poignard drinks the victim's gore,
The crimson torrent streams from ev'ry pore;
His blade drops useless from his palsied hand,
He reels—he falls extended on the sand—
Toward his dead Florence turns his wand'ring eyes,
Half rears his feeble hand to heaven—and dies!

NOTES

CANTO THE FIRST

Note 1, *page* 3, *line* 1

" The sun has risen "

I take this opportunity of introducing a short sketch of the massacre of St. Bartholomew. It may be thought by many an unnecessary task, and some will not fail to deem it as presuming, to suppose that our learned University is unacquainted with the full particulars. This I thought myself, when I published the First Canto; but an earnest and attentive canvassing of the opinions of those who have done me the honour to peruse my publication has convinced me of my mistake; and since I have done my best to please, I hope I shall be pardoned if I be in error.—The year of our Lord 1572 will ever be branded with infamy and recollected with horror, as the date of this most barbarous and cold-blooded massacre. The Queen mother, Catherine de' Medici, actuated by zeal or ambition, conceived this design, so pleasing to the Court of Rome; and her weak and ill-fated son, Charles the Ninth, was made the tool of her bloodthirsty intentions. The hour of twelve, according to Voltaire, of three, according to Sully, was the time appointed for the commencement of the assassination, and the clock of the church of St.

Germain l'Auxerrois awakened the pious Catholics of Paris to deeds of treachery and murder. Coligny, Lord High Admiral of France, was one of the first that were * martyred, 30,000 Huguenots shared his fate throughout the Empire, and it was only a motive of policy that spared the Protestant King of Navarre, afterwards the famous Henry the Fourth, who had lately married the King's sister. Charles died, not long after, a victim to a most miserable disease; his dying moments were haunted with the visions of a distempered imagination or a guilty conscience, and he seemed to wish to atone for his conduct towards the Protestants by appointing his brother-in-law of Navarre his successor. The poetry of Voltaire, and the prose of Sully, exhibit two Frenchmen speaking in abhorrence of the deeds of their countrymen; and this single circumstance is perhaps more convincing, in respect to the atrocity of the massacre, than the most laboured declamation of the historian.

[J. H. N.]

Note 2, page 3, line 1.

"Belleville's lengthen'd height."

The heights of Belleville are situated on the east of Paris. It was from this place that Sir Charles Stewart dated the despatches which announced the surrender of Paris to the allied forces.

[J. W. B.]

---

* Corrected in pencil to "was" in Dr. Bloxam's copy in British Museum.

CANTO THE SECOND

Note 1, *page* 19, *line* 9.

" In vain thy bravest strew'd Moncontour's shore,
And Jarnac's plain was dyed with Condé's gore : "

In the long civil wars which preceded the massacre, Moncontour and Jarnac were the scenes of two most bloody battles between the Catholics and Protestants.—*Vide* Notes to " Henriade."

[J. W. B.]

Note 2, *page* 19, *line* 20.

" Austrasian Charles arose "

Charles, surnamed Martel, or " the hammer," also defeated the Arabian army near Jours, and drove them beyond the Pyrenees.—*Vide* Gibbon, vol. x. p. 23.

[J. H. N.]

Note 3, *page* 19, *line* 22.

" Thy sainted Louis dar'd the Moslem's pride ?
O'er Barca's deserts spread thy sceptre's fame,
And wav'd 'neath Afric's skies thy oriflamme ? "

" In complete armour, the oriflamme waving before him, Louis leaped foremost on the beach " (Gibbon). For a fuller account of this hero, *vide* that historian. The oriflamme was the sacred standard of the French monarchy.

[J. H. N.]

Note 4, page 21, *line* 1.

"Through this the Arab's kindling thoughts expand,
When circling skies on all sides kiss the sand."

"The wandering life of the Arabs, Tartars, and Turkomans will be found detailed in any book of Eastern travels. That it possesses a charm peculiar to itself, cannot be denied. A young French renegado confessed to Chateaubriand, that he never found himself alone, galloping in the desert, without a sensation approaching to rapture, which was indescribable" (Notes to the "Bride of Abydos"). It may be said that, in the above instance, it was the sublimity of the waste, rather than the stillness of the solitude, that produced the rapturous feelings; perhaps it will be more just to pronounce them as proceeding from both together. Paley, in his "Moral Philosophy," supposes that the happiness of the lower and sedentary orders of animals, as of oysters, periwinkles, etc., consists in perfect health; I should prefer to say, it consists in the silence they enjoy. And I am in part borne out by that author himself, who seems to be of opinion that happiness is independent of any particular outward gratification whatever, and a feeling of which we can give no account.

[J. H. N.]

MEMORIALS OF THE PAST

[1832]

The Title-page of this volume reads as follows—

MEMORIALS / OF / THE PAST. /

Procul O procul este profani !/ The voices of the dead, and songs of other years. / Oxford / MDCCCXXXII. /

And on the back of the title are these lines—

Strains, framed in youth, in our life's history
Stand as Antiquities; and so we love them.—
Each has its legend, and bespeaks its times.

J. H. N.

MEMORIALS OF THE PAST

SUMMER
AN ECLOGUE

Damon.

MY breath is spent;—Menalcas, check your pace!
Must I incessant urge this noon-tide chase?
From yonder hill I saw you cross the mead,
And mount the stile;—hence all this toilsome speed.

Menalcas.

'Tis well:—the face of nature blooms so fair,
I sought a friendly mind, my thoughts to share.
See richest green yon hanging wood adorn,
And the ripe fields stand thick with golden corn.
The clear blue skies to bright Italia given
We envy not, so radiant smiles our heaven.

Damon.

How hot the day! a lassitude invades
My sinking limbs, e'en mid these sylvan
  shades.

Menalcas.

'Tis meet your voice should fail, your step
  should lag;
A chase at noon is wont the limbs to fag!
There, where the hill a steeper fall displays,
And its sweet scent the latent thyme betrays,
Where beeches ranged in clumps to grace the
  scene
Cherish the freshness of the grass's green,
There sit we down.

Damon.

Agreed.   How swift has past
The time since I this calm view greeted last!
Yet nine whole weeks their lengthened course
  have run,
In which fair Athens held her duteous son.

Menalcas.

Athens your theme! in dull and tiresome
  sound
Her eager praises from your mouth resound.

Damon.

City of Attic fame and Attic grace,
Fit seat for sages of Cecropian race,
Nurse of the brave, the wise, the good, the
    great,
A fairer Athens in a happier state !—
He who can view thy awe-inspiring towers,
Thy solemn halls, thy academic bowers,
Nor feels his breast with secret ardour glow,
—A thrill how sweet, who feel alone can
    know—
Is kindred to the surge that sweeps the shore,
Or the hard rock which stems that surge's roar.

Menalcas.

Yet while you praise the art-ennobled plain,
Where bright Athena holds her learned reign,
The candid verse let green Arcadia share ;
Clear are her streams, her dells for ever fair.
What, tho' no tasselled cap and formal gown
Roam o'er our fields, or loiter in our town ?
We have not, safe from academic strife,
The cares, the contests of a lettered life ;
The brilliant prize, the effort to be great,
Envy from rival, from the vanquished hate.
No pallid student walks the unvaried round,
No footstep falls with big proctorial sound ;
The ruddy ploughboy whistles as he goes,
He knows no Don, no despot Proctor knows.

Damon.

True :—choicest gifts a country life adorn ;
Do any scorn them ? idiots ! let them scorn.
Not great Olympia's self, tho' famed she be,
Shall be preferred, dear rural cot, to thee !
Truer the joys that lowly Scyllus crown
Than all the splendours of the neighbouring town.

Menalcas.

O blest retreat ! where, bursting on the eye,
The vine-clad cot detained the passer-by.
By groves embellished, sheltered in the dale,
Scenting with endless sweets the sportive gale,
It was a place that might have soothed the breast,
By gloomy thought and feverish cares opprest.
How oft have we upon the lawn displayed
Our frolicks, changed as changing humour bade !
Or thro' the fields prolonged the breathless race,
Or thro' the shrubberies wound the joyous chase,
Now hid and hushed, now hallooing from our lair,
Now starting sudden into open air !

Damon.

Fresh in my mind that last sad morn I view,
When to its lowly walks I bade adieu.—
" No more," thought I, " shall Damon see these bowers,
" And say, with beating heart, 'that cot is ours.'
" Ne'er, as thro' Scyllus' dear retreats I stroll,
" Behold our smoke from yonder chimnies roll;
" Nor see the sheep, that range yon hills' green side,
" Bear N upon their fleecy honors dyed!"
Well, 'tis all o'er! yet will not I repine,
Tho' Scyllus' lawns for me no longer shine.
Her scenes were fair—but fairer far the mead,
Where vagrant Ophis feeds her waving reed;
And grander views and richer copses rise,
And hills of bolder swell, and clearer skies.
O! what could Scyllus boast, that might compare
With this cool wood, so large, so lone, so fair!
So prodigal of hill and silent dale,
Of clumps of trees that court the balmy gale,
Of sloping stair, straight terrace, winding walk,
And hazel shades for philosophic talk,
That in gay fancy's vision may be seen
Shy Fauns and Dryads peeping thro' the green,

Or merry Comus and his jovial crew
Starting upon the unwary stranger's view.

MENALCAS.

Enough! let's rise, and wind our homeward course,
Where reedy Ophis finds its humble source.

ALTON, *July*, 1818.

AUTUMN
AN ECLOGUE

CHILL blows the wind ;—the Sun's enfeebled power
Warms with its radiance but the noon-tide hour.
Autumn has tanned the flaunting summer-hues ;
Spent is the nightly store of drenching dews ;
The early sportsman summons me to yield
Words to his music of the wood and field.—
Such suits me not ;—and, though to such consigned,
On calmer themes falls back my lagging mind.

Not far from lowly Maera's rural nest,
There swells a mount, conspicuous o'er the rest.
Climb to the top, and on the stroller's eyes,
Hills, clustering woods, and sacred spires will rise.
With oaks its brow is crowned ; and O ! how gay
Their foliage glitters in the autumnal ray !
When all the colours of the varying bow
Upon the leaves in quick succession glow.
Here mid the shrubs the squirrel loves to spring,
And here the pheasant plumes his golden wing,

And here the furtive noose, with wiry snare,
Cuts short the boundings of the heedless hare.

Along the path, which up the slanting plain
Long lingers onward, ere the height it gain ;
What time the red sun shot his western ray,
Two youths I spied drag on their weary way.
The first's keen eye, and vest in rustic sort,
And murderous tube, bespoke the man of sport.
His friend, in studious garb, strange sight, arrayed,
Boasted no weapons of the deadly trade.
A bag, with strap across his shoulders braced,
Laden with spoils, depended from his waist.
E'en his right hand with sylvan deaths was stored,—
A future banquet for the festive board.
True to the scent, in many a mazy round,
Two dogs in front surprise the tainted ground.
Lone was the spot, the winds in frolic mood
Conveyed their converse through the echoing wood ;
And, as they paced along the hill's steep side,
Thus Damon spoke, and Thyrsis thus replied :

DAMON.

Yes—so it is—inconstant as this wind,
Light as these feathers, is the human mind.
Each, his own good, as Horace sings, forgot,
Sighs for the blessings of his neighbour's lot ;

From what he is, in fancy loves to roam,
Regrets the past, or sighs for the to-come.
Around the past fond memory's soft tints play,
And hope's gay falsehoods gild the future day.
So to our minds in lovelier garb appears
The faded landscape of departed years;
On happy hours at school we pensive dwell
On those we fought so brave, or loved so well.

Thyrsis.

Then, while we muse on pleasures now gone by,
No vain regret shall dim the clouded eye;
We'll hope to be, in life's succeeding scene,
As happy as we are, and we have been.
—Sad thoughts, away! rather let memory smile,
Painting that hospitable hall the while,
Where Greeks, Scots, Romans, and the tuneful
    Nine,
Spoke the same tongue, and shared the same
    design;
Where laughing Swaran uttered his last joke,
And dark Ulysses vanished into smoke,
And Clio marked the royal eagle's flight,
And Oscar mounted in his car of light.

Damon.

Or let us celebrate the real debate,
The chair of office and the throne of state;
The siege, the tussle, and our remnant hope
Snapped in the snapping of the treacherous rope.

Thyrsis.

There is a fragment fame to you assigns,
My shallow head but ill retains the lines.
It sang, " how hostile tumult dared prophane
" Awful St. Laurence mid his client train ;
" Aimed at the sacred tools, the treasured store,
" The purple cushion with its tassels four ;
" The mace, the tomes in which recorded lay
" The strange events of many a well-fought day ;
" E'en the saint's gridiron, and the ribbons blue,
" Meet furniture of that mysterious crew."

Damon.

I know one portion of those fragment strains,
My tongue shall utter what my mind retains.
" First he, the Treasurer, rears his awful form,
" And moves the mighty semblance of a storm ;
" Frowns angrily upon the snarling foe,
" And feels his bosom for the conflict glow.
" And next, more noted in the wordy war,
" Marches the chief, conspicuous by the star ;
" The downcast look, dissembling proud disdain,
" Bespeaks the leader of the undaunted train.
" Then comes the hero of the yellow hair,
" The glossy curl his solitary care,
" And then, far blazing in the lists of fame,
" He who from ' Mild.' derives his peaceful
        name ;

" With prudent skill he calms the Treasurer's rage,
" A man in wisdom, while a youth in age.
" Next from Ierne's meads, their birthplace dear,
" The brothers haste, and raise the associate spear.
" His dark hair notes the first, our constant grief ;
" His floating gold proclaims the younger chief,
" And last their gallant warriors march behind ;
" Various in lineage they, but one in mind,
" With steady gaze the hostile bands they view,
" True to their secret, to their party true ! "

THYRSIS.

Enough ! yon cloud with gold and purple bright
Heralds the near approach of dusky night.
Yon peeping star disturbs this idle talk,
And chides the slowness of our homeward walk.
Between yon trees the pale moon casts her ray,
And seems to warn us, " Loiterers, haste away."

ALTON, *September*, 1818.

SPRING

AN ECLOGUE

Damon.

NOW that the dreary cold of winter flies,
And Taurus reigns the monarch of the skies,
And earth, inviting song, in fairest vest,
And richest gems, as Maro tells, is drest,
Come let us play the rhymster's part, and sing
The opening beauties of the verdant spring.
That look pleads inability;—such plea
May weigh with others, but is lost on me.
For erst you tuned your lyre, nor tuned in vain;
And larks and robins have adorned your strain.
A brother's wish what sister can refuse?
The plaintive mastered, dare the pastoral muse.

Amaryllis.

Hard task! for who but sings the spring by rule?
Its "verdant views"—its "fountains clear and cool"—

"The lark's brisk carol"—"Philomela's trill"—
"The painted mead"—"the gently-purling rill"—
"The industrious bee"—"the silken butterfly"—
"The frisking lambkins"—and "the smiling sky."—
Hail! commonplaces of the pastoral strain!
Which, once endured, we ne'er endure again;
Where down the stanza tuneful dulness flows,
Or ponderous truisms stalk in measured prose.
Leave them! the flippant toil let others take,
Feel without heart, and talk for talking's sake.

DAMON.

True;—blame the folly, but the purpose spare;
Praise we or not, the Spring *is* passing fair.
'Tis we, who feebly read, or ill express,
Her chastened mirth, her thoughtful tenderness.
From sober truth your tasteless rhymster flies
To read romance and soft monstrosities.
Strange fearful feats in every verse are done,
And earth is dazzled with an Eden's sun.
The crocus flames while jasmine scents the air,
Tulips and lilies grace the same parterre;
Mid ripening ears the heedless rustic ploughs,
And bulbuls sigh on grape-enclustered boughs.
For us, albeit we own our colours faint,
The scenes before us we may *try* to paint;

Be unambitious truth alone our pride,
Nature our pattern, common-sense our guide.

AMARYLLIS.

You then begin ;—while I attempt to frame
The verse responsive, such my humbler aim.

DAMON.

Spring ! fairest season of the sunborn four,
Gifts of the year, dispensers of its store :—
The young prefer thee, for the smiles they see
Give back the image of their own light glee.
The old prefer thee, for thy bloom displays,
To memory dear, the scenes of former days ;
When hope poured brightest visions on their view,
And all things pleased, for all things then were new.

AMARYLLIS.

The sportive Zephyr, rousing with the spring,
In viewless frolics fans his odorous wing ;
Sighs o'er the modest violet's mild perfume,
And drinks the teardrops from the rose's bloom ;
See how those soft thin limes, with golden hair,
Shrink from the rudeness of the busy air ;
While yon slight ash and willow-flowrets white
Sleep in the hollow, in the wind's despite.

Damon.

Mark the gay varying of the cloud, as chance
Curls its bright form, or smooths its dark
    expanse ;
First calm and soft, when soberest colours tinge,
Then waving fleecy with translucent fringe,
Now a bright robe flung o'er the orb of day,
And last impassive to the searching ray.
So change,—unless comparisons may seem
To mar the line and dim the glorious theme,
And critics frown and shake the head, and
    name
The great Martinus and his sinking fame,—
So change, as some astonished peasant views,
The gay calidoscope's transparent hues ;
In endless dance the melting colours glide,
Till fancy's every whim is gratified.

Amaryllis.

Nor shall the tale be hid, these columns tell,
If Amaryllis may interpret well ;
Whether true scenes in the blue distance rise,
Or brain-born splendours deck the unconscious
    skies.
There wondrous castles frown with shadowy
    towers,
And magic domes the toil of fairy powers ;
The skiff winds up the visionary rill,
And nodding forests glitter on the hill ;

Or long processions wind their airy train,
And coursers prance, impatient of the rein;
Or warring armies, fearful sight, advance,
Shake the thin shield and hurl a phantom
    lance.

Damon.

Calm mid the vale reclines our lowly town,
Safe from the thousand perils of renown.
No solemn mace, the portent of the Mayor,
No awe-inspiring Aldermen are there;
Not e'en that first big requisite of state,
The well-lined stomach of a magistrate.
Smile not, ye strangers, nor with listless eyes
Our gabled roof and ill-paved streets despise.
What though your city boasts in massive stone
Wonders of art and greatness all her own?
Tho' proud Olympia glitter from afar,
The mart of nations and the queen of war,
With ceaseless anger bid her thunders roll,
And spread dismay at will from pole to pole?
Think of your lives, to care and strife a prey;
Prove, ere from joys like ours you turn away.

Amaryllis.

Yes, here the boor contented runs his race,
Too proud to wander from his native place.
Peace to their honest souls! tho' at four score
They scarce have passed two furlongs from
    their door;

Some barbarous shape and voice to strangers give,
—If men in truth in foreign countries live—
And deem a hero in his small abode,
Whoso has roughed it on the King's high-road,
With bosom steeled * left Maera's green retreats,
Nor stopped till lost in vast Olympia's streets.

DAMON.

But see how Corydon, with many a bound,
Darts thro' the shrubs and mounts the crum-
    bling ground.
The slender plants, his rapid passage shakes,
Startling and trembling track the path he takes.
—Poor honest Argus! thou with greater speed
Hast climbed the ascent and gained the level
    mead;
And has[t] thou, faithful servant, hastened here,
To tell the news that Corydon is near?
That panting side, those limbs with toil opprest,
Bespeak thy age, and thou shouldest give it rest.

CORYDON.

What winning theme enchains you grave and
    still,
Like two stiff statues stuck upon the hill?
With rude forgetfulness the hour you slight,
When hunger and the fragrant board invite;
Not without cause this unaccustomed stay,
Some secrets have beguiled the time away.

    ALTON, *April,* 1819.

---

    * Illi robur et aes triplex, etc.

ON MY BIRTHDAY

LET the sun summon all his beams to hold
    Bright pageant in his court, the cloud-paved sky;
Earth trim her fields and leaf her copses cold;
    Till the dull month with summer-splendour vie.
    It is my birthday;—and I fain would try,
Albeit in rude, in heartfelt strains to praise
    My God, for He hath shielded wondrously
From harm and envious error all my ways,
And purged my misty sight, and fixed on heaven my gaze.

II.

Far be that mood, in which the insensate crowd
    Of wealthy folly hail their natal day,—
With riot throng, and feast, and greetings loud,
    Chasing all thoughts of God and heaven away.
    Poor insect! feebly daring, madly gay,
What, joy because the fulness of the year
    Marks thee for greedy death a riper prey?
Is not the silence of the grave too near?
Viewest thou the end with glee, meet scene for harrowing fear?

III.

Go then, infatuate! where the festive hall,
    The curious board, the oblivious wine invite;
Speed with obsequious haste at pleasure's call,
    And with thy revels scare the far-spent night.
    Joy thee, that clearer dawn upon thy sight
The gates of death;—and pride thee in thy sum
    Of guilty years, and thy increasing white
Of locks;—in age untimely frolicksome,
Make much of thy brief span, few years are yet to come!

IV.

Yet wiser such, than he whom blank despair
    And fostered grief's ungainful toil enslave;
Lodged in whose furrowed brow thrives fretful care,
    Sour graft of blighted hope; who, when the wave
    Of evil rushes, yields,—yet claims to rave
At his own deed, as the stern will of heaven.
    In sooth against his Maker idly brave,
Whom e'en this creature-world has tossed and driven,
Cursing the life he mars, "a boon so kindly given." *

---

* "Is life a boon so kindly given?" etc., *vide* "Childe Harold," Can. ii.

V.

He dreams of mischief; and that brainborn ill
   Man's open face bears in his jealous view.
Fain would he fly his doom ; that doom is still
   His own black thoughts, and they must aye
      pursue.
Too proud for merriment, or the pure dew
Soft glistening on the sympathising cheek ;
   As some dark, lonely, evil-natured yew,
Whose poisonous fruit—so fabling poets speak—
Beneath the moon's pale gleam the midnight
      hag doth seek.

VI.

No ! give to me, Great Lord, the constant soul
   Nor fooled by pleasure nor enslaved by
      care ;
Each rebel-passion (for Thou can'st) control,
   And make me know the tempter's every
      snare.
   What, tho' alone my sober hours I wear,
No friend in view, and sadness o'er my mind
   Throws her dark veil ?—Thou but accord
      this prayer,
And I will bless Thee for my birth, and find
That stillness breathes sweet tones, and loneli-
      ness is kind.

VII.

Each coming year, O grant it to refine
    All purer motions of this anxious breast ;
Kindle the steadfast flame of love divine,
    And comfort me with holier thoughts possest ;
    Till this worn body slowly sink to rest,
This feeble spirit to the skies aspire,—
    As some long-prisoned dove toward her nest—
There to receive the gracious full-toned lyre,
Bowed low before the throne mid the bright
    seraph choir.

OXFORD, *February* 21, 1819.

PROLOGUE

To the Masque of Amyntor

IN times of old, ere Learning's dawning beam
    Roused slumbering Genius from her Gothic dream,
Magic, of Ignorance and Fancy born,
With wonders peopled every waste forlorn,
And told how soft the sprightly fairy trod
The dewy verdure of the midnight sod.

Taught in her love, the traveller-knight descried
The unearthly castle vaunt its portal wide,
While the gay flood of hospitable light
Blazed high and low, and scared the gazing wight,
And festive voices floating on the gale
In full accordance bade the stranger hail!

To those, who thus, in measure rich and full,
Feasted on wonders till the truth was dull,
The smiling word of Chawton might appear
A haunted grove of Magic's orgies drear,

This home a fort, fenced round with cautious ditch,
Yon dames enchanted, and myself a witch.

Ah ! were it true ! so might I earn the power
To fix you mine one fa[s]cinating hour !
So might the scene yon curtain furled will show
Spellbind each care and charm to sleep each woe,
Win the dull spirits with sweet-mannered art,
And be a mightier magic o'er the heart-!

ALTON, *July*, 1819.

PARAPHRASE

Of Ecclesiastes, Ch. xii. vv. 1–7

WHILE life's young dawnings o'er the
    meads diffuse
Hope's radiant mist and pleasure's
    fragrant dews,
Ere angry frowns the sunbright sky deform,
And cloud on cloud prolongs the unyielding
    storm,
Remember God.—There comes an awful hour,
When bows each guardian of the ancient
    tower,
The strong ones faint, the vassals lose their
    might,
And each dim window yields a fading light,
The unsocial door sends forth no festive train,
And music's daughters hush their wonted
    strain.

Poor helpless being! his straggling locks
    assume
The chilling whiteness of the almond's bloom.
Mark how he dreads, his frame with sickness
    bent,
The tedious effort of the steep ascent.

Unstrung each nerve, he starts! he has but
 heard
The whizzing locust, or the warbling bird.

Desire has failed; the world's choice pleasures
 seem
As some dull jest, or scarce-remembered dream.
He sinks—he fails—he quits this mortal state—
The home of ages opes her silent gate,
And marshalled mourners, while the bier moves
 slow,
Display the tearless pomp of studied woe.

Weep! for the silver chord has loosed its hold,
For ever broken lies that bowl of gold,
No more the urn will search the deep-lodged
 rill,
The fount is dried, the busy wheel is still.
The body crumbles to its ancient clay,
The soul to God, who gave it, wings its way.

OXFORD, *May*, 1821.

PARAPHRASE

Of Isaiah, Ch. lxiv.

THAT Thou wouldest rend the breadth of sky,
  That veils Thy presence from the sons of men !
O that, as erst Thou camest from on high
  Sudden in strength, Thou so wouldest come again !
Tracked out by judgments was Thy fiery path,
Ocean and mountain withering in Thy wrath !

Then would Thy name—the Just, the Merciful—
  Strange dubious attributes to human mind,
Appal Thy foes ; and kings who spurn Thy rule
  Then, then would quake to hopeless doom consigned.
See, the stout bow, and totter the secure,
While pleasure's bondsman hides his head impure !

Come down ! for then shall from its seven bright springs
  To him who thirsts the draught of life be given ;

Eye hath not seen, ear hath not heard the
    things
  Which He hath purposed for the heirs of
    'heaven;—
A God of love, guiding with gracious ray
Each meek rejoicing pilgrim on his way.

Yea, tho' we err, and Thine averted face
  Rebukes the folly in Thine Israel done,
Will not that hour of chastisement give place
  To beams, the pledge of an eternal sun?
Yes! for His counsels to the end endure;
We shall be saved, our rest abideth sure.

Lord, Lord! our sins . . . our sins . . . un-
    clean are we,
  Gross and corrupt; our seeming-virtuous
    deeds
Are but abominate; all, dead to Thee,
  Shrivel, like leaves when summer's green
    recedes;
While, like the autumn blast, our lusts arise,
And sweep their prey where the fell serpent lies.

None, there is none to plead with God in
    prayer,
  Bracing his laggart spirit to the work
Of intercession; conscience-sprung despair,
  Sin-loving still, doth in each bosom lurk.
Guilt calls Thee to avenge;—Thy risen ire
Sears like a brand, we gave and we expire.

F

But now, O Lord, our Father! we are Thine—
   Design and fashion ; senseless while we lay,
Thou, as the potter, with a hand divine,
   Mouldest Thy vessels of the sluggish clay.
See not our guilt, Thy word of wrath recal,
Lo, we are Thine by price, Thy people all !

Alas for Zion ! 'tis a waste ;—the fair,
   The holy place in flames ;—where once our sires
Kindled the sacrifice of praise and prayer,
   Far other brightness gleams from Gentile fires.
Low lies our pride ;—and wilt Thou self-deny
Thy rescuing arm unvexed amid Thine Israel's cry ?

BRIGHTON, *September*, 1821.

TO M. S. N.

On her Birthday

MY sister, on a day so dear,
   That ushers in the thirteenth year
     Of life to one I love,
   Permit a brother's heart to pay
The tribute of a humble lay,
Thinking of thee, tho' far away,
     In learning's classic grove.

" Pay " was my word ;—it is a debt ;
For I have not forgotten yet,
     When last thy birthday came.
My purpose was to write to Strand,
But other cares were then on hand
—Philosophers, a crabbed band,
Grave annalists from ancient land,
Bards, waving high the spell-fraught wand,
All joined that purpose to withstand,
Forbad the letter I had planned
     And urged a sovereign claim.

That time is past ; I groan no more
Chained to the literary oar.
In midnight dreams before my eyes
No ghosts of mangled metres rise,

No limping anapaests advance,
No dochmees trail the doleful dance ;
E'en critics lose their power to scare,
Schneider, Bos, Erfurdt, Wesseling, Valckenaer,
Brunck, Schutz, Schweighaeuser,—no for none
    I care !

Young Isis timorously pours
Her slender stream thro' Oxford's bowers ;
Yet soon her waters broader grow,
Deepen and swell, and proudly flow ;
I see them now their course pursue
To Richmond's heights and royal Kew,—
Passing the well-known windows, as they gleam
A watch-tower on the Strand, high-jutting o'er
    the stream.

See, I have whispered, as they flow,
    A message for my sister's ear,
And their bright ripple laughs, as though
    In token they that message hear ;
So when the light wave lifts its head
Impatient from the river's bed,
Or close at hand is seen to leap,
And chafe the bank's opposing steep,
Deem it a tongueless messenger to be,
That longs to wish thee joy from me.

How shall we keep this glad birthday ?
    Shall mirth unveil her sparkling eye,
Shall pomp her waving plumes display,
    And pleasure weave a crown of flowers,
        which die,

Leaving no fruit to grace their memory?
—No! to affection's hallowed shrine I bear
  A purer offering than the world can boast,
Kind serious thoughts of love, the full heart's prayer,
  Which speaks the least whene'er it means the most.

All grace, all blessing on thy head
  May He rain down, the Mighty One;
By His good Spirit onward led,
  Until the holy prize be won.
O! may faith fix thy brightening eye
On blissful scenes beyond the sky;
May sacred love be seen to speak
In the warm transport of thy cheek;
And hope so sweet a smile inspire,
That e'en the angels might admire.
May gentle peace, and joy divine,
Content, and charity, be thine,
And each fair grace, whose mounting flame
Points to the heaven from whence it came.

Bold heart forbear!—a strain so high
  Needs angel's voice, or prophet's tongue of fire;
Think o'er its music silently,
  Lest thou prophane it by a tuneless lyre.
I cease. Adieu till next I see
Thy face, dear Mary, smile on me.

Time speeds; the post will soon demand
This letter from my hurrying hand;
And all my labours would be lost,
Were I to miss this evening's post.

OXFORD, *November* 9, 1821.

TO C. R. N.

On his Birthday

A YEAR and more has fled,
   Since first, dear Charles, I read
   Your lines set forth to grace my
     natal day;
Yet from me no answer came,
—I own it to my shame,—
To thank the kindness and applaud the lay.

   Yet deem it not neglect;
   The ready pen that checked,
Nor dull reluctance, nor unkind disdain;
   Free tho' my heart, my mind
   In studious cell confined
Felt the long rigor of a tightened chain.

   But now my thoughts are free,
   Farewell, constraint, to thee!
Seize on the lyre, and tune each jarring string;
   And, sure, that slighted lyre
   Much tuning will require,
So long a while debarred its vibrating.

And, say, what happier time
To fit the pliant rhyme,
With merry fingers searching the sweet wires,
Than when your star of birth,
The beacon of our mirth,
Darts the sly twinkling of its annual fires?

"Annual" is not the word;
Our tongue does not afford
Some compound adjective of twenty-one;
Which neatly may express,
What I mean should have the stress,
"O'er Charles's head, years three times seven have run!"

Why not in bathos strive
Of Helicon to dive?
Come, let us revel—no cold-hearted slave
To crouch before the chaste
And peevish rules of taste—
In its dark depth, the vast poetic wave!

March winds have moaned away,
Wet April had his day,
Now the young year, in gaily plaited bower,
Her greenest garment weareth,
While every slim bough beareth
The juicy fruit or sweetly-breathing flower.

What month along the year
More kindly might appear
To hold remembrance of our day of birth,
Than when the summer-sun,
Fresh armed his course to run,
Unsheaths his beams and strikes the new-fledged earth?

Snow-bleached is December's morn,
When H. E. N. was born;
Chill fog and drizzle is November's best;
And the sun amid the Fishes
Unquestionably wishes
To leave the sea and dry his dripping vest.

But this dainty month of June
All nature puts in tune,
Winning true concord from the sounding spheres;
No ill-tempered minor third
Is in hail or thunder heard,
No blast's diminished seventh wails on our shrinking ears.

O! may the lark this morn,
On heaven's own pinion borne,
Chant gratulation mid the aerial plain!
O! may the rose bloom sweetest,
When thou, Philomela, greetest
Dim Hesper's presence with thy melting strain!

O! may the stars dispense
   Their holiest influence,
Their silent-sinking dews of soothing balm!
   O! may to-day's sun bring
   A blessing on its wing,
The pledge of good in store, the gift of present
   calm!

OXFORD, *June* 16, 1823.

TO H. E. N.

On her Birthday

THE Muse has sway in the truant mind,
    And the heart from care set free,
    In the thoughts that wanton un-
        confined,
That range o'er the earth, and float on the wind,
    And dive in the boundless sea.

To the Muse alone Nature's stores are known,
    And she compounds them well;
For she can draw from the scenes around
That nameless charm, which is never found
Out of the range of the magic ground
    In which she loves to dwell.

The Muse is Nature's Alchemist,
    And she fashions it at her will,
And 'tis hers to mould the sunset gold,
    And the draught of life distil.

—Why then resume her fairy wand,
    And why renew the strain?
Ill 'seems it the devoted hand,
That has touched the plough, to trifle now
    With the toys of verse again.

Yet be there a time may claim a rhyme,
   Tho' weightier thoughts engage,
It is, dear Harriet, when away
From home and thee upon the day
When thou art . . . hold! I must not say
   Aloud a lady's age.

Some there are born to ample lands,
   And mansions tall and fair,
And fortune stands with laden hands
   To greet the eager heir.

Thro' youth's long grove and the vista green
   Of summers twenty-one,
Is dimly seen the bounteous queen
   Beckoning her favourite son.

Wealth's golden key displayeth she,
   And robes of state she weareth,
And the jewelled star of high degree
   Fixed at her bosom flareth.

But others find a nobler lot
   Than earthly heirs obtain;
The sons of pleasure court them not,
   Nor fashion's painted train.

Their food is sent them from above,
   And they drink of the morning dew;
No mortal loom their raiment wove,
   Nor fading is its hue.

For them the earth to sights gave birth
  The many cannot know ;
All things combine on them to shine,
And rude forms melt into groups divine,
  Where'er their footsteps go.

Tales from the East of cities tell,
Which start to view at the potent spell
  Gained from the wizard's teaching,
Where the dull hind discerns alone
The silent pool, and the desert stone,
  And the dusky heath far-reaching.

And the Muse, I said, had learned to shed
  (As poets oft have shown)
O'er Nature's face a nameless grace
  And a radiance all her own.

But vain is Magic's fabled power,
  And vain the Muse's skill,
To charm the heart in its gloomy hour,
  Or to fix the vagrant will.

But souls, from off whose grosser sight
  The film is cleared away,
Thrive on the pure and strange delight
  Of that bright inward day.

Before their eyes high domes arise,
  With spacious halls within,
To skreen the heat of summer skies,
  Or the storm's tumultuous din.

And there they rove in the balmy grove
   And to fountains clear repair;
Or pace the flower-entwined alcove,
While the plaintive note of the lonely dove
   Floats on the listening air.

So high a call, so rich a prize,
   So blest a lot is thine;
Mayest thou the birthright ne'er despise,
   And ne'er thy hope resign!

So when the great day comes at last,
And life's long infancy is past,
   Thou mayest securely go,
Thine own inheritance to claim,
Pleading the all-prevailing Name
   Thou servedst here below.

OXFORD, *December* 30, 1824.

TO J. C. N.

On her Birthday

I AM a tree, whose spring is o'er,
    Whose summer is not come ;
    My viol must be struck no more,
    My voice of song is dumb.
Flowers deck the spring ; and fruits instead
    Summer's rich hand supplies ;
But fancy's blossoms, they are shed
    Ere years proclaim me wise.—
    Green fruit and faded flower,
    Shrub unfit for lady's bower!

And thou, sweet May, art young and gay,
    Thy life is in its bloom ;
Bright are the hues thy gown display,
    Sense-piercing their perfume,
Taste, genius, fancy, all are thine
    Which nature can bestow ;
Meekness and goodness, plants divine,
    Deep in thy garden grow.—
Hail, dearest, for to-day
Is thine own, my merry May !

Thy sisters, they will join with me
In this my deed of courtesy,
For they have been on former days
Meet subjects of a brother's praise;
And verse has told, by truth inspired,
How much I loved, how much admired.
But thou hast had, my sister fair,
No wreath of song to deck thy hair;
'Tis tardy justice now to bring
This poor but honest offering.

Yet have I chosen happier time
To send to thee, dear May, my rhyme.
Clouds there have been and storms, but they
Had April course, and past away.
Bright Harriet's, gentle Mary's, strain
Was saddened by a recent pain;
But now it moves in different mood,
My verse, the harbinger of good.
Its wings they play, as it skims its way
   From the groves of Rhedycine;
And glancing bright in the clear sun-light,
   Its glorious feathers shine.
A name it knows; but it must wait
E'er it has leave to intimate
   The secret it would tell;
Yet sign and gesture may supply
Some silent hint at victory
   And trial answered well.

"Well done! the prize is won!
"A budding wreath behold!
"Some flowers full grown, some partly blown—
"Last but this fair and favoring sun,
"And all will soon unfold."

  * * * *

... Ah! whence is this? ... Why fails
 my hand,
 Why falters on the ready string? ...
My time of song is past. ... I stand
 'Twixt summer's fruit and flowers of spring.
Rest thou, my lyre, thy day is o'er;
 Not often shall I task thy skill;
And yet thy tones, tho' heard no more,
 On memory's ear will linger still.—
Fleeting pleasures! place give
To works that last and joys that live!

... What, Muse, impatient? nay, but why
That burning cheek, that flashing eye?
For shame! compose with modest care
Thy tresses of disordered hair.
Thy decent vest will start aside;
Its curious flounces, erst thy pride,
Now mark thy perturbation.
Enough! resume thy task begun;
—Thy sister, May, is looking on—
Come, end thy gratulation.

All hail, all hail, my light of May,
    Queen of the early spring !
The wide world's store, I will run it o'er
    For a birthday offering.
Rich to thy soul as the fruitful earth ;
    And as the wild wind free ;
As the sun's ray bright, in the noontide height;
    And pure as the summer sea.
Keen as the lightning on its way,
    When the red tempest lours ;
Yet mild as is the morn of day,
    Fresh banquetted on flowers.
Thy birthday dress be the soft rainbow,
    If mercy pledged the sign ;
And the gracious stars upon thy brow
    As a diadem shall shine.
Farewell, farewell, my merry May,
    Light of the young spring be !
The world's choice store, from its quarters four,
    In blessing I pour,—on thee.

OXFORD, *May* 19, 1826.

TO F. W. N.

ON HIS BIRTHDAY

DEAR Frank, this morn has ushered in
    The manhood of thy days;
A boy no more, thou must begin
    To choose thy future ways;
To brace thy arm, and nerve thy heart,
For maintenance of a noble part.

And thou a voucher fair has[t] given,
    Of what thou wilt atchieve,
Ere age has dimmed thy sun-lit heaven,
    In weary life's chill eve;
Should Sovereign Wisdom in its grace
Vouchsafe to thee so long a race.

My brother, we are link'd with chain
    No time shall e'er destroy;
Together we have been in pain,
    Together now in joy;
For duly I to share may claim
The present brightness of thy name.

My brother, 'tis no recent tie
    Which binds our fates in one ;
E'en from our tender infancy
    The twisted thread was spun ;—
Her deed, who stored in her fond mind
Our forms, by sacred love enshrined.

In her affection all had share,
    All six, she loved them all ;
Yet on her early-chosen Pair
    Did her full favour fall ;
And we became her dearest theme,
Her waking thought, her nightly dream.

Ah ! brother, shall we e'er forget
    Her love, her care, her zeal ?
We cannot pay the countless debt,
    But we must ever feel ;
For thro' her earnestness were shed
Prayer-purchased blessings on our head.

Tho' in the end of days she stood,
    And pain and weakness came,
Her force of thought was unsubdued,
    Her fire of love the same ;
And e'en, when memory fail'd its part,
We still kept lodgment in her heart.

And when her Maker from the thrall
    Of flesh her spirit freed,
No suffering companied the call.
    —In mercy 'twas decreed,—
One moment here, the next she trod
The viewless mansion of her God.

Now then, at length she is at rest,
    And, after many a woe,
Rejoices in that Saviour blest,
    Who was her hope below ;
Kept till the day when He shall own
His saints before His Father's throne.

So it is left for us to prove
    Her prayers were not in vain ;
And that God's grace-according love
    Has fallen as gentle rain,
Which, sent in the due vernal hour,
Tints the young leaf, perfumes the flower.

Dear Frank, we both are summon'd now
    As champions of the Lord ;—
Enrolled am I, and shortly thou
    Must buckle on thy sword ;
A high employ, nor lightly given,
To serve as messengers of heaven !

Deep in my heart that gift I hide ;
    I change it not away,
For patriot-warrior's hour of pride,
    Or statesman's tranquil sway ;
For poet's fire, or pleader's skill
To pierce the soul and tame the will.

O ! may we follow undismayed
    Where'er our God shall call !
And may His Spirit's present aid
    Uphold us lest we fall !
Till in the end of days we stand,
As victors in a deathless land.

STRAND-ON-THE-GREEN, *June* 27, 1826.

NATURE AND ART

For a Lady's Album

"Man goeth forth" with reckless trust
    Upon his wealth of mind,
As if in self a thing of dust
    Creative skill might find ;
He schemes and toils ; stone, wood, and ore
Subject or weapon of his power.

By arch and spire, by tower-girt heights,
    He would his boast fulfil ;
By marble births, and mimic lights,—
    Yet lacks one secret still ;
Where is the master-hand shall give
To breathe, to move, to speak, to live ?

O take away this shade of might,
    The puny toil of man,
And let great Nature in my sight
    Unfold her varied plan ;
I cannot bear those sullen walls,
Those eyeless towers, those tongueless halls.

Art's labour'd toys of highest name
    Are nerveless, cold, and dumb;
And man is fitted but to frame
    A coffin or a tomb;
Well suit, when sense is past away,
Such lifeless works the lifeless clay.

Here let me sit where wooded hills
    Skirt yon far-reaching plain;
While cattle bank its winding rills,
    And suns embrown its grain;
Such prospect is to me right dear,
For freedom, health, and joy are here.

There is a spirit ranging through
    The earth, the stream, the air;
Ten thousand shapes, garbs ever new,
    That restless One doth wear;
In colour, scent, and taste, and sound
The energy of life is found.

The leaves are rustling in the breeze,
    The bird chants forth her song;
From field to brook, o'er heath, o'er trees,
    The sunbeam glides along;
The insect, happy in its hour,
Floats softly by, or sips the flower.

Now dewy rain descends, and now
    Brisk showers the welkin shroud;
I care not, tho' with angry brow
    Frowns the red thunder-cloud;

Let hail-storm pelt, and lightning harm,
'Tis Nature's work, and has its charm.

Ah! lovely Nature! others dwell
    Full favoured in thy court;
I of thy smiles but hear them tell,
    And feed on their report,
Catching what glimpse an Ulcombe yields
To strangers loitering in her fields.

I go where form has ne'er unbent
    The sameness of its sway;
Where iron rule, stern precedent,
    Mistreat the graceful day;
To pine as prisoner in his cell,
And yet be thought to love it well.

Yet so His high dispose has set,
    Who binds on each his part;
Though absent, I may cherish yet
    An Ulcombe of the heart;
Calm verdant hope divinely given,
And suns of peace, and scenes of heaven;—

—A soul prepared His will to meet,
    Full fix'd His work to do;
Not laboured into sudden heat,
    But inly born anew.—
So living Nature, not dull Art,
Shall plan my ways and rule my heart.

    ULCOMBE, *September*, 1826.

INTRODUCTION

To my Sisters' Album

I AM a harp of many chords, and each
   Strung by a separate hand;—most musical
My notes, discoursing with the mental sense,
Not the outward ear. Try them, for they bespeak
Mild wisdom, graceful wit, and high-wrought taste,
Fancy, and hope, and decent gaiety.
   Come, add a string to my assort of sounds;
Widen the compass of my harmony;
And join thyself in fellowship of name
With those whose courteous labour and fair gifts
Have given me voice, and made me what I am.

BRIGHTON, *April*, 1827.

SNAPDRAGON

A Riddle for a Lady's Flower Book

I AM rooted in the wall
Of buttressed tower or ancient hall;
Mortared in an art-wrought bed,
Cased in cement, cramped with lead;
Of a living stock alone
Brother of the lifeless stone.

Else unprized, I have my worth
On the spot that gives me birth;
Nature's vast and varied field
Braver flowers than me will yield,
Bold in form and rich in hue,
Children of a purer dew;
Smiling lips and winning eyes
Meet for earthly paradise.
Choice are such,—and yet thou knowest
Highest he whose lot is lowest.
They, proud hearts, a home reject
Framed by human architect;
Humble I—can bear to dwell
Near the pale recluse's cell,

And I spread my crimson bloom,
Mingled with the cloister's gloom. *

Life's gay gifts and honors rare,
Flowers of favor win and wear!
Rose of beauty, be the queen
In pleasure's ring and festive scene.
Ivy, venturous plant, ascend
Where lordly oaks a bold stair lend.
Vaunt, fair lily, stately dame,
Pride of birth and pomp of name.
Miser crocus, starved with cold,
Hide in earth thy timid gold.
Travell'd dahlia, thine the boast
Of knowledge brought from foreign coast.
Pleasure, wealth, birth, knowledge, power,
These have each an emblem flower;
So for me alone remains
Lowly thought and cheerful pains.

Be it mine to set restraint
On roving wish and selfish plaint;
And for man's drear haunts to leave
Dewy morn and balmy eve.
Be it mine the barren stone
To deck with green life not its own,

---

* Snapdragon fringed the wall opposite the rooms in which I spent my first solitary three weeks at College in June, 1817.

So to soften and to grace
Of human works the rugged face.
Mine, the Unseen to display
Where crowds choke up truth's languid ray,
Where life's busy arts combine
To shut out the Hand Divine.

Ah! no more a scentless flower,
By approving heaven's high power,
Suddenly my leaves exhale
Fragrance of the Syrian gale.
Ah! 'tis timely comfort given
By the answering breath of Heaven!
May it be! then well might I
In College cloister live and die.

ULCOMBE, *October 2, 1827.*

TIME ENTRANCED

For my Sisters' Album

"Felix, qui potuit rerum cognoscere causas,
Atque metus omnes, et inexorabile fatum
Subjecit pedibus, strepitumque Acherontis avari!"

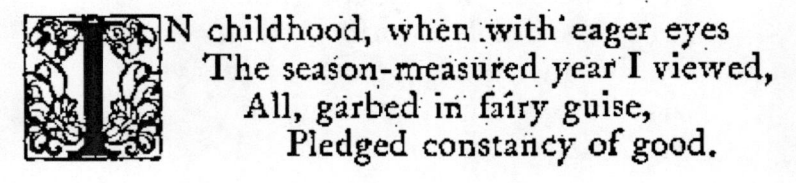

IN childhood, when with eager eyes
   The season-measured year I viewed,
     All, garbed in fairy guise,
       Pledged constancy of good.

Spring sang of heaven; the summer flowers
   Let me gaze on, and did not fade;
     Even suns o'er autumn's bowers
       Heard my strong wish, and stayed.

They came and went, the short-lived four,
   Yet, as their varying dance they wove,
     To my young heart each bore
       Its own sure claim of love.

Far different now;—the whirling year
   Vainly my dizzy eyes pursue;
     And its fair tints appear
       All blent in one dusk hue.

Why dwell on rich autumnal lights,
   Spring-time, or winter's social ring?
     Long days are fire-side nights,
        Brown autumn is fresh spring.

Then what this world to thee, my heart?
   Its gifts nor feed thee nor can bless.
     Thou hast no owner's part
        In all its fleetingness.

The flame, the storm, the quaking ground,
   Earth's joy, earth's terror, nought is thine,
     Thou must but hear the sound
        Of the still voice divine.

O princely lot! O blissful art!
   E'en while by sense of change opprest,
     Thus to forecast in heart
        Heaven's age of fearless rest.

HIGHWOOD, *October*, 1827.

[This poem, to which no title was assigned in the "Lyra Apostolica," bore, in the 1853 volume, the title "Changes," and was eventually styled "The Trance of Time." The quotation at the head, from the Georgics, gave place in 1853 to the text "cum essem parvulus, sapiebam ut parvulus; quando factus sum vir, evacuavi quae erant parvuli," but the author eventually reverted to the Virgilian quotation.]

COMFORT IN BEREAVEMENT

DEATH was full urgent with thee,
    Sister dear,
      And startling in his speed;
    —Brief pain, then languor till thy
    end came near—
Such was the path decreed,
    The hurried road
To lead thy soul from earth to thy own God's abode.

Death wrought with thee, sweet girl, impatiently:—
    Yet merciful the haste
That baffles sickness;—dearest, thou didst die,
    Thou wast not made to taste
      Death's bitterness,
Decline's slow-wasting charm, or fever's fierce distress.

Death came unheralded:—but it was well;
    For so thy Savior bore
Kind witness, thou wast meet at once to dwell
    On His eternal shore;
      All warning spared,
For none He gives where hearts are for prompt change prepared.

Death wrought in mystery; both complaint
    and cure
        To human skill unknown :—
God put aside all means, to make us sure
        It was His deed alone ;
            Lest we should lay
Reproach on our poor selves, that thou wast
    caught away.

Death urged as scant of time :—lest, Sister
    dear,
        We many a lingering day
Had sicken'd with alternate hope and fear,
        The ague of delay ;
            Watching each spark
Of promise quenched in turn, till all our sky
    was dark.

Death came and went :—that so thy image
    might
        Within our fond hearts glow,
Associate with such pleasant thoughts and
    bright,
        As health and peace bestow ;
            No theme of sorrow
From thy soft comforting name ought like
    itself can borrow.

Joy of sad hearts, and light of downcast eyes !
        Dearest thou art enshrined

In all thy fragrance in our memories;
    For we must ever find
        Bare thought of thee
Kindle our sluggish souls, from care and gloom
    set free.

OXFORD, *April*, 1828.

A PICTURE

"The maiden is not dead, but sleepeth."

SHE is not lost;—still in our sight
    That dearest saint shall live,
In form as true, in tints as bright,
    As breath and health could give.

Still, still is ours the modest eye;
    The smile unwrought by art;
The glance that shot so piercingly
    Affection's keenest dart;

The thrilling voice, I ne'er could hear
    But felt a joy and pain;—
A pride that she was ours, a fear
    Ours she might not remain;

Whether the page divine called forth
    Its clear, sweet, tranquil tone,
Or cheerful hymn, or seemly mirth
    In sprightlier measure shown;

The meek inquiry on that face,
    Musing on wonders found,
As 'mid dim paths she sought to trace
    The truth on sacred ground;

The thankful sigh we witnessed rise,
　　When ought her doubts removed,
Full set the explaining voice to prize
　　Admiring while she loved;

The pensive brow, the world might see
　　When she in crowds was found;
The burst of heart, the o'erflowing glee
　　When only friends were round;

Hope's warmth of promise, prompt to fill
　　The thoughts with good in store,
Matched with content's deep stream, which still
　　Flowed on, when hope was o'er;

That peace, which with its own bright day
　　Made cheapest sights shine fair;
That purest grace, which track'd its way
　　Safe from ought earthly there.—

Such was she in the sudden hour
　　That brought her Maker's call,—
Proving her heart's self-mastering power
　　Blithely to part with all,

Her eye e'er loved, her hands e'er pressed
　　With true affection's glow,
The voice of friends, all pleasures best
　　All dearest thoughts below.

From friend-lit hearth, from social board,
    All duteously she rose ;
For weal or suffering, on His word
    Faith found assured repose.

Gay dress, bright trinkets, braided hair,
    She put them all aside,—
E'en nature's garb of beauty rare
    'Seemed not heaven's chosen bride,—

Then waited for the solemn spell,
    Her tranced soul to steep
In blissful dreams of breaking well
    That brief-enduring sleep.

Such was she then ; and such she is
    Shrined in each mourner's breast ;
Such shall she be, and more than this
    In promised glory blest ;

When in due lines her Savior dear
    His scattered saints shall range,
And knit in love souls parted here,
    Where cloud is none, nor change.

OXFORD, *August*, 1828.

REVERIE ON A JOURNEY

To my Mother

THE coachman was seated, with ribbons
    in hand,
    And they cried me to haste in a
    tone of command;
The porter I paid; and plunged thro' the
    coach door
In a cold bath of faces I ne'er saw before.

A dip in the morning will brace, if you please;
But to dawdle six hours, is to stay till you
    freeze.
And the sluggard's down bed has its charms
    for another,
But these huge living bolsters press close till
    they smother.

Well, in bath or in bed, nestled up, or plunged
    deep,
I will dive from myself, or I'll dream as I sleep.
From all notice of sight my mind's tablet I'll
    clear,
The *then* shall be *now*, and the *there* shall be
    here.

When once a man gains philosophical views,
Between coach and coach there is little to
 choose ;
And oft have I proved, seen in truth's purest
 beam,
That space is a name, and that time is a dream.

This dark stifling closet expands on my eyes !
Its sides they recede, and its windows they rise !
Its seats become chairs ; and a table is made
Of the shawls and great coats, on our knees
 that are laid !

That gentleman opposite melts into you,
The fat dame rolls into Jemima and Lou ;
Two Harriets arise where there nobody sat,—
I am brother to this, and I'm cousin to that.

We travel with speed ! 'tis the sun as it goes ;
—'Twas breakfast,—'tis noon,—now 'tis lunch,
 I suppose.
(That child is Tinpot,)—who's for walking
 to-day ?
The large woman snores ! so time passes away.

'Tis dinner,—'tis tea,—hear the coach's dull
 drone !
'Tis the reading that humdrums its equable tone.
The wheels, how they rumble ! that rumbling
 must be
Beethoven's Quintette, or Mynheer's Zuyderzee.

We speed it! we speed it! the town-fogs are
    rising!
Our love-lighted converse the night is sur-
    prising;
The stones, how they clatter! the crowds, how
    they hum!
Our journey is o'er, chamber-candles are come.

BRIGHTON COACH, *January* 23, 1829.

MY LADY NATURE AND HER DAUGHTERS

Given to my Sisters

LADIES, well I deem, delight
    In comely tire to move;
    Soft, and delicate, and bright,
    Are the robes they love.
Silks, where hues alternate play,
Shawls, and scarfs, and mantles gay,
Gold, and gems, and crisped hair,
Fling their light o'er lady fair.
'Tis not waste, or sinful pride,
—Name them not, nor fault beside,—
But her very cheerfulness
Prompts and weaves the curious dress;
While her holy * thoughts still roam
Mid birth-friends and scenes of home.
Pleased to please whose praise is dear,
Glitters she? she glitters there;—
And she has a pattern found her
In Nature's glowing world around her.

---

* *Vide* 1 Pet. iii. 5; and cf. Gen. xxiv. 22, 28-30.

Nature loves, as lady bright,
    In gayest guise to shine,
All forms of grace, all tints of light,
    Fringe her robe divine.
Sun-lit heaven, and rain-bow cloud,
Changeful main, and mountain proud.
Branching tree, and meadow green,
All are deck'd in broidered sheen.
Not a bird on bough-propp'd tower,
Insect slim, nor tiny flower.
Stone, nor spar, nor shell of sea,
But is fair in its degree.
'Tis not pride, this vaunt of beauty;
Well she 'quits her trust of duty;
And, amid her gorgeous state,
Bright, and bland, and delicate,
Ever beaming from her face
Praise of a Father's love we trace.

Ladies, shrinking from the view
    Of the prying day,
In tranquil diligence pursue
    Their heaven-appointed way.
Noiseless duties, silent cares,
Mercies lighting unawares,
Modest influence working good,
Gifts, by the keen heart understood,
Such as viewless spirits might give,
These they love, in these they live.—
Mighty Nature speeds her through
Her daily toils in silence too.

Calmly rolls her giant spheres,
Sheds by stealth her dew's kind tears;
Cheating sage's vexed pursuit,
Churns the sap, matures the fruit,
And, her deft hand still concealing,
Kindles motion, life, and feeling.

Ladies love to laugh and sing,
    To rouse the chord's full sound,
Or to join the festive ring
    Where dancers gather round.
Not a sight so fair on earth,
As a lady's graceful mirth;
Not a sound so chasing pain,
As a lady's thrilling strain.—
Nor is Nature left behind
In her lighter moods of mind;
Calm her duties to fulfil,
In her glee a prattler still.
Bird and beast of every sort
Hath its antic and its sport;
Chattering brook, and dancing gnat,
Subtle cry of evening bat,
Moss uncouth, and twigs grotesque,
These are Nature's picturesque.

Where the birth of Poesy?
    Its fancy and its fire?
Nature's earth, and sea, and sky,
    Fervid thoughts inspire.

Where do wealth and power find rest,
When hopes have failed, and toil opprest?
Parks, and lawns, and deer, and trees,
Nature's work, restore them ease.—
Few are gifted, few are great!
Where shall guileless souls retreat,
Unennobled, unrefined,
From the rude world and unkind?
Who shall friend their lowly lot?
High-born Nature answers not.
Leave her in her star-gemmed dome,
Seek we lady-lighted home.
Nature mid the spheres has sway,
Ladies rule where hearts obey.

OXFORD, *February*, 1829.

OPUSCULUM

To H. F.

For a very Small Album

[N.B.—These lines are jointed in five, according to a new patent, and folded up for easy packing.]

1. FAIR Cousin, thy page
is small to encage
the vast thoughts which
engage
the mind of a sage,
such as I am;

2. 'Twere in teaspoon to take
the whole Genevese lake,
or a lap-dog to make
the white Elephant sac-
-red in Siam.

3. Yet inadequate tho'
to the terms strange and so-
-lemn that figure in po-
-lysyllabical row
in a treatise;

4. Still, true words and plain,
of the heart, not the brain,
in affectionate strain,
this book to contain
very meet is.

5. So I promise to be
a good Cousin to thee,
and to keep safe the se-
cret I heard, although e-
-v'ry one know it ;

6. With a lyrical air
my kind thoughts I would dare,
my joy, and whate'er
beseems the news, were
I a poet.

BRIGHTON, *April*, 1829.

A VOICE FROM AFAR

WEEP not for me :—
    Be blithe as wont, nor tinge with gloom
    The stream of love that circles home,
        Light hearts and free !
Joy in the gifts heaven's bounty lends ;
  Nor miss my face, dear friends !

    I still am near ;—
Watching the smiles I prized on earth,
Your converse mild, your blameless mirth ;
    Now too I hear
Of whispered sounds the tale complete,
  Low prayers, and musings sweet.

    A sea before
The Throne is spread :—its pure still glass
Pictures all earth-scenes as they pass.
    We, on its shore,
Share, in the bosom of our rest,
  God's knowledge, and are blest.

HORSEPATH, *September* 29, 1829.

THE HIDDEN ONES

For a Lady

"Your life is hid with Christ in God."

HID are the saints of God ;—
Uncertified by high angelic sign ;
Nor raiment soft, nor empire's golden
  rod
    Marks them divine.
Theirs but the unbought air, earth's parent sod
  And the sun's smile benign ;—
Christ rears His throne within the secret heart,
  From the haughty world apart.

They gleam amid the night,
Chill sluggish mists stifling the heavenly ray ;
Fame chants the while,—old history trims his
  light,
    Aping the day ;
In vain ! staid look, loud voice, and reason's
  might
    Forcing its learned way,
Blind characters ! these aid us not to trace
  Christ and His princely race.

  Yet not all-hid from those
Who watch to see ;—'neath their dull guise of
    earth,
Bright bursting gleams unwittingly disclose
    Their heaven-wrought birth.
Meekness, love, patience, faith's serene repose ;
  And the soul's tutor'd mirth,
Bidding the slow heart dance, to prove her
    power
  O'er self in its proud hour.

  These are the chosen few,
The remnant fruit of largely scatter'd grace,
God sows in waste, to reap whom He foreknew
  Of man's cold race ;
Counting on wills perverse, in His clear view
  Of boundless time and space,
He waits, by scant return for treasures given,
  To fill the thrones of heaven.

  Lord ! who can trace but Thou
The strife obscure, 'twixt sin's soul-thralling spell
And Thy sharp Spirit, now quench'd, reviving
    now ?
  Or who can tell,
Why pardon's seal stands sure on David's brow,
  Why Saul and Demas fell ?
Oh ! lest our frail hearts in the annealing break,
  Help, for Thy mercy's sake !

HORSEPATH, *September*, 1829.

A THANKSGIVING

"Thou in faithfulness hast afflicted me."

LORD, in this dust Thy sovereign voice
 First quicken'd love divine;
I am all Thine,—Thy care and
 choice,
 My very praise is Thine.

I praise Thee, while Thy providence
 In childhood frail I trace,
For blessings given, ere dawning sense
 Could seek or scan Thy grace;

Blessings in boyhood's marvelling hour,
 Bright dreams, and fancyings strange;
Blessings, when reason's awful power
 Gave thought a bolder range;

Blessings of friends, which to my door
 Unask'd, unhoped, have come;
And, choicer still, a countless store
 Of eager smiles at home.

Yet, Lord, in memory's fondest place
    I shrine those seasons sad,
When, looking up, I saw Thy face
    In kind austereness clad.

I would not miss one sigh or tear,
    Heart-pang, or throbbing brow;
Sweet was the chastisement severe,
    And sweet its memory now.

Yes! let the fragrant scars abide,
    Grace-tokens in Thy stead,
Faint shadows of the spear-pierced side
    And thorn-encompass'd head.

And such Thy loving force be still,
    Mid life's fierce shifting fray,
Shaping to truth self's froward will
    Along Thy narrow way.

Deny me wealth; far, far remove
    The lure of power or name;
Hope thrives in straits, in weakness love,
    And faith in this world's shame.

OXFORD, *October*, 1829.

MONKS

To L. E. F.

For a very Small Album

[N.B.—These lines are put on hinges on a rival patent to the former, so as to fold up and pack closely, if required.]

DEAR Louisa, . . why
    Ask for verses, . . when a poet's . .
      fount of song is . . dry?
    Or, if ought be . . there,
Harsh and chill, it . . ill may bathe the . .
      hand of lady . . fair.
    Who can . . perfumed waters . . bring
      From a convent . . spring?

    " Monks in the olden . . time,
" They were rhymsters?"— . . I will own
      it, . . but in latin . . rhyme.
    Monks in the days of . . old
Lived in secret, . . in the church's . . kindly
      sheltering . . fold;
    No bland . . meditators . . they
      Of a courtly . . lay.

"They had visions . . bright?"—
Well I wot it, . . yet not sent in . . slumbers
    soft and . . light.
    No! a lesson . . stern
First by vigils, . . fast, and penance, . . 'twas
    their choice to . . learn.
    This their . . soul-ennobling . . gain,
    Joys wrought out by . . pain.

    "When from home they . . stirred
"Sweet their voices?"— . . still, a blessing
    . . closed their merriest . . word;
    And their gayest . . smile
Told of musings . . solitary, . . and the
    hallowed . . aisle.
    "Songsters?"— . . hark! they answer!
    . . round
    Plaintive chantings . . sound!"

    Grey his cowled . . vest,
Whose strong heart has . . pledged his service
    . . to the cloister . . blest.
    Duly garbed is . . he,
As the frost-work . . decks the branches . .
    of yon stately . . tree.
    'Tis a . . danger-thwarting . . spell,
    And it fits me . . well!

OXFORD, *December*, 1829.

EPIPHANY-EVE:

A Birthday Offering

"God said, Let there be light: and there was light."
"Awake thou that sleepest, and arise from the dead; and Christ shall give thee light!"

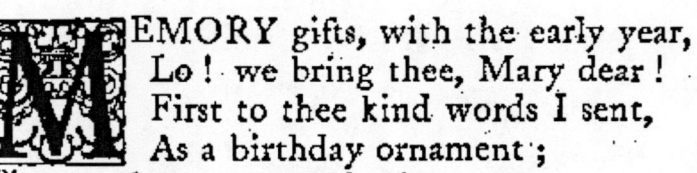

MEMORY gifts, with the early year,
Lo! we bring thee, Mary dear!
First to thee kind words I sent,
As a birthday ornament;
First to thee my verse is given
Hymning thy second birth in heaven.
Christmas snow, for maiden's bloom
Blenched in winter's sudden tomb;
Christmas berries, His red token,
Who that grave's stern seal hath broken;
These to thee the thoughtful heart,
Symbol-offerings, set apart.

'Twas a fast, that Eve of sorrow,
Herald veiled of glorious morrow.
Speechless we sat; and watched, to know
How it would be;—but time moved slow
Along that day of sacred woe.

... A pause ... then faith in mystery
  viewed
Christ's Epiphany renewed.

Dearest, gentlest, purest, fairest!
Strange half-being now thou sharest;
Wrapt around in peaceful bed
Conscience-whispered hope hath spread,
Mid those other gems, that shine
Paradised in the inmost shrine.
There thou liest, and in thy slumber
Times and changes thou dost number;
Deeds and joys of earth o'er summing
Visioning forth the glories coming
When thy soul shall re-awaken
Those soft looks and form forsaken.

Thinkest of us, dearest, ever?
Ah! so be it nought can sever
Spirit and life, the past and present,
Still we yield thee musings pleasant.
—God above, and we below;—
So thought ranges, to and fro.
We at times; but He always
Prompts the full chant of thy praise,
He, in sooth, by tutorings mild,
From the rude clay shaped His child,
Fiery trial, anguish chill,
Served not here His secret will;
But His love in whispers drew,
And thy vigorous soul so grew,

That the work in haste was done,
Grace and nature blent in one.—
Harmless this, and not unmeet,
To kiss the dear prints of thy feet,
Tracing thus the narrow road
Saints must tread, and Christ has trod.

Loveliest, meekest, blithest, kindest!
Lead! we seek the home thou findest!
Though thy name to us most dear,
Go! we would not have thee here.
Lead, a guiding beacon bright
To travellers on the Eve of Light.
Welcome aye thy Star before us,
Bring it grief or gladness o'er us;—
Keen regret and tearful yearning,
Whiles unfelt, and whiles returning;—
Or more gracious thoughts abiding,
Fever-quelling, sorrow-chiding;—
Or, when day-light blessings fail,
Transport fresh as spice-fraught gale,
Sparks from thee, which oft have lighted
Weary heart and hope benighted.

I this monument would raise,
Sacred from the public gaze.
Few will see it;—few e'er knew thee;
But their beating hearts pursue thee,—
And their eyes fond thoughts betoken,
Tho' thy name be seldom spoken.

Pass on, stranger, and despise it !
These will read, and these will prize it.

OXFORD, *January* 5, 1829.

Manibus date lilia plenis ;
Purpureos spargam flores, animamque nepotis
His saltem accumulem donis, et fungar inani
Munere.

Παύετε θρήνων, παῖδες· ἐν οἷς γὰρ
χάρις ἡ χθονία νῦν ἀπόκειται,
πενθεῖν οὐ χρή· νέμεσις γάρ.

THE WINTER FLOWER

(For Music)

BLOOM, beloved Flower!—
 Unknown;—'tis no matter.
Courts glitter brief hour,
Crowds can but flatter.

Plants in the garden
 See best the Sun's glory;
They lose the green sward in
 A conservatory.

—PRIZED WHERE'ER KNOWN.—
Sure this is a blessing,
Outrings the loud tone
 Of the dull world's caressing.

OXFORD, *December* 30, 1830.

KIND REMEMBRANCES

To A. M. F.

(From an Unknown Friend)

'TIS long, dear Annie, since we met,
    Yet deem not that my heart,
For all that absence, can forget
    A kinsman's pious part.

How oft on thee, a sufferer mild,
    My kindly thoughts I turn,
He knows, upon whose altar piled
    The prayers of suppliants burn.

I love thy name, admiring all
    Thy sacred heaven-sent pain;
I love it, for it seems to call
    The Lost to earth again.

Can I forget, She to thy need
    Her ministry supplied,
Who now, from mortal duty freed,
    Serves at the Virgin's side?

What wouldest thou more ? Upon thy head
 A two-fold grace is pour'd ;—
Both in thyself, and for the dead,
 A witness of thy Lord !

OXFORD, *March*, 1831.

STRAY SEEDS OF POESY

For a Lady's Album

Igneus est ollis vigor, et cœlestis origo
Seminibus.

COULD I hit on a theme
    To fashion my verse on,
Not long would I seem
    A lack-courtesy person.
But I have not the skill,
    Nor talisman strong,
To summon at will
    The Spirit of song.—
Bright thoughts are roaming
    Unseen in the air;
Like comets, their coming
    Is sudden and rare.
They strike, and they enter,
    And light up the brain,
Which thrills to its centre
    With rapturous pain.
Where the chance-seed
    Is piously nursed,
Brighter succeed
    In the path of the first.—

  One sighs to the Muse,
   One speaks to his heart,
  One sips the night-dews
   Which moon-beams impart.
  All this is a fiction ;
   I never could find
  A suitable friction
   To frenzy my mind.
  What use are empirics?
   No gas on their shelf
  Can make one spout lyrics
   In spite of oneself!

DARTINGTON, *July* 18; 1831.

THE PILGRIM

THERE strayed awhile, amid the woods
    of Dart,
  One who could love them, but who
    durst not love.
A vow had bound him, ne'er to give his heart
  To streamlet bright, or soft secluded grove.
  'Twas a hard humbling task, onwards to
    move
His easy-captured eyes from each fair spot,
  With unattached and lonely step to rove
O'er happy meads, which soon its print forgot;—
Yet kept he safe his pledge, prizing his pilgrim-
    lot.

DARTINGTON, *July* 21, 1831.

The following dedication, printed in capitals, appears at the end of " Memorials of the Past":—

TO MY DEAREST MOTHER,

TO MY SWEET SISTERS,

HARRIET AND JEMIMA,

WHO REMAIN,

THESE ;—

THE SHADOWS OF PAST BLESSINGS,

WHICH SHALL ONE DAY RETURN

MORE GLORIOUS

TO ABIDE WITH US FOR EVER.

J. H. N.

Jan. 25, 1832.

From LYRA APOSTOLICA

[1836]

LYRA / APOSTOLICA. /

Γνοῖεν δ', ὡς δὴ δῆρον ἐγὼ πολέμοιο πέπαυμαι.

Derby : / Henry Mozley and Sons, / and J. G. and F. Rivington, / St. Paul's Church Yard, and Waterloo Place, London. / 1836. /

THE "Lyra Apostolica" was largely the work of Newman, but contained also contributions from John Keble, Isaac Williams, Richard Hurrell Froude, J. W. Bowden, and Robert Isaac Wilberforce. Naturally, only the contributions of Newman appear in the present volume.

From LYRA APOSTOLICA

HOME

WHERE'ER I roam in this fair English
        land,
    The vision of a temple meets my
        eyes :
Modest without ; within, all glorious rise
Its love-enclustered columns, and expand
Their slender arms. Like olive-plants they
        stand,
    Each answering each, in home's soft sympathies,
    Sisters and brothers. At the Altar sighs
Parental fondness, and with anxious hand
Tenders its offering of young vows and prayers.
The same and not the same, go where I will,
The vision beams ! ten thousand shrines, all one.
Dear fertile soil ! what foreign culture bears
Such fruit ? And I through distant climes
        may run
My weary round, yet miss thy likeness still.

ERE yet I left home's youthful shrine,
    My heart and hope were stored
Where first I caught the rays divine,
    And drank the Eternal Word.

I went afar; the world unrolled
    Her many-pictured page;
I stored the marvels which she told,
    And trusted to her gage.

Her pleasures quaff'd, I sought awhile
    The scenes I priz'd before:
But parent's praise and sisters' smile
    Stirred my cold heart no more.

So ever sear, so ever cloy,
    Earth's favours as they fade,
Since Adam lost for one fierce joy
    His Eden's sacred shade.

My home is now a thousand mile away ;
　Yet in my thoughts its every image fair
Rises as keen, as I still lingered there,
And, turning me, could all I loved survey.
And so upon Death's unaverted day,
　As I speed upward, I shall on me bear,
　And in no breathless whirl, the things that were,
And duties given, and ends I did obey.
And, when at length I reach the Throne of Power,
Ah ! still unscared, I shall in fulness see
The vision of my past innumerous deeds,
My deep heart-courses, and their motive-seeds,
So to gaze on till the red dooming hour.
Lord ! in that strait, the Judge ! remember me !

HOW can I keep my Christmas feast
  In its due festive show,
Reft of the sight of the High Priest
  From whom its glories flow?

I hear the tuneful bells around,
  The blessed towers I see;
A stranger on a foreign ground,
  They peal a fast for me.

O Britons! now so brave and high,
  How will ye weep the day
When Christ in judgment passes by,
  And calls the Bride away!

Your Christmas then will lose its mirth,
  Your Easter lose its bloom :—
Abroad, a scene of strife and dearth;
  Within, a cheerless home!

BANISHED the House of sacred rest,
   Amid a thoughtless throng,
At length I heard its creed confessed,
   And knelt the Saints among.

Artless his strain and unadorned,
   Who spoke Christ's message there ;
But what at home I might have scorned,
   Now charmed my famished ear.

Lord, grant me this abiding grace,
   Thy Word and Sons to know,
To pierce the veil on Moses' face,
   Although his speech be slow !

SHAME

I BEAR upon my brow the sign
    Of sorrow and of pain :
Alas ! no hopeful cross is mine,
    It is the mark of Cain.

The course of passion, and the fret
    Of godless hope and fear—
Toil, care, and guilt—their hues have set,
    And fixed that sternness there.

Saviour ! wash out the imprinted shame ;
    That I no more may pine,
Sin's martyr, though not meet to claim
    Thy cross, a Saint of Thine.

BONDAGE

OH, prophet, tell me not of peace,
    Or Christ's all-loving deeds;
Death only can from sin release,
    And death to judgment leads.

Thou from thy birth hast set thy face
    Towards thy Redeemer Lord,
To tend and deck His holy place,
    And note His secret word.

I ne'er shall reach Heaven's glorious path;
    Yet haply tears may stay
The purpose of His instant wrath,
    And slake the fiery day.

Then plead for me, thou blessed saint,
    While I in haste begin,
All man e'er guessed of work or plaint
    To wash away my sin.

TERROR

FATHER, list a sinner's call!
  Fain would I hide from man my fall—
  But I must speak, or faint—
I cannot wear guilt's silent thrall:
  Cleanse me, kind Saint!

"Sinner ne'er blunted yet sin's goad;
Speed thee, my son, a safer road,
  And sue His pardoning smile
Who walked woe's depths, bearing man's load
  Of guilt the while."

Yet raise a mitigating hand,
And minister some potion bland,
  Some present fever-stay!
Lest one for whom His work was planned
  Die of dismay.

"Peace cannot be, hope must be thine;
I can but lift the Mercy-sign.
  This wouldst thou? It shall be!
Kneel down, and take the word divine,
  ABSOLVO TE."

RESTLESSNESS

ONCE, as I brooded o'er my guilty state,
   A fever seized me, duties to devise
   To buy me interest in my Saviour's
     eyes :
Not that His love I would extenuate,
But scourge and penance, and perverse self-hate,
   Or gift of cost, served by an artifice
   To quell my restless thoughts and envious sighs
And doubts, which fain heaven's peace would
    antedate.
Thus, as I tossed, He said :—" Even holiest
    deeds
Shroud not the soul from God, nor soothe its
    needs ;
Deny thee thine own fears, and wait the end ; "
Stern lesson ! Let me con it day by day,
And learn to kneel before the Omniscient Ray,
Nor shrink, while Truth's avenging shafts
    descend !

THE PAINS OF MEMORY

WHAT time my heart unfolded its fresh
    leaves,
    In spring-time gay, and scatter'd
    flowers around,
A whisper warned of earth's unhealthy
    ground,
And all that there faith's light and pureness
    grieves ;
    Sun's ray and canker-worm,
    And sudden-whelming storm :—
But, ah! my self-will smiled, nor recked the
    gracious sound.

So now defilement dims life's morning springs ;
    I cannot hear an early-cherished strain,
    But first a joy, and then it brings a pain—
Fear, and self-hate, and vain remorseful stings :
    Tears lull my grief to rest,
    Not without hope, this breast
May one day lose its load, and youth yet bloom
    again.

DREAMS

OH! miserable power
   To dreams allowed, to raise the
      guilty past,
   And back awhile the illumined spirit
      to cast
   On its youth's twilight hour:—
In mockery guiling it to act again
The revel or the scoff in Satan's frantic train!

   Nay, hush thee, angry heart!
An Angel's grief ill fits a penitent;
Welcome the thorn—it is divinely sent,
   And with its wholesome smart
Shall pierce thee in thy virtue's home serene,
And warn thee what thou art, and whence thy
      wealth has been.

CONFESSION

MY smile is bright, my glance is free,
    My voice is calm and clear;
Dear friend, I seem a type to thee
    Of holy love and fear.

But I am scanned by eyes unseen,
    And these no saint surround;
They mete what is by what has been,
    And joy the lost is found.

Erst my good Angel shrank to see
    My thoughts and ways of ill;
And now he scarce dare gaze on me,
    Scar-seamed and crippled still.

AWE

I BOW at Jesus' Name, for 'tis the Sign
    Of awful mercy towards a guilty
        line.—
Of shameful ancestry, in birth defiled,
        And upwards from a child
Full of unlovely thoughts and rebel aims,
        As hastening judgment flames,
How can I lightly view my Means of life?—
The Just assailing sin, and death-strained in
    the strife!

And so, albeit His woe is our release,
Thought of that woe aye dims our earthly
    peace;
The Life is hidden in a Fount of Blood!—
        And this is tidings good,
But in the Angel's reckoning, and to those
        Who Angel-wise have chose
And kept, like Paul, a virgin course, content
        To go where Jesus went;
But for the many laden with the spot
And earthly taint of sin, 'tis written, "Touch
    Me not."

THE CROSS OF CHRIST

"Ad omnem progressum atque promotum, ad omnem aditum et exitum, ad vestitum ad calciatum, ad lavacra, ad mensas, ad lumina, ad cubilia, ad sedilia, quacunque nos conversatio exercet, frontem Crucis signaculo terimus."—Tertull. de Corona, § 3.

WHENE'ER across this sinful flesh of mine
    I draw the Holy Sign,
All good thoughts stir within me, and collect
    Their slumbering strength divine :
Till there springs up that hope of God's elect,
    My faith shall ne'er be wrecked.

And who shall say, but hateful spirits around,
    For their brief hour unbound,
Shudder to see, and wail their overthrow?
    While on far heathen ground
Some lonely Saint hails the fresh odour, though
    Its source we cannot know.

DAVID AND JONATHAN

"Thy love to me was wonderful, passing the love
of women."

HEART of fire ! misjudged by wilful
man,
Thou flower of Jesse's race !
What woe was thine, when thou and
Jonathan
Last greeted face to face !
He doomed to die, thou on us to impress
The portent of a blood-stained holiness.

Yet it was well :—for so, mid cares of rule
And crime's encircling tide,
A spell was o'er thee, zealous one, to cool
Earth-joy and kingly pride ;
With battle scene and pageant, prompt to blend
The pale calm spectre of a blameless friend.

Ah ! had he lived, before thy throne to stand,
Thy spirit keen and high,
Sure it had snapped in twain love's slender band,
So dear in memory ;
Paul's strife unblest * its serious lesson gives,
He bides with us who dies, he is but lost who
lives.

---

* Acts xv. 39.

"Blessed be ye poor."

I HAVE been honoured and obeyed,
   I have met scorn and slight;
And my heart loves earth's sober shade
   More than her laughing light.

For what is rule but a sad weight
   Of duty and a snare?
What meanness, but with happier fate
   The Saviour's Cross to share?

This my hid choice, though not from heaven,
   Moves on the heavenward line;
Cleanse it, good Lord, from sinful leaven,
   And make it simply Thine.

MOSES

MOSES, the patriot fierce, became
    The meekest man on earth,
To show us how love's quicken-
    ing flame
    Can give our souls new birth.

Moses, the man of meekest heart,
    Lost Canaan by self-will,
To show where grace has done its part,
    How sin defiles us still.

Thou who hast taught me in Thy fear,
    Yet seest me frail at best,
O grant me loss with Moses here,
    To gain his future rest!

"And we indeed justly; for we receive the due
	reward of our deeds."

MORTAL! if e'er thy spirits faint,
    By grief or pain opprest,
    Seek not vain hope, or sour complaint,
    To cheer or ease thy breast;

But view thy bitterest pangs as sent
    A shadow of that doom,
Which is thy soul's just punishment
    In its own guilt's true home.

Be thine own judge: hate thy proud heart;
    And while the sad drops flow,
E'en let thy will attend the smart,
    And sanctify thy woe.

DAVID NUMBERING THE PEOPLE

"I am in a great strait: let me fall now into the hand of the Lord."

IF e'er I fall beneath Thy rod,
    As through life's snares I go,
Save me from David's lot, O God!
    And choose Thyself the woe.

How should I face Thy plagues?—which scare,
    And haunt, and stun, until
The heart or sinks in mute despair,
    Or names a random ill.

If else . . . then guide in David's path,
    Who chose the holier pain;
Satan and man and tools of wrath,
    An Angel's scourge is gain.

ABRAHAM

THE better portion didst thou choose, Great Heart,
   Thy God's first choice, and pledge of Gentile-grace!
Faith's truest type, he with unruffled face
Bore the world's smile, and bade her slaves depart;
Whether, a trader, with no trader's art,
   He buys in Canaan his first resting-place,—
   Or freely yields rich Siddim's ample space,—
Or braves the rescue and the battle's smart,
Yet scorns the heathen gifts of those he saved.
O happy in their soul's high solitude,
Who commune thus with God and not with earth!
Amid the scoffings of the wealth-enslaved,
A ready prey, as though in absent mood
They calmly move, nor hear the unmannered mirth.

"Unto the godly there ariseth up light in the darkness."

LEAD, kindly Light, amid the encircling gloom,
    Lead Thou me on!
The night is dark, and I am far from home—
    Lead Thou me on!
Keep Thou my feet; I do not ask to see
The distant scene,—one step enough for me.

I was not ever thus, nor prayed that Thou
    Shouldst lead me on.
I loved to choose and see my path; but now,
    Lead Thou me on!
I loved the garish day, and, spite of fears,
Pride ruled my will: remember not past years.

So long Thy power hath blest me, sure it still
    Will lead me on,
O'er moor and fen, o'er crag and torrent, till
    The night is gone;
And with the morn those Angel faces smile
Which I have loved long since, and lost awhile.

"It is I : be not afraid."*

WHEN I sink down in gloom or fear,
  Hope blighted or delayed,
Thy whisper, Lord, my heart shall cheer,
  "'Tis I : be not afraid!"

Or, startled at some sudden blow,
  If fretful thoughts I feel,
"Fear not, it is but I!" shall flow,
  As balm my wound to heal.

Nor will I quit Thy way, though foes
  Some onward pass defend;
From each rough voice the watchword goes,
  "Be not afraid! . . . a friend!"

And O! when judgment's trumpet clear
  Awakes me from the grave,
Still in its echo may I hear,
  "'Tis Christ! He comes to save."

---

* *Vide* Bishop Wilson's "Sacra Privata" for Friday. The above lines were written before the appearance of Mr. Lyte's elegant Poem on the same text.

"The Lord stood with me, and strengthened me."

SAY not thou art left of God,
    Because His tokens in the sky
Thou canst not read ; this earth He trod
    To teach thee He was ever nigh.

He sees, beneath the fig-tree green,
    Nathaniel con His sacred lore ;
Shouldst thou the closet seek, unseen
    He enters through the unopened door.

And, when thou liest, by slumber bound,
    Outwearied in the Christian fight,
In glory, girt with Saints around,
    He stands above thee through the night.

When friends to Emmaus bend their course,
    He joins, although He holds their eyes ;
Or, shouldst thou feel some fever's force,
    He takes thy hand, He bids thee rise.

Or, on a voyage, when calms prevail,
    And prison thee upon the sea,
He walks the wave, He wings the sail,
    The shore is gained, and thou art free.

JAMES AND JOHN

TWO brothers freely cast their lot,
  With David's royal Son ;
The cost of conquest counting not,
  They deem the battle won.

Brothers in heart, they hope to gain
  An undivided joy,
That man may one with man remain,
  As boy was one with boy.

Christ heard ; and willed that James should fall
  First prey of Satan's rage ;
John linger out his fellows all,
  And die in bloodless age.

Now they join hands once more above,
  Before the Conqueror's throne ;
Thus God grants prayer ; but in His love
  Makes times and ways His own.

"Whither I go, thou canst not follow Me now,
but thou shalt follow Me afterwards."

DID we but see,
    When life first opened, how our journey lay
    Between its earliest and its closing day;
Or view ourselves, as we one time shall be,
Who strive for the high prize, such sight would break
The youthful spirit, though bold for Jesus' sake.

    But Thou, dear Lord!
Whilst I traced out bright scenes which were to come,
Isaac's pure blessings, and a verdant home,
    Didst spare me, and withhold Thy fearful word;
Wiling me year by year, till I am found
A pilgrim pale, with Paul's sad girdle bound.

GUARDIAN ANGELS

ARE these the tracks of some unearthly
    Friend,
    His footprints, and his vesture-
    skirts of light,
Who, as I talk with men, conforms aright
Their sympathetic words, or deeds that blend
With my hid thought;—or stoops him to
    attend
    My doubtful-pleading grief;—or blunts the
    might
Of ill I see not;—or in dreams of night
Figures the scope in which what is will end?
Were I Christ's own, then fitly might I call
That vision real; for to the thoughtful mind
That walks with Him, He half unveils His
    face;
But when on common men such shadows fall,
These dare not make their own the gifts they
    find,
Yet, not all hopeless, eye His boundless grace.

WARNINGS

(For Music)

WHEN Heaven sends sorrow,
    Warnings go first,
    Lest it should burst
    With stunning might
    On souls too bright
        To fear the morrow.

Can science bear us
    To the hid springs
    Of human things?
    Why may not dream,
    Or thought's day gleam,
        Startle, yet cheer us?

Are such thoughts fetters,
    While faith disowns
    Dread of earth's tones,
    Recks but Heaven's call,
    And on the wall
        Reads but Heaven's letters?

DISCIPLINE

WHEN I look back upon my former race,
    Seasons I see, at which the Inward Ray
More brightly burned, or guided some new way;
Truth, in its wealthier scene and nobler space,
Given for my eye to range, and feet to trace,
    And next I mark, 'twas trial did convey,
    Or grief, or pain, or strange eventful day,
To my tormented soul such larger grace.
So now, whene'er, in journeying on, I feel
The shadow of the Providential Hand,
Deep breathless stirrings shoot across my breast,
Searching to know what He will now reveal,
What sin uncloak, what stricter rule command,
And girding me to work His full behest.

WHENE'ER I seek the Holy Altar's
    rail,
    And kneel to take the grace there
    offered me,
It is no time to task my reason frail,
    To try Christ's words, and search how they
    may be ;
Enough, I eat His Flesh and drink His Blood,
More is not told—to ask it is not good.

I will not say with these, that bread and wine
    Have vanish'd at the consecration prayer ;
Far less with those deny that aught divine
    And of immortal seed is hidden there.
Hence, disputants ! The din, which ye admire,
Keeps but ill measure with the Church's choir.

*" He is not the God of the dead, but of the living;
for all live unto Him."*

"THE Fathers are in dust, yet live to
God;"
So says the Truth; as if the motionless clay
Still held the seeds of life beneath the sod,
  Smouldering and struggling till the judgment-day.

And hence we learn with reverence to esteem
  Of these frail houses, though the grave confines;
Sophist may urge his cunning tests, and deem
  That they are earth;—but they are heavenly shrines.

"The effectual fervent prayer of a righteous man
        availeth much."

THERE is not on the earth a soul so
        base
    But may obtain a place
    In covenanted grace ;
So that forthwith his prayer of faith obtains
        Release of his guilt-stains,
And first-fruits of the second birth, which rise
From gift to gift, and reach at length the
    eternal prize.

All may save self ;—but minds that heavenward
    tower
        Aim at a wider power,
        Gifts on the world to shower.—
And this is not at once ;—by fastings gained,
        And trials well sustained,
By pureness, righteous deeds, and toils of love,
Abidance in the Truth, and zeal for God above.

JOSEPH

PUREST semblance of the Eternal Son!
Who dwelt in thee as in some blessed shrine,
To draw hearts after thee and make them thine;
Not parent only by that light was won,
And brethren crouched who had in wrath begun,
E'en heathen pomp abased her at the sign
Of a hid God, and drank the sound divine,
Till a king heard, and all thou bad'st was done.
Then was fulfill'd Nature's dim augury,
That, "Wisdom, clad in visible form, would be
So fair, that all must love and bow the knee;" *
Lest it might seem, what time the Substance came,
Truth lacked a sceptre, when It but laid by
Its beaming front, and bore a willing shame.

---

* Ἡ φρόνησις οὐχ ὁρᾶται· δεινοὺς γὰρ ἂν παρεῖχεν ἔρωτας, εἰ τοιοῦτον ἑαυτῆς ἐναργὲς εἴδωλον παρείχετο εἰς ὄψιν ἰόν.

PLAT. Phæd.

THE HAVEN

WHENCE is this awe, by stillness spread
    O'er the world-fretted soul?
  Wave reared on wave its boastful head,
While my keen bark, by breezes sped,
Dash'd fiercely through the ocean bed,
    And chafed towards its goal.

But now there reigns so deep a rest,
    That I could almost weep.
Sinner! thou hast in this rare guest
Of Adam's peace a figure blest;
'Tis Eden seen, but not possessed,
    Which cherub flames still keep.

THE DESERT

TWO sinners have been grace-endued,
    Unwearied to sustain
For forty days a solitude
    On mount and desert plain.

But feverish thoughts the breasts have swayed,
    And gloom or pride is shown,
If e'er we seek the garden's shade,
    Or walk the world, alone.

For Adam e'en, before his sin,
    His God a help-meet found;
Blest with an Angel's heart within,
    Paul wrought with friends around.

Lone saints of old, of purpose high!
    On Syria's sands ye claim,
Mid heathen rage, our sympathy,
    In peace ye force our blame.

DEATH

WHENE'ER goes forth Thy dread
    command,
  And my last hour is nigh,
Lord, grant me in a Christian land,
  As I was born, to die.

I pray not, Lord, that friends may be
  Or kindred standing by;
Choice blessing! which I leave to Thee,
  To give me, or deny.

But let my failing limbs beneath
  My mother's smile recline;
My name in sickness and in death
  Heard in her sacred shrine.

And may the Cross beside my bed
  In its meet emblems rest;
And may the absolving words be said,
  To ease a laden breast.

Thou, Lord! where'er we lie, canst aid;
  But He, who taught His own
To live as one, will not upbraid
  The dread to die alone.

"Man walketh in a vain shadow, and disquieteth
    himself in vain."

THEY do but grope in learning's
    pedant round,
  Who on the fantasies of sense bestow
  An idol substance, bidding us bow
    low
Before those shades of being which are found
Stirring or still on man's brief trial ground;
  As if such shapes and moods, which come
    and go,
  Had aught of Truth or Life in their poor
    show,
To sway or judge, and skill to sain or wound.
Son of immortal Seed, high destined Man!
Know thy dread gift,—a creature, yet a cause;
Each mind is its own centre, and it draws
Home to itself, and moulds in its thought's span
All outward things, the vassals of its will,
Aided by Heaven, by earth unthwarted still.

MELCHIZEDEK

"Without father, without mother, without descent, having neither beginning of days, nor end of life."

THRICE blest are they who feel their
  loneliness;
 To whom nor voice of friend nor
  pleasant scene
 Brings that on which the saddened heart
  can lean;
Yea, the rich earth, garbed in its daintiest dress
Of light and joy, doth but the more oppress,
 Claiming responsive smiles and rapture high:
 Till, sick at heart, beyond the vail they fly,
Seeking His presence, who alone can bless.
Such, in strange days, the weapons of Heaven's
  grace
When, passing o'er the high-born Hebrew line,
He forms the vessel of his vast design;
Fatherless, homeless, reft of age and place,
Severed from earth, and careless of its wreck,
Born through long woe His rare Melchizedek.

SIREN ISLES

CEASE, Stranger, cease those piercing
    notes,
  The craft of Siren choirs;
Hush the seductive voice, that floats
  Upon the languid wires.

Music's ethereal fire was given,
  Not to dissolve our clay,
But draw Promethean beams from Heaven,
  And purge the dross away.

Weak self! with thee the mischief lies,
  Those throbs a tale disclose;
Nor age nor trial have made wise
  The Man of many woes.

MESSENA

WHY, wedded to the Lord, still yearns
   my heart
      Upon these scenes of ancient
      heathen fame?
Yet legend hoar, and voice of bard that came
Fixing my restless youth with its sweet art,
And shades of power, and those who bore their
   part
   In the mad deeds that set the world in flame,
   So fret my memory here,—ah! is it blame—
That from my eyes the tear is fain to start?
Nay, from no fount impure these drops arise;
'Tis but the sympathy with Adam's race,
Which in each brother's history reads its own.
So, let the cliffs and seas of this fair place
Be named man's tomb and splendid record-
   stone,
High hope pride-stained, the course without
   the prize.

TAUROMINIUM

"And Jacob went on his way, and the Angels of
God met him."

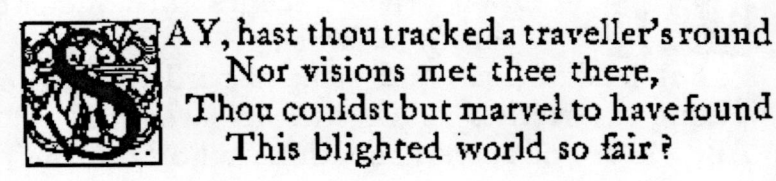

SAY, hast thou tracked a traveller's round
   Nor visions met thee there,
Thou couldst but marvel to have found
   This blighted world so fair?

And feel an awe within thee rise,
   That sinful man should see
Glories far worthier Seraph's eyes
   Than to be shared by thee?

Store them in heart! thou shalt not faint
   'Mid coming pains and fears,
As the third heaven once nerved a Saint
   For fourteen trial years.

CORCYRA

I SAT beneath an olive's branches grey
    And gazed upon the site of a lost
        town,
    By sage and poet chosen for renown ;
Where dwelt a Race that on the sea held sway,
And, restless as its waters, forced a way
    For civil strife a thousand states to drown.
That multitudinous stream we now note down,
As though one life, in birth and in decay.
Yet, is their being's history spent and run,
Whose spirits live in awful singleness,
Each in his self-formed sphere of light or
        gloom ?
Henceforth, while pondering the fierce deeds
        then done,
Such reverence on me shall its seal impress,
As though I corpses saw, and walked the tomb.

REMOVAL

DEAR sainted Friends, I call not you
    To share the joy serene
Which flows upon me from the view
    Of crag and steep ravine.

Ye, on that loftier mountain old,
    Safe lodged in Eden's cell,
Whence run the rivers four, behold
    This earth, as ere it fell.

Or, when ye think of those who stay,
    Still tried by the world's fight,
'Tis but in looking for the day
    Which shall the lost unite.

Ye rather, elder Spirits strong!
    Who from the first have trod
This nether scene, man's race among,
    The while ye live to God.

Ye hear, and ye can sympathize—
    Vain thought! those eyes of fire
Pierce thro' God's works, and duly prize;
    Ye smile when we admire.

Ah, Saviour Lord! with Thee my heart
    Angel nor Saint shall share;
To Thee 'tis known, for man Thou art,
    To soothe each tumult there.

REST

THEY are at rest:
    We may not stir the heaven of their repose
By rude invoking voice, or prayer addrest
    In waywardness to those
Who in the mountain grots of Eden lie,
And hear the fourfold river as it murmurs by.

    They hear it sweep
In distance down the dark and savage vale;
But they at rocky bed, or current deep,
    Shall never more grow pale;
They hear, and meekly muse, as fain to know
How long untired, unspent, that giant stream shall flow.

    And soothing sounds,
Blend with the neighbouring waters as they glide;
Posted along the haunted garden's bounds,
    Angelic forms abide,
Echoing, as words of watch, o'er lawn and grove
The verses of that hymn which Seraphs chant above.

PRAYER

WHILE Moses on the Mountain lay,
Night after night, and day by day,
    Till forty suns were gone,
  Unconscious, in the Presence bright,
Of lustrous day and starry night,
As though his soul had flitted quite
    From earth, and Eden won;

The pageant of a kingdom vast,
And things unutterable, past
    Before the Prophet's eye;
Dread shadows of the Eternal Throne,
The fount of Life, and Altar-stone,
Pavement, and them that tread thereon,
    And those who worship nigh.

But lest he should his own forget,
Who in the vale were struggling yet,
    A sadder vision came,
Announcing all that guilty deed
Of idol rite, that in her need
He for the Church might intercede,
    And stay Heaven's rising flame.

ISAAC

MANY the guileless years the Patriarch
        spent,
    Blessed in the wife a father's fore-
        sight chose ;
Many the prayers and gracious deeds which
    rose,
Daily thank-offerings from his pilgrim tent.
Yet these, though written in the heavens, are
    rent
    From out truth's lower roll, which sternly
        shows
    But one sad trespass at his history's close,
Father's, son's, mother's, and its punishment.
Not in their brightness, but their earthly stains
Are the true seed vouchsafed to earthly eyes.
Sin can read sin, but dimly scans high grace ;
    So we move heavenward with averted face,
Scared into faith by warning of sin's pains ;
And Saints are lowered, that the world may rise.

THE CALL OF DAVID

"And the Lord said, Arise, anoint him : for this is he."

LATEST born of Jesse's race,
Wonder lights thy bashful face,
While the prophet's gifted oil
Seals thee for a path of toil.
We, thy Angels, circling round thee,
Ne'er shall find thee as we found thee,
When thy faith first brought us near
In thy lion-fight severe.

Go ! and mid thy flocks awhile,
At thy doom of greatness smile ;
Bold to bear God's heaviest load,
Dimly guessing of the road,—
Rocky road, and scarce ascended,
Though thy foot be angel-tended ;
Double praise thou shalt attain,
In royal court and battle plain ;
Then comes heart-ache, care, distress,
Blighted hope, and loneliness ;
Wounds from friend and gifts from foe,
Dizzied faith, and guilt, and woe,
Loftiest aims by earth defiled,
Gleams of wisdom sin-beguiled,

Sated power's tyrannic mood,
Counsels shared with men of blood,
Sad success, parental tears,
And a dreary gift of years.

Strange, that guileless face and form
To lavish on the scarring storm!
Yet we take thee in thy blindness,
And we harass thee in kindness ;
Little chary of thy fame,—
Dust unborn may bless or blame.—
But we mould thee for the root
Of man's promised healing fruit,
And we mould thee hence to rise
As our brother to the skies.

"They glorified God in me."

I SAW thee once, and nought discerned
    For stranger to admire;
A serious aspect, but it burned
    With no unearthly fire.

Again I saw, and I confessed
    Thy speech was rare and high;
And yet it vexed my burdened breast,
    And scared, I knew not why.

I saw once more, and awe-struck gazed
    On face, and form, and air;
God's living glory round thee blazed—
    A Saint—a Saint was there!

"I fear, lest, when I come, I shall not find you such as I would, and that I shall be found unto you such as ye would not."

I DREAMED that, with a passionate complaint,
   I wished me born amid God's deeds of might ;
And envied those who saw the presence bright
Of gifted Prophet and strong-hearted Saint,
Whom my heart loves, and fancy strives to paint.
   I turned, when straight a stranger met my sight,
   Came as my guest, and did awhile unite
His lot with mine, and lived without restraint.
Courteous he was, and grave,—so meek in mien,
It seemed untrue, or told a purpose weak ;
Yet in the mood, he could with aptness speak,
Or with stern force, or show of feelings keen,
Marking deep craft, methought, or hidden pride :
Then came a voice—" St. Paul is at thy side ! "

"Him that escapeth from the sword of Jehu shall Elisha slay."

CHRIST bade His followers take the sword,
    And yet He chid the deed,
When Peter seized upon His word,
    And made a foe to bleed.

The Gospel Creed, a sword of strife,
    Meek hands alone may rear;
And ever Zeal begin its life
    In silent thought and fear.

Ye, who would weed the Vineyard's soil,
    Treasure the lesson given;
Lest in the judgment-books ye toil
    For Satan, not for heaven.

"Come with me, and see my zeal for the Lord."

THOU to wax fierce
   In the cause of the Lord,
  To threat and to pierce
   With the heavenly sword ;
Anger and Zeal,
  And the Joy of the brave,
Who bade *thee* to feel,
  Sin's slave.

The Altar's pure flame
  Consumes as it soars ;
Faith meetly may blame,
  For it serves and adores.
Thou warnest and smitest !
  Yet Christ must atone
For a soul that thou slightest—
  Thine own.

THY words are good and freely given,
    As though thou felt them true;
Friend, think thee well, to hell or heaven
    A serious heart is due.

It pains thee sore man's will should swerve
    In his true path divine;
And yet thou venturest not to serve
    Thy neighbour's weal nor thine.

Beware! such words may once be said,
    Where shame and fear unite;
But, spoken twice, they mark instead
    A sin against the light.

DEEDS NOT WORDS

PRUNE thou thy words, the thoughts
    control
  That o'er thee swell and throng;
They will condense within thy soul,
  And change to purpose strong.

But he, who lets his feelings run
  In soft luxurious flow,
Shrinks when hard service must be done,
  And faints at every woe.

Faith's meanest deed more favour bears,
  Where hearts and wills are weighed,
Than brightest transports, choicest prayers,
  Which bloom their hour and fade.

"I have need to be baptized of Thee, and comest
       Thou to me?"

How didst thou start, Thou Holy
       Baptist, bid
   To pour repentance on the Sinless
       Brow!
Then all thy meekness, from thy hearers hid
   Beneath the Ascetic's port and Preacher's fire,
Flowed forth, and with a pang thou didst
       desire
   He might be chief, not thou.

And so on us, at whiles, it falls to claim
   Powers that we fear, or dare some forward
       part;
Nor must we shrink as cravens from the blame
   Of pride, in common eyes, or purpose deep;
But with pure thoughts look up to God, and
       keep
   Our secret in our heart.

SLEEP

UNWEARIED God! before whose face
    The night is clear as day,
  Whilst we, poor worms, o'er life's
    brief race
  Now creep, and now delay;
We with death's foretaste alternate
Our labour's dint and sorrow's weight,
Save in that fever-troubled state
    When pain and care hold sway.

Dread Lord! Thy glory, watchfulness,
   Is but disease in man:
Oh! hence upon our hearts impress
   Our place in the world's plan!
Pride grasps the powers by Heaven displayed;
But ne'er the rebel effort made
But fell beneath the sudden shade
    Of nature's withering ban.

THE ELEMENTS

πολλὰ τὰ δεῖνα, κοὐδὲν
ἀνθρώπου δεινότερον πέλει.

MAN is permitted much
    To scan and learn
    In Nature's frame ;
    Till he well-nigh can tame
Brute mischiefs, and can touch
Invisible things, and turn
All warring ills to purposes of good.
    Thus as a God below,
    He can control,
And harmonize what seems amiss to flow
    As severed from the whole
    And dimly understood.

    But o'er the elements
      One Hand alone,
      One Hand has sway.
    What influence day by day
    In straiter belts prevents
The impious Ocean, thrown
Alternate o'er the ever-sounding shore ?

Or who has eye to trace
   How the Plague came?
Forerun the doublings of the Tempest's race?
   Or the Air's weight and flame
   On a set scale explore!

   Thus God has willed
That man, when fully skilled,
Still gropes in twilight dim;
Encompassed all his hours
   By fearfullest powers
   Inflexible to him;
That so he may discern
   His feebleness,
And e'en for earth's success
To Him in wisdom turn,
Who holds for us the Keys of either home,
   Earth and the world to come.

"Freely ye have received : freely give."

"GIVE any boon for peace!
    Why should our fair-eyed Mother
      e'er engage
    In the world's course and on a
      troubled stage,
From which her very call is a release?
      No! in thy garden stand,
      And tend with pious hand
      The flowers thou findest there,
      Which are thy proper care,
O man of God! in meekness and in love,
And waiting for the blissful realms above."

      Alas! for thou must learn,
Thou guileless one! rough is the holy hand;
Runs not the Word of Truth through every land,
A sword to sever, and a fire to burn?
      If blessed Paul had stayed
      In cot or learned shade,
      With the priest's white attire,
      And the saints' tuneful choir,
Men had not gnashed their teeth, nor risen to
      slay,
But thou hadst been a heathen in thy day.

TIME was, I shrank from what was
    right,
  From fear of what was wrong;
I would not brave the sacred fight,
  Because the foe was strong.

But now I cast that finer sense
  And sorer shame aside;
Such dread of sin was indolence,
  Such aim at heaven was pride.

So, when my Saviour calls, I rise,
  And calmly do my best;
Leaving to Him, with silent eyes
  Of hope and fear, the rest.

I step, I mount where He has led;
  Men count my haltings o'er;—
I know them; yet, though self I dread,
  I love His precept more.

ΠΑΥΛΟΥ ΜΙΜΗΤΗΣ

LORD! when sin's close marshalled line
  Urges Thy witness on his way,
How should he raise Thy glorious Sign,
  And how Thy will display?

Thy holy Paul, with soul of flame,
  Rose on Mars'-hill a soldier lone;
Shall I thus speak the Atoning Name
  Though with a heart of stone?

"Not so," He said:—"hush thee, and seek,
  With thoughts in prayer and watchful eyes,
My seasons sent for thee to speak,
  And use them as they rise."

THE SAINT AND THE HERO

AGED Saint! far off I heard
　The praises of thy name;
Thy deed of power, thy skilful word,
　Thy zeal's triumphant flame.

I came and saw; and, having seen,
　Weak heart, I drew offence
From thy prompt smile, thy simple mien,
　Thy lowly diligence.

The Saint's is not the Hero's praise;—
　This have I found, and learn
Nor to profane Heaven's humblest ways,
　Nor its least boon to spurn.

JONAH

"But Jonah rose up to flee unto Tarshish, from the presence of the Lord."

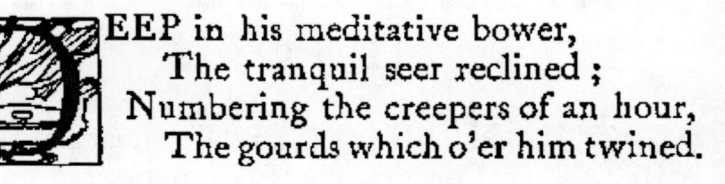

DEEP in his meditative bower,
    The tranquil seer reclined;
Numbering the creepers of an hour,
    The gourds which o'er him twined.

To note each plant, to rear each fruit
    Which soothes the languid sense,
He deemed a safe refined pursuit,—
    His Lord, an indolence.

The sudden voice was heard at length,
    "Lift thou the prophet's rod!"
But sloth had sapped the prophet's strength,
    He feared, and fled from God.

Next, by a fearful judgment tamed,
    He threats the offending race;
God spares;—he murmurs, pride-inflamed,
    His threat made void by grace.

What?—pride and sloth! man's worst of foes!
    And can such guests invade
Our choicest bliss, the green repose
    Of the sweet garden shade?

JEREMIAH

"Oh that I had in the wilderness a lodging-place
of wayfaring men; that I might leave my people,
and go from them."

"WOE'S me!" the peaceful prophet
   cried,
 "Spare me this troubled life;
To stem man's wrath, to school his
   pride,
 To head the sacred strife!

"O place me in some silent vale,
 Where groves and flowers abound;
Nor eyes that grudge, nor tongues that rail,
 Vex the truth-haunted ground!"

If his meek spirit erred, opprest
 That God denied repose,
What sin is ours, to whom Heaven's rest
 Is pledged to heal earth's woes?

ST. PAUL AT MELITA

"And when Paul had gathered a bundle of sticks, and laid them on the fire, there came a viper out of the heat."

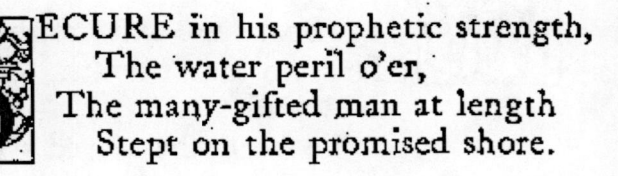

SECURE in his prophetic strength,
    The water peril o'er,
The many-gifted man at length
    Stept on the promised shore.

He trod the shore; but not to rest,
    Nor wait till Angels came;
Lo! humblest pains the Saint attest,
    The firebrands and the flame.

But when he felt the viper's smart,
    Then instant aid was given:
Christian! hence learn to do thy part,
    And leave the rest to Heaven.

"Am I my brother's keeper?"

THE time has been, it seemed a precept plain
   Of the true faith, Christ's tokens to display;
And in life's commerce still the thought retain,
   That men have souls, and wait a judgment-day;
Kings used their gifts as ministers of heaven,
Nor stripped their zeal for God of means which God had given.

'Tis altered now;—for Adam's eldest born
   Has trained our practice in a selfish rule;
Each stands alone, Christ's bonds asunder torn,
   Each has his private thought, selects his school,
Conceals his creed, and lives in closest tie
Of fellowship with those who count it blasphemy.

Brothers! spare reasoning;—men have settled long
  That ye are out of date, and they are wise;
Use their own weapons; let your words be strong,
  Your cry be loud, till each scared boaster flies;
Thus the Apostles tamed the pagan breast,
They argued not, but preached; and conscience did the rest.

ZEAL BEFORE LOVE

AND wouldst thou reach, rash scholar mine,
    Love's high unruffled state?
Awake! thy easy dreams resign:
    First learn thee how to hate.

Hatred of sin, and Zeal, and Fear,
    Lead up the Holy Hill;
Track them, till Charity appear
    A self-denial still.

Feeble and false the brightest flame
    By thoughts severe unfed;
Book-lore ne'er served, when trial came,
    Nor gifts, where Faith was dead.

THE WRATH TO COME

WHEN first God stirred me, and the
   Church's word
      Came as a theme of reverent search
      and fear,
   It little cost to own the lustre clear
O'er rule she taught, and rite, and doctrine
   poured ;
For conscience craved, and reason did accord.
   Yet one there was that wore a mien austere,
   And I did doubt, and, troubled, asked to
      hear
Whose mouth had force to edge so sharp a
   sword.
My Mother oped her trust, the Holy Book,
And healed my pang. She pointed, and I found
Christ on Himself, considerate Master, took
The utterance of that doctrine's fearful sound.
The fount of Love His servants sends to tell
Love's deeds ; Himself reveals the sinner's hell.

THE COURSE OF TRUTH

"Him God raised up the third day, and showed Him openly, not to all the people, but unto witnesses chosen before of God."

WHEN royal Truth, released from
    mortal throes,
  Burst His brief slumber, and triumphant rose,
  Ill had the Holiest sued
  A patron multitude,
Or courted Tetrarch's eye, or claimed to rule
By the world's winning grace, or proofs from
  learned school.

But, robing Him in viewless air, He told
His secret to a few of meanest mould;
  They in their turn imparted
  The gift to men pure-hearted.
While the brute many heard His mysteries
  high,
As some strange fearful tongue, they crouched
  they knew not why.

Still is the might of Truth, as it has been:
Lodged in the few, obeyed, and yet unseen.
   Reared on lone heights, and rare,
   His Saints their watch-flame bear,
And the mad world sees the wide-circling blaze,
Vain-searching whence it streams, and how to quench its rays.

THE WATCHMAN

"Quit you like men, be strong."

FAINT not, and fret not, for threatened woe,
    Watchman on Truth's grey height !
Few though the faithful, and fierce though the foe,
    Weakness is aye Heaven's might.

Infidel Ammon and niggard Tyre,
    Ill-attuned pair, unite ;
Some work for love, and some work for hire,
    But weakness shall be Heaven's might !

Eli's feebleness, Saul's black wrath,
    May aid Ahitophel's spite :
And prayers from Gerizim, and curses from Gath . . .
    Our weakness shall be Heaven's might.

Quail not, and quake not, thou Warder bold,
    Be there no friend in sight ;
Turn thee to question the days of old,
    When weakness was aye Heaven's might.

Moses was one, yet he stayed the sin
    Of the host, in the Presence bright ;
And Elias scorned the Carmel-din,
    When Baal would scan Heaven's might.

Time's years are many, Eternity one,
    And one is the Infinite ;
The chosen are few, few the deeds well done,
    For scantness is still Heaven's might.

VEXATIONS

EACH trial has its weight; which whoso bears,
    Knows his own woe, and need of succouring grace;
The martyr's hope half wipes away the trace
Of flowing blood; the while life's humblest cares
Smart more, because they hold in Holy Writ no place.

    This be my comfort, in these days of grief
        Which is not Christ's, nor forms heroic tale.
        Apart from Him if not a sparrow fail,
    May not He pitying view, and send relief
When foes or friends perplex, and peevish thoughts prevail?

    Then keep good heart; nor take the self-wise course
        Of Thomas, who must see ere he would trust.
        Faith will fill up God's word, not poorly just
    To the bare letter, heedless of its force,
But walking by its light amid earth's sun and dust.

THE GREEK FATHERS

LET others sing thy heathen praise,
Fallen Greece! the thought of holier
days
In my sad heart abides;
For sons of thine in Truth's first hour
Were tongues and weapons of his power,
Born of the Spirit's fiery shower,
Our fathers and our guides.

All thine is Clement's varied page;
And Dionysius, ruler sage
In days of doubt and pain;
And Origen, with eagle eye;
And saintly Basil's purpose high
To smite imperial heresy,
And cleanse the Altar's stain.

From thee the glorious preacher came
With soul of zeal and lips of flame,
A court's stern martyr-guest;
And thine, O inexhaustive race;
Was Nazianzen's heaven-taught grace;
And royal-hearted Athanase,
With Paul's own mantle blest.

ATHANASIUS

WHEN shall our northern Church her
    champion see,
    Raised by divine decree,
To shield the Ancient Truth at his
    own harm ? . . .
Like him who stayed the arm
Of tyrannous power, and learning's sophist-tone,
    Keen-visioned Seer, alone.

The many crouched before an idol-priest,
    Lord of the world's rank feast.
In the dark night, mid the saints' trial sore,
    He stood, then bowed before
The Holy Mysteries,—he their meetest sign,
    Weak vessel, yet divine.*

Cyprian is ours, since the high-souled primate laid
    Under the traitorous blade
His silvered head. And Chrysostom we claim
    In that clear eloquent flame
And deep-taught zeal in the same woe, which
    shone
    Bright round a Martyr's throne.

---

* *Vide* the account of Syrianus breaking into his Church, Theodoret Hist., ii. 13.

And Ambrose reared his crosier as of old,
    Less honoured, but as bold,
When in dark times our champion crossed a king :—
    But good in everything
Comes as ill's cure. Dim Future! shall we need
    A prophet for Truth's Creed?

GREGORIUS THEOLOGUS

PEACE-LOVING man, of humble
    heart and true !
      What dost thou hear ?
   Fierce is the city's crowd ; the lordly
    few
      Are dull of ear !
Sore pain it was to thee, till thou didst quit
Thy patriarch-throne at length, as though for
    power unfit.

So works the All-wise ! our services dividing
     Not as we ask :
For the world's profit, by our gifts deciding
     Our duty-task.
See in king's courts loth Jeremiah plead ;
And slow-tongued Moses rule by eloquence of
    deed !

Yes ! thou, bright Angel of the East, didst rear
     The Cross divine,
Borne high upon thy clear-voiced accents, where
     Men mocked the Sign ;
Till that cold city heard thy battle-cry,
And hearts were stirred, and deemed a Pentecost
    was nigh.

Thou couldst a people raise, but couldst not
    rule :—
        So, gentle one,
Heaven broke at last the consecrated tool
    Whose work was done ;
According thee the lot thou lovedst best,—
To muse upon times past, to serve, yet be at
    rest.

WHEN I would search the truths that in me burn,
   And mould them into rule and argument,
A hundred reasoners cried :—" Hast thou to learn
   " Those dreams are scattered now, those fires are spent ? "
And, did I mount to simpler thoughts and try
Some theme of peace, 'twas still the same reply.

Perplexed, I hoped my heart was pure of guile,
   But judged me weak in wit, to disagree ;
But now I see, that men were mad awhile,
   And joy the age to come will think with me ;
'Tis the old history ;—Truth without a home,
Despised and slain—then, rising from the tomb.

"I saw all Israel scattered upon the hills as sheep
that have not a shepherd."

POOR wanderers, ye are sore distrest
To find that path which Christ has
blest,
 Tracked by His saintly throng;
Each claims to trust his own weak will,
Blind idol!—so ye languish still,
 All wranglers, and all wrong.

He saw of old, and met your need,
Granting you prophets of His creed,
 The throes of fear to suage;
They fenced the rich bequest He made,
And sacred hands have safe conveyed
 Their charge from age to age.

Wanderers! come home! when erring most
Christ's Church aye kept the faith, nor lost
 One grain of Holy Truth:
She ne'er has erred as those ye trust,
And now shall lift her from the dust,
 And reign as in her youth!

PATRIARCHAL FAITH

We are not children of a guilty sire,
    Since Noe stepped from out his
        wave-tossed home,
    And a stern baptism flushed earth's
        faded bloom.
Not that the heavens then cleared, or cherub's
    fire
From Eden's portal did at once retire ;
    But thoughts were stirred of Him who was
        to come,
    Whose rainbow hues so streaked the o'er-
        shadowing gloom,
That faith could e'en that desolate scene
    admire.
The Lord has come and gone ; and now we
    wait
The second substance of the deluge type,
When our slight ark shall cross a molten
    surge ;
So, while the gross earth melts, for judgment
    ripe,
Ne'er with its haughty turrets to emerge,
We shall mount up to Eden's long lost gate.

HEATHENISM

MID Balak's magic fires
The Spirit spake clear as in Israel;
With prayers untrue and covetous desires
Did God vouchsafe to dwell;
Who summoned dreams, His earlier word to bring
To holy Job's vexed friends and Gerar's guileless king.

If such o'erflowing grace
From Aaron's vest e'en on the Sibyl ran,
Why should we fear the Son now lacks His place,
Where roams unchristened man?
As tho', when faith is keen, He cannot make
Bread of the very stones, or thirst with ashes slake.

JUDAISM

PITEOUS race!
Fearful to look upon;
Once standing in high place,
　Heaven's eldest son.
　　O aged blind
Unvenerable! as thou flittest by,
I liken thee to him in pagan song,
　　In thy gaunt majesty,
The vagrant King, of haughty-purposed mind,
　　Whom prayer nor plague could bend;*
Wronged, at the cost of him who did the wrong,
Accursed himself, but in his cursing strong,
　　And honoured in his end.

　　O Abraham! sire
　　Shamed in thy progeny;
　　Who to thy faith aspire,
　　　Thy hope deny.
　　　Well wast thou given
From out the heathen an adopted heir,
Raised strangely from the dead, when sin had slain
　Thy former-cherished care.

---

* *Vide* the "Œdipus Coloneus" of Sophocles.

O holy men, ye first-wrought gems of heaven !
    Polluted in your kin,
Come to our fonts, your lustre to regain !
O Holiest Lord ! . . . but thou canst take no
        stain
    Of blood, or taint of sin.

        Twice in their day
        Proffer of precious cost
        Was made, Heaven's hand to stay
        Ere all was lost.
        The first prevailed ;
Moses was outcast from the promised home
    For his own sin, yet taken at his prayer
        To change his people's doom.
    Close on their eve, one other asked and failed,
        When fervent Paul was fain
The accursed tree, as Christ had borne, to bear ;
No hopeful answer came—a Price more rare
        Already shed in vain.

SUPERSTITION

LORD, and Christ, Thy Churches
    of the South
So shudder, when they see
The two-edged sword sharp-issuing
    from Thy mouth,
As to fall back from Thee,
And seek to charms of man, or saints above,
To aid them against Thee, Thou Fount of
    grace and love !

But I before Thine awful eyes will go,
    And firmly fix me there
In my full shame ; not bent my doom to know,
    Not fainting with despair ;
Not fearing less then they, but deeming
    sure,
If e'en Thy Name shall fail, nought my base
    heart can cure.

SCHISM

OH, rail not at our brethren of the
        North,
    Albeit Samaria finds her likeness
        there ;
A self-formed Priesthood, and the Church cast
        forth
    To the chill mountain air.

What though their fathers sinned, and lost the
        grace
    Which seals the Holy Apostolic Line?
Christ's love o'erflows the bounds His Prophets
        trace
    In His revealed design.

Israel had Seers ; to them the Word is nigh ;
    Shall not that Word run forth, and gladness
        give
To many a Shunamite, till in His eye
    The full Seven thousand live?

LIBERALISM

"Jehu destroyed Baal out of Israel. Howbeit from the sins of Jeroboam Jehu departed not from after them, to wit, the golden calves that were in Bethel, and that were in Dan."

WE cannot halve the gospel of God's
    grace ;
      Men of presumptuous heart! I
        know you well.
Ye are of those who plan that we should
    dwell,
Each in his tranquil home and holy place :
Seeing the Word refines all natures rude,
And tames the stirrings of the multitude.

And ye have caught some echoes of its lore,
    As heralded amid the joyous choirs ;
    Ye heard it speak of peace, chastised desires,
Good-will and mercy,—and ye heard no more ;
But, as for zeal and quick-eyed sanctity,
And the dread depths of grace, ye pass them by.

And so ye halve the Truth ; for ye in heart,
    At best, are doubters whether it be true,
    The theme discarding, as unmeet for you,
Statesmen or sages. O new-ventured art
Of the ancient Foe !—but what if it extends
O'er our own camp, and rules amid our friends ?

APOSTACY

FRANCE! I will think of thee, as what
    thou wast,
    When Poictiers showed her zeal
    for the true creed;
Or in that age, when holy truth, tho' cast
    On a rank soil, yet was a thriving seed
Thy schools within, from neighbour countries
    chased;
    E'en of thy pagan day I bear to read,
Thy Martyrs sanctified the guilty host,
The sons of blessed John, reared on a western
    coast.

I dare not think of thee, as what thou art,
    Lest thoughts too deep for man should trouble
    me.
It is not safe to place the mind and heart
    On brink of evil, or its flame to see;
Lest they should dizzy, or some taint impart,
    Or to our sin a fascination be.
And so by silence I will now proclaim
Hate of thy present self, and scarce will sound
    thy name.

CONVERSION

ONCE cast with men of language strange
    And foreign-moulded creed,
  I marked their random converse
    change,
    And sacred themes succeed.

O how I coveted the gift
    To thread their mingled throng
Of sounds, then high my witness lift!
    But weakness chained my tongue.

Lord! has our earth of faith and prayer
    Lost us this power once given;
Or is it sent at seasons rare,
    And then flits back to Heaven?

"Many shall run to and fro, and knowledge shall
 be increased."

THERE is one only Bond in the wide
 earth
   Of lawful use to join the earth in
    one;
But in these weary times, the restless run
E'en to its distant verge, and so give birth
To other friendships, and joint-works to bind
Their hearts to the unclean whom there they
 find.

And so is cast upon the face of things
   A many webs to fetter down the Truth;
   While the vexed Church, which gave in her
    fair youth
Prime pattern of the might which order brings,
But dimly signals to her distant seed,
There strongest found, where darkest in her
 creed.

O shame! that Christian joins with Infidel
   In learned search and curious-seeming art!
   Burn we our book, if Christ's we be in heart,
Sooner than heaven should court the praise of
 hell!
Self-flattering age! to whom shall I not seem
Pained with hot thoughts, the preacher of a
 dream?

"I have a few things against thee, because thou sufferest that woman Jezebel, which calleth herself a prophetess, to teach and to seduce My servants to commit fornication, and to eat things sacrificed unto idols."

WEEP, Mother mine, and veil thine
        eyes with shame!
    What was thy sin of old,
That men now give thy awful-sound-
        ing name
    To the false prophet's fold?
    Whose flock thy crosier claim.

Sure thou hast practised in the tongues unclean
    Which Babel-masters teach;
Slighting the Paraclete's true flame serene,
    The inimitative speech,
    Which throned thee the world's queen.

But, should earth-dust, from court or school of
        men,
    Have dimmed thy bridal gear,
When Wrath next walks his rounds, and in
        Heaven's ken
    Thy charge and works appear . . .
    Ah! thou must *suffer* then!

THE BEASTS OF EPHESUS

"My soul is among lions; and I lie even among the children of men that are set on fire, whose teeth are spears and arrows, and their tongue a sharp sword."

HOW long, O Lord of grace,
    Must languish Thy true race,
  In a forced friendship linked with
      Belial here;
With Mammon's brand of care,
    And Baal pleading fair,
And the dog-breed who at thy Temple jeer?

  How long, O Lord, how long
    Shall Cæsar do us wrong,
Laid but as steps to throne his mortal power?
    While e'en our Angels stand
      With helpless voice and hand,
Scorned by proud Haman, in his triumph-hour.

    'Tis said our seers discern
      The destined bickerings stern,
In the dim distance, of Thy fiery train.
      O nerve us in that woe!
      For, where Thy wheels shall go,
We must be tried, the while Thy foes are slain.

"I will give power unto My two witnesses, and
they shall prophesy."

HOW shall a child of God fulfil
His vow to cleanse his soul from ill,
And raise on high his baptism-light,
Like Aaron's seed in ritual white,
And holy tempered Nazarite?

First let him shun the haunts of vice,
Sin-feast, or heathen sacrifice;
Fearing the board of wealthy pride,
Or heretic, self-trusting guide,
Or where the adulterer's smiles preside.

Next, as he threads the maze of men,
Aye must he lift his witness, when
A sin is spoke in Heaven's dread face,
And none at hand of higher grace
The Cross to carry in his place.

But if he hears and sits him still,
First he will lose his hate of ill;
Next, fear of sinning; after, hate;
Small sins his heart then desecrate,
And last, despair persuades to great.

AUTUMN

NOW is the Autumn of the Tree of
    Life ;
    Its leaves are shed upon the unthank-
    ful earth,
Which lets them whirl, a prey to the winds'
    strife,
    Heartless to store them for the months of
    dearth
    Men close the door, and dress the cheerful
    hearth,
Self-trusting still ; and in his comely gear,
Of precept and of rite, a household Baal rear.

But I will out amid the sleet, and view
    Each shrivelling stalk and silent-falling leaf ;
Truth after truth, of choicest scent and hue,
    Fades, and in fading stirs the Angels' grief,
    Unanswered here ; for she, once pattern chief
Of faith, my country, now gross-hearted grown,
Waits but to burn the stem before her idol's
    throne.

"Quiescere faciamus omnes dies festos Dei â terra."

WHEN first earth's rulers welcomed home
    The Church, their zeal impressed
Upon the seasons, as they come,
    The image of their guest.

Men's words and works, their hopes and fears,
    Henceforth forbid to rove,
Paused, when a Martyr claimed her tears,
    Or Saint inspired her love.

But craving wealth, and feverish power,
    Such service now discard;
The loss of one excited hour
    A sacrifice too hard!

And e'en about the holiest day,
    God's own in every time,
They doubt and search, lest aught should stay
    The cataract of crime.

Where shall this cease; must Crosiers fall,
    Shrines suffer touch profane,
Till, cast without His vineyard wall,
    The Heaven-sent Heir is slain?

CHRIST'S Church was holiest in her
        youthful days
    Ere the world on her smiled;
So now, an outcast, she would pour
        her rays
    More keen and undefiled;
Yet would I not that hand of force were mine,
Which thrusts her from her awful ancient
        shrine.

'Twas duty bound each convert-king to rear
        His Mother from the dust,
And pious was it to enrich, nor fear
        Christ for the rest to trust;
But who shall dare make common or unclean
What once has on the Holy Altar been?

Dear Brothers!—hence, while ye for ill prepare,
        Triumph is still your own;
Blest is a pilgrim Church!—yet shrink to share
        The curse of breaking down.
So will we toil in our old place to stand,
Still calmly looking for the spoiler's hand.

UZZAH AND OBED-EDOM

Μὴ κίνει Καμαρίναν· ἀκίνητος γὰρ ἀμείνων.

THE ark of God has hidden strength,
    Who reverence or profane,
They, or their seed, shall find at length
    The penalty or gain.

While as a sojourner it sought
    Of old its destined place,
A blessing on the home it brought
    Of one who did it grace.

But there was one, outstripping all
    The holy-vestured band,
Who laid on it, to save its fall,
    A rude corrective hand.

Read, who the Church would cleanse, and mark
    How stern the warning runs:
There are two ways to aid her ark,
    As patrons and as sons.

PROSPERITY

"When they shall say, Peace and safety, then sudden destruction cometh upon them."

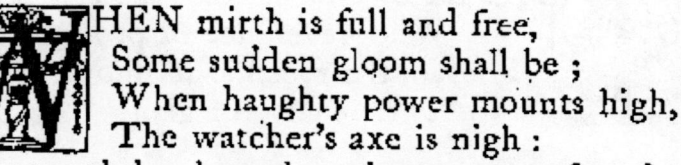

WHEN mirth is full and free,
   Some sudden gloom shall be;
   When haughty power mounts high,
   The watcher's axe is nigh :
All growth has bound : when greatest found,
     It hastes to die.

   When the rich town, that long
   Has lain its huts among,
   Builds court and palace vast,
   And vaunts,—it shall not last!
Bright tints that shine are but a sign
     Of summer past.

   And when thine eye surveys,
   With fond adoring gaze,
   And yearning heart, thy friend,—
   Love to its grave doth tend.
All gifts below, save Truth, but grow
     Towards an end.

FAITH AGAINST SIGHT

" As it was in the days of Lot, so shall it be also in the days of the Son of man."

THE world has cycles in its course, when all
    That once has been, is acted o'er again :
Not by some fated law, which need appal
    Our faith, or binds our deeds as with a chain ;
But by men's separate sins, which blended still
    The same bad round fulfil.

Then fear ye not, though Gallio's scorn ye see,
    And soft-clad nobles count you mad, true hearts !
These are the fig-tree's signs ; rough deeds must be,
    Trials and crimes ; so learn ye well your parts :
Once more to plough the earth it is decreed,
    And scatter wide the seed.

ENGLAND

TYRE of the West, and glorying in the name
    More than in Faith's pure fame!
O' trust not crafty fort nor rock renowned
    Earned upon hostile ground;
Wielding Trade's master-keys, at thy proud will
To lock or loose its waters, England! trust not still.

Dread thine own power! since haughty Babel's prime
    High towers have been man's crime.
Since her hoar age, when the huge moat lay bare,
    Strongholds have been man's snare.
Thy nest is in the crags; ah! refuge frail!
Mad council in its hour, or traitors will prevail.

He who scanned Sodom for His righteous men,
    Still spares thee for thy ten;
But should vain hands defile the temple wall,
    More than His Church will fall:
For, as Earth's kings welcome their spotless guest,
So gives He them by turn, to suffer or be blest.

"Instead of thy fathers thou shalt have children,
whom thou mayest make princes in all lands."

SAY, who is he in deserts seen,
 Or at the twilight hour;
Of garb austere, and dauntless mien,
Measured in speech, in purpose keen,
Calm as in heaven he had been,
 Yet blithe when perils lower?

My holy Mother made reply,
 "Dear Child, it is my priest.
The world has cast me forth, and I
Dwell with wild earth and gusty sky;
He bears to men my mandates high,
 And works my sage behest.

Another day, dear Child, and thou
 Shalt join his sacred band.
Ah! well I deem, thou shrinkest now
From urgent rule and severing vow;
Gay hopes flit round, and light thy brow;—
 Time hath a taming hand!"

THE AFFLICTED CHURCH

τλῆθι, λέων, ἄτλητα παθών, τετληότι θυμῷ.

BIDE thou thy time!
    Watch with meek eyes the race of
        pride and crime
    Sit in the gate, and be the heathen's
        jest,
      Smiling and self-possest.
O thou, to whom is pledg'd a victor's sway,
      Bide thou the victor's day!

      Think on the sin
That reaped the unripe seed, and toiled to win
Foul history-marks at Bethel and at Dan,
      No blessing, but a ban;
Whilst the wise Shepherd * hid his heaven-told
        fate,
      Nor recked a tyrant's hate.

      Such need is gain;
Wait the bright Advent that shall loose thy
        chain!
E'en now the shadows break, and gleams divine
      Edge the dim distant line.
When thrones are trembling, and earth's fat
        ones quail,
      True Seed! thou shalt prevail!

---

        * David.

THE BACKWARD CHURCH

"Can a woman forget her sucking child, that she should not have compassion on the son of her womb? Yea, they may forget, yet will I not forget thee."

WAKE, Mother dear, the foes are near,
    A spoiler claims thy child;
This the sole refuge of my fear,
    Thy bosom undefiled.

What spells of power, in this strange hour,
    My Mother's heart enslave?
Where is thy early bridal dower,
    To suffer and to save?

Thee then I sue, Sleepless and True,
    Dread Maker reconciled!
Help ere they smite, Thy shrine in view,
    The Mother with the child.

THE CHURCH IN PRAYER

"Thou meetest him that rejoiceth and worketh righteousness, those that remember Thee in Thy ways."

WHY loiterest within Simon's walls,
    Hard by the barren sea,
Thou Saint! when many a sinner calls
    To preach and set him free?

Can this be he, who erst confessed
    For Christ affection keen,
Now truant in untimely rest,
    The mood of an Essene?

Yet He who at the sixth hour sought
    The lone house-top to pray,
There gained a sight beyond his thought—
    The dawn of Gentile day.

Then reckon not, when perils lower,
    The time of prayer mis-spent;
Nor meanest chance, nor place, nor hour,
    Without its heavenward bent.

THE CHURCH IN BONDAGE

"Remember my bonds."

COMRADE bold of toil and pain !
   Thy trial how severe,
When severed first by prisoner's chain
   From thy loved labour-sphere.

Say, did impatience first impel
   The heaven-sent bond to break ?
Or couldst thou bear its hind'rance well,
   Loitering for Jesu's sake ?

O might we know ! for sore we feel
   The languor of delay,
When sickness lets our fainter zeal
   Or foes block up our way.

Lord ! who Thy thousand years dost wait,
   To work the thousandth part
Of Thy vast plan, for us create
   With zeal a patient heart !

THE PROSPECTS OF THE CHURCH

" And He said, It is finished."

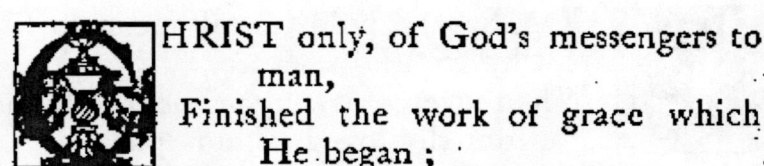

CHRIST only, of God's messengers to man,
    Finished the work of grace which He began ;
E'en Moses wearied upon Nebo's height,
    Though loth to leave the fight
With the doomed foe, and yield the sun-bright land
    To Joshua's armed hand.

And David wrought in turn a strenuous part,
Zeal for God's house consuming him in heart ;
And yet he might not build, but only bring
    Gifts for the heavenly King ;
And these another reared, his peaceful son,
    Till the full work was done.

List, Christian warrior ! thou, whose soul is fain
To rid thy Mother of her present chain ;—
Christ will unloose His Church ; yea, even now
    Begins the work, and thou
Shalt spend in it thy strength ; but, ere He save,
    Thy lot shall be the grave.

ROME

Far sadder musing on the traveller falls
    At sight of thee, O Rome !
Than when he views the rough sea-
    beaten walls
Of Greece, thought's early home ;
For thou wast of the hateful Four, whose doom
    Burdens the Prophet's scroll ;
But Greece was clean, till in her history's gloom
    Her name and sword a Macedonian stole.

And next a mingled throng besets the breast
    Of bitter thoughts and sweet ;
How shall I name thee, Light of the wide West,
    Or heinous error-seat ?
O Mother erst, close tracing Jesus' feet !
    Do not thy titles glow
In those stern judgment-fires, which shall com-
    plete
      Earth's strife with Heaven, and ope the
        eternal woe ?

THE CRUEL CHURCH

MOTHER Church of Rome! why has thy heart
　　Beat so untruly towards thy northern child?
Why give a gift, nor give it undefiled,
Drugging the blessing with a step-dame's art?
Why bare thy sword? beneath thy censure's smart
　　Long days we writhed, who would not be beguiled;
　　While thy keen breath, like blast of winter wild,
Froze, till it crumbled, each sublimer part
Of rite or work, devotion's flower and prime.
Thus have we lain, thy charge, a dreary time,
Christ's little ones, torn from faith's ancient home,
To dogs a prey. And now thou sendest foes,
Bred from thy womb, lost Church! to mock the throes
Of thy free child, thou cruel-natured Rome!

THE GOOD SAMARITAN

OH THAT thy creed were sound!
  For thou dost soothe the heart, Thou
    Church of Rome,
    By thy unwearied watch and varied
      round
Of service, in thy Saviour's holy home.
  I cannot walk the city's sultry streets,
    But the wide porch invites to still retreats,
Where passion's thirst is calmed, and care's
    unthankful gloom.

    There, on a foreign shore,
The homesick solitary finds a friend :
    Thoughts, prisoned long for lack of speech,
      outpour
Their tears ; and doubts in resignation end.
  I almost fainted from the long delay,
    That tangles me within this languid bay,
When comes a foe, my wounds with oil and
    wine to tend.

WHEN I am sad, I say,
    "What boots it me to strive,
And vex my spirit day by day
    Dead memories to revive?

Alas! what good will come,
    Though we our prayer obtain,
To bring old times triumphant home,
    And Heaven's lost sword regain?

Would not our history run
    In the same weary round,
And service, in meek faith begun,
    One time in forms be bound?

Union would give us strength,—
    That strength the earth subdue;
And then comes wealth, and pride at length,
    And sloth, and prayers untrue."

Nay, this is worldly wise;
    To reason is a crime,
Since the Lord bade His Church arise,
    In the dark ancient time.

He wills that she should shine;
    So we her flame must trim
Around His soul-converting Sign,
    And leave the rest to Him.

MOSES SEEING THE LAND

MY Father's hope! my childhood's dream
    The promise from on high!
Long waited for! its glories beam
    Now when my death is nigh.

My death is come, but not decay;
    Not eye nor mind is dim;
The keenness of youth's vigorous day
    Thrills in each nerve and limb.

Blest scene! thrice welcome after toil—
    If no deceit I view;
O might my lips but press the soil
    And prove the vision true!

Its glorious heights, its wealthy plains,
    Its many-tinted groves,
They call! but He my steps restrains
    Who chastens whom He loves.

Ah! now they melt . . . they are but
    shades . . .
I die!—yet is no rest,
O Lord! in store, since Canaan fades
    But seen, and not possest!

ISRAEL

"And all his sons and all his daughters rose up to comfort him: but he refused to be comforted."

SPECIOUS sin, and Satan's subtle snare,
    That urges sore each gentlest, meekest heart,
When its kind thoughts are crushed and its wounds smart,
World-sick to turn within and image there
Some idol dream, to lull the throbbing care!
    So felt reft Israel, when he fain would part
    With living friends; and called on memory's art
    To raise the dead and soothe him by despair.
Nor err they not, although that image be
God's own, nor to the dead their thoughts be given—
Earth-hating sure, but yet of earth enthralled;
For who dare sit at home, and wait to see
High Heaven descend, when man from self is called
Up through this thwarting outward world to Heaven?

DO not their souls, who 'neath the
    Altar wait
      Until their second-birth,
    The gift of patience need, as separate
From their first friends of earth?
Not that earth's blessings are not all outshone
    By Eden's Angel flame,
But that earth knows not yet, the Dead has won
    That crown, which was his aim.
For when he left it, 'twas a twilight scene
    About his silent bier,
A breathless struggle, faith and sight between,
    And Hope and sacred Fear.
Fear startled at his pains and dreary end,
    Hope raised her chalice high,
And the twin-sisters still his shade attend,
    Viewed in the mourner's eye.

So day by day for him from earth ascends,
    As dew in summer-even,
The speechless intercession of his friends,
    Toward the azure heaven.
Ah! dearest, with a word he could dispel
    All questioning, and raise
Our hearts to rapture, whispering all was well,
    And turning prayer to praise.

And other secrets too he could declare,
    By patterns all divine,
His earthly creed retouching here and there,
    And deepening every line.
Dearest! he longs to speak, as I to know,
    And yet we both refrain:
It were not good; a little doubt below,
    And all will soon be plain.

From
TRACTS FOR THE TIMES
[1836]

TRACTS FOR THE TIMES.

By Members of the University of Oxford. / Vol. III. / for / 1835-6. / "If the trumpet give an uncertain sound, who shall prepare himself to the / battle?" / London: / Printed for J. G. & F. Rivington, / St. Paul's Church Yard, and Waterloo Place, Pall Mall; / & J. H. Parker, Oxford. / 1836. /

No. 75, from which the following poems are extracted, was by Newman, and was entitled "On the Roman Breviary as embodying the Substance of the Devotional Services of the Church Catholic."

From
TRACTS FOR THE TIMES

MATINS—SUNDAY

Nocte surgentes.

LET us arise, and watch by night
    And meditate always;
And chant, as in our Maker's sight,
    United hymns of praise.

So singing with the Saints in bliss,
    With them we may attain
Life everlasting after this,
    And heaven for earthly pain.

Grant it to us, O Father, Son,
    And Spirit, God of grace,
To whom all worship shall be done
    In every time and place.

LAUDS—SUNDAY

Ecce jam noctis.

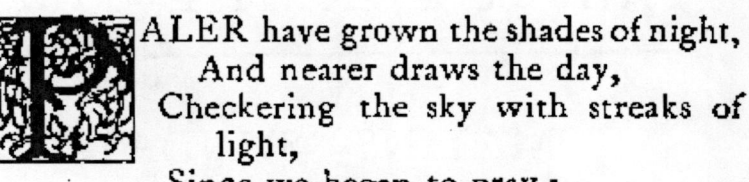

PALER have grown the shades of night,
    And nearer draws the day,
Checkering the sky with streaks of
    light,
    Since we began to pray:

To pray for mercy when we sin,
    For cleansing and release,
For ghostly safety, and within
    For everlasting peace.

Grant this to us, O Father, Son,
    And Spirit, God of grace,
To whom all worship shall be done
    In every time and place.

PRIME—SUNDAY

THE star of morn to night succeeds,
   We therefore meekly pray,
May God in all our words and deeds
   Keep us from harm this day.

May He in love restrain us still
From tones of strife and words of ill,
And wrap around and close our eyes
To earth's absorbing vanities.

May wrath and thoughts that gender shame
   Ne'er in our breasts abide,
And painful abstinences tame
   Of wanton flesh the pride;
So when the weary day is o'er
And night and stillness come once more,
Blameless and clean from spot of earth,
We may repeat, with reverent mirth,

Praise to the Father as is meet,
   Praise to the only Son,
Praise to the Holy Paraclete
   While endless ages run.

[The last two lines of the second stanza were altered in the 1853 volume to—

   Strong in self-conquering purity,
     We may proclaim with choirs on high,]

TERCE—SUNDAY

Nunc sancte nobis Spiritus.

COME, Holy Ghost, who ever One
Art with the Father and the Son,
Come, Holy Ghost, our souls possess
With Thy full flood of holiness.

Let mouth, and heart, and flesh combine
To herald forth our creed divine ;
And love so wrap our mortal frame,
Others may catch the living flame.

This grace on Thy redeemed confer,
Father, Co-equal Son,
And Holy Ghost, the Comforter,
Eternal Three in One.

SEXT—SUNDAY

Rector potens, verax Deus.

GOD, the Lord of place and time,
    Who orderest all things prudently,
Brightening with beams the opening
    prime,
    And burning in the mid-day sky,

Quench Thou the fires of hate and strife,
    The wasting fever of the heart :
From perils guard our feeble life,
    And to our souls Thy peace impart.

This grace on Thy redeemed confer,
    Father, Co-equal Son,
And Holy Ghost, the Comforter,
    Eternal Three in One.

NONE—SUNDAY

Rerum Deus tenax vigor.

GOD, unchangeable and true,
   Of all the Life and Power,
Dispensing light in silence through
   Every successive hour,

Lord, brighten our declining day,
   That it may never wane,
Till death, when all things round decay,
   Brings back the morn again.

This grace on Thy redeemed confer,
   Father, Co-equal Son,
And Holy Ghost, the Comforter,
   Eternal Three in One.

VESPERS—SUNDAY

Lucis Creator optime.

FATHER of Lights, by whom each day
    Is kindled out of night,
  Who, when the heavens were made, didst lay
    Their rudiments in light ;
Thou, who didst bind and blend in one
  The glistening morn and evening pale,
Hear Thou our plaint, when light is gone,
  And lawlessness and strife prevail.

Hear, lest the whelming weight of crime
  Wreck us with life in view ;
Lest thoughts and schemes of sense and time
  Earn us a sinner's due.
So may we knock at Heaven's door,
  And strive the prize of life to win,
Continually and evermore
  Guarded without and pure within.

This grace on Thy redeemed confer,
  Father, Co-equal Son,
And Holy Ghost, the Comforter,
  Eternal Three in One.

COMPLINE—SUNDAY

Te lucis ante terminum.

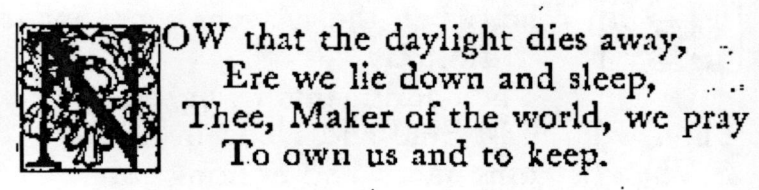

NOW that the daylight dies away,
 Ere we lie down and sleep,
Thee, Maker of the world, we pray
 To own us and to keep.

Let dreams depart and visions fly,
 The offspring of the night,
Keep us, like shrines, beneath Thine eye,
 Pure in our foe's despite.

This grace on Thy redeemed confer,
 Father, Co-equal Son,
And Holy Ghost, the Comforter,
 Eternal Three in One.

THE TRANSFIGURATION—
MATINS

Quicunque Christum quæritis.

YE who seek the Lord,
    Lift up your eyes on high,
For there He doth the Sign accord
    Of His bright majesty.

We see a wondrous sight
    That shall outlive all time,
Older than depth and starry height,
    Limitless and sublime.

'Tis He for Israel's fold
    And heathen tribes decreed,
The King to Abraham pledged of old
    And his unfailing seed.

Prophets foretold His birth,
    And witnessed when He came,
The Father speaks to all the earth
    To hear, and fear His name.

To Jesus, who displays
    To babes His beaming face,
Be, with the Father, endless praise,
    And with the Spirit of grace.

THE TRANSFIGURATION—
LAUDS

Lux alma Jesu.

LIGHT of the anxious heart,
   Jesu, Thy suppliants hear,
  Bid Thou the gloom of guilt depart,
   And shed Thy sweetness here.

Happy the man, whose breast
   Thou makest thy residence ;
From God's right hand a radiant guest ;
   Unseen by fleshly sense.

Brightness of God above !
   Unfathomable grace !
Vouchsafe a present fount of love
   To cleanse Thy chosen place.

To Thee whom children see,
   The Father ever blest,
The Holy Spirit, One and Three,
   Be endless praise addrest.

FIRST VESPERS — FEAST OF ST. LAURENCE

MARTYR of Christ, thy fight is won,
Following the Father's only Son;
O'er thy fall'n foes thou triumphest
In heavenly courts a risen guest.
Use thou for us thy gift of prayer
To cleanse thy brethren's sin,
To sweeten earth's infectious air,
And gain us peace within.

For ever broken is the chain
That bound thy body's hallowed fane;
As God hath given thee, break the tie
Which links our hearts to vanity.
To God the Father, God the Son,
And God the Paraclete,
Be praise, while circling ages run
Beneath the Eternal's feet.

MATINS—FEAST OF ST. LAURENCE

Deus tuorum militum.

GOD, of Thy soldiers
    the Portion and Crown,
Spare sinners who hymn
    the praise of the Blest;
Earth's bitter joys,
    its lures and its frown,
He scann'd them and scorn'd,
    and so is at rest.

The Martyr he ran
    all valiantly o'er
A highway of blood
    for the prize Thou hast given.
We kneel at Thy feet,
    and meekly implore,
That our pardon may wait
    on his triumph in heaven.

Honour and praise
  To the Father and Son,
  And the Spirit be done
Now and always.

From
THE CHURCH OF THE FATHERS
[1840]

The Church / of / the Fathers. /

Who is she that looketh forth as the morning, / fair as the morn, clear as the sun, and terrible as an / army with banners? / London : / Printed for J. G. F. & J. Rivington, / St. Paul's Church Yard, / and Waterloo Place, Pall Mall. / 1840. /

The translations, all from St. Gregory Nazianzen, occur in the sections entitled respectively "Basil and Gregory" and "Rise and Fall of Gregory."

From THE CHURCH OF THE FATHERS

[Gregory thus describes, in after life, his early intimacy with Basil.]

ATHENS and letters followed on my
    stage ;
    Others may tell how I encountered
    them ;—
How in the fear of God, and foremost found
Of those who knew a more than mortal lore ;—
And how, amid the venture and the risk
Of maddened youth with youth in rivalry,
My tranquil course ran like some fabled spring,
Which bubbles fresh beneath the turbid brine ;
Not drawn away by those who lure to ill,
But drawing dear ones to the better part.
There, too, I gained a further gift of God,
Who made me friends with one of wisdom high,
Without compeer in learning and in life.
Ask ye his name ?—in sooth, 'twas Basil, since
My life's great gain,—and then my fellow dear

In home, and studious search, and knowledge
    earned.
May I not boast how in our day we moved
A truest pair, not without name in Greece;
Had all things common, and one only soul
In lodgement of a double outward frame?
Our special bond, the thought of God above,
And the high longing after holy things.
And each of us was bold to trust in each,
Unto the emptying of our deepest hearts,
And then we loved the more, for sympathy
Pleaded in each, and knit the twain in one.

[Gregory describes the life which was the common choice of Basil and himself.]

FIERCE was the whirlwind of my storm-toss'd mind,
   Searching, 'mid holiest ways, a holier still.
Long had I nerved me, in the depths to sink
Thoughts of the flesh, and then more strenuously.
Yet, while I gazed upon diviner aims,
I had not wit to single out the best:
For, as is aye the wont in things of earth,
Each had its evil, each its nobleness.
I was the pilgrim of a toilsome course,
Who had o'erpast the waves, and now look'd round,
With anxious eye, to track his road by land.
Then did the awful Tishbite's image rise,
His highest Carmel, and his food uncouth ;
The Baptist wealthy in his solitude ;
And the unencumbered sons of Jonadab.
But soon I felt the love of holy books,
The spirit beaming bright in learned lore ;
Which deserts could not hear, nor silence tell.
Long was the inward strife, till ended thus :—
I saw, when men lived in the fretful world,
They vantaged other men, but wrong'd the while

Their own calm hearts, which straight by
 storms were tried.
They who retired held an uprighter port,
And raised their eyes with quiet strength
 towards God ;
Yet served self only on moroser plan.
And so, 'twixt these and those, I struck my
 path,
To meditate with the free solitary,
Yet to live secular, and serve mankind.

[Gregory passed the whole of one Lent without speaking, with a view of gaining command over his tongue, in which he felt his deficiency. The following passages allude to this or to similar infirmities.]

I LOST, O Lord, the use of yesterday;
Anger came on, and stole my heart away.
O may I find this morn some inward-piercing ray!

* * * * *

The serpent comes anew! I hold thy feet.
O David! list, and strike thy harp-strings sweet!
Hence! choking spirit, hence! for saintly minds unmeet.

MORNING

I RISE and yield my clasped hands to Thee!
Henceforth, no deed of dark 'shall trouble me,
Thy sacrifice this day;
Calm, stationed at my post, and with free soul
Stemming the waves of passion as they roll.
Ah! should I from thee stray,
My hoary head, Thy table where I bow,
Will be my shame, which are mine honour now.
Thus I set out;—Lord! lead me on my way!

EVENING

O HOLIEST Truth! how have I lied
    to Thee!
This day I vowed Thy festival should
    be;
    Yet I am dim ere night.
Surely I made my prayer, and I did deem
That I could keep me in Thy morning beam,
    Immaculate and bright.
But my foot slipped, and, as I lay, he came,
My gloomy foe, and robbed me of heaven's flame.
Help Thou my darkness, Lord, till I am light.

[Gregory refers to his priesthood.]

IN service o'er the mystic feast I stand,
   I cleanse Thy victim-flock, and bring
     them near
   In holiest wise, and by a bloodless rite.
O bounteous blaze ! O gushing Fount of Light !
(As best I know, who need Thy cleansing hand,)
Dread office this, bemired souls to clear
Of their defilement, and again make bright.

[Gregory contrasts the spirit and the letter.]

As viewing sin, e'en in its faintest trace,
    Murder in wrath, and in the wanton oath
    The perjured tongue, and therefore shunning them,
So deem'd I safe a strict virginity.
And hence our ample choir of holiest souls
Are followers of the unfleshly seraphim,
And Him who 'mid them reigns in lonely light.
These, one and all, rush towards the thought of death,
And hope of second life, with single heart,
Loosed from the law and chain of marriage-vow.
For I was but a captive at my birth,
Sin my first being, till its base discipline
Revolted me towards a nobler path,
Then Christ drew near me, and the Virgin-born
Spoke the new call to join His virgin-train.
So now towards highest heaven my innocent brow
I raise exultingly, sans let or bond,
Leaving no heir of this poor tabernacle
To ape me when my proper frame is broke;
But solitary with my only God,
And truest souls to bear me company.

[Gregory contrasts the married and the single estates.]

As when the hand some mimic form would paint,
It marks its purpose first in shadows faint,
And next its store of varied hues applies,
Till outlines fade, and the full limbs arise ;
So the Lord's holy choice, the virgin heart,
Once held in duty but a lesser part,
When the Law swayed us in Religion's youth,
Tracing, with lustre pale, the angelic truth,
But, when the Christ came by a Virgin-birth,—
His radiant chariot-course from heaven to earth,—
And, spurning father for His mortal state,
Did Eve and all her daughters consecrate ;
Solved fleshly laws, and in the letter's place
Gave us the Spirit and the Word of Grace,
Then shone the glorious Celibate at length,
Robed in the dazzling lightnings of its strength,
Surpassing spells of earth and marriage vow,
As soul the body, heaven this world below,
The eternal peace of saints life's troubled span,
And the high throne of God the haunts of man.
So now there circles round the King of Light
A heaven on earth, a blameless court and bright,

Aiming as emblems of their God to shine,
Christ in their heart, and on their brow His
  Sign,—
Soft funeral lights in the world's twilight dim,
Seeing their God, and ever one with Him.

Ye countless brethren of the marriage-band,
Slaves of the enfeebled heart and plighted hand,
I see you bear aloft your haughty gaze,
Gems deck your hair, and silk your limbs arrays;
Come, tell the gain which wedlock has conferred
On man; and then the single shall be heard.

The married many thus might plead, I ween;
Full glib their tongue, full confident their
  mien :—
" Hear, all who live! to whom the nuptial rite
Has brought the privilege of life and light.
We who are wedded, but the law obey
Stamped at creation on our blood and clay,
What time the Demiurge our line began,
Oped Adam's side, and out of man drew man.
Thenceforth let children of a mortal sod
Honour the law of earth, the primal law of God.

  " List, you shall hear the gifts of price that lie
Gathered and bound within the marriage-tie.
Who taught the arts of life, the truths that sleep
In earth, or highest heaven, or vasty deep?
Who raised the town? who gave the type and
  germ

Of social union, and of sceptre firm?
Who filled the mart, and urged the vessel brave
To link in one far countries o'er the wave?
Who the first husbandman the glebe to plough,
And rear the garden, but the marriage vow?

"Nay, list again! Who seek its kindly chain,
A second self, a double presence gain;
Hands, eyes, and ears, to act or suffer here,
Till e'en the weak inspire both love and fear,—
A comrade's sigh, to soothe when ears annoy,
A comrade's smile, to elevate his joy.

"Nor say it binds to an ungodly life,
When want is urgent, prayers and vows are rife.
Light heart he bears, who has no yoke at home,
Scant need of blessings, as the seasons come;
But wife, and offspring, and the treasured hoard,
Raise us in dread and faith towards the Lord.
Take love away, and life would be defaced,
A ghastly vision on the mountain-waste,
Heartless and stern, bereft of the soft charm
Which steals from age its woes, from passion's
  sting its harm.
No child's sweet pranks, once more to make
  us young;
No ties of place about our heart-strings flung;
No public haunts to cheer; no festive tide
Where harmless mirth and smiling wit preside;
A life which scorns the gifts by heaven assign'd,
Nor knows the sympathy of human kind.

"Prophets and teachers, priests and victor
    kings,
Decked with each grace which heaven-taught
    nature brings,
These were no giant offspring of the earth,
But to the marriage-promise owe their birth :—
Moses and Samuel, David, David's Son,
The blessed Tishbite, and more blessed John,
The sacred Twelve in apostolic choir,
Strong-hearted Paul, instinct with seraph fire,
And others, now or erst, who to high heaven
    aspire.
Bethink ye ; should the single state be best,
Yet who the single, but my offspring blest ?
My sons, be still, nor with your parents
    strive :
They coupled in their day, and so ye live."

    Thus marriage pleads.   Now let her rival
        speak—
Dim is her downcast eye, and pale her
    cheek ;
Untrimm'd her gear ; no sandals on her feet ;
A sparest form for austere tenant meet.
She drops her veil her modest face around,
And her lips open, but we hear no sound.
I will address her :—" Hail, O child of Heaven,
Glorious within ! to whom a post is given
Hard by the Throne where angels bow and
    fear,
E'en while thou hast a name and mission here,

O deign thy voice, unveil thy brow and see
Thy ready guard and minister in me.
Oft hast thou come heaven-wafted to my breast,
Bright Spirit! so come again, and give me rest."

. . . "Ah, who has hither drawn my backward feet,
Changing for worldly strife my lone retreat?
Where, in the silent chant of holy deeds,
I praise my God, and tend the sick soul's needs;
By toils of day, and vigils of the night,
By gushing tears, and blessed lustral rite.
I have no sway amid the crowd, no art
In speech, no place in council or in mart.
Nor human law, nor judges throned on high,
Smile on my face, and grant my words reply.
Let others seek earth's honours; be it mine
One law to cherish, and to track one line;
Straight on towards heaven to press with single bent,
To know and love my God, and then to die content."

[These stanzas give an account of the place and circumstances of Gregory's retirement.]

SOME one whispered yesterday
   Of the rich and fashionable,
"Gregory, in his own small way,
   Easy was, and comfortable.

"Had he not of wealth his fill,
   Whom a garden gay did bless,
And a gently trickling rill,
   And the sweets of idleness?"

I made answer, "Is it ease,
   Fasts to keep, and tears to shed?
Vigil hours and wounded knees,
   Call you such a pleasant bed?

"Thus a veritable monk
   Does to death his fleshly frame;
Be there who in sloth are sunk,
   They have forfeited the name."

From
VERSES ON RELIGIOUS SUBJECTS
[1853]

VERSES / ON / RELIGIOUS SUBJECTS. /

Dublin : / James Duffy, 7, Wellington Quay. /
MDCCCLIII.

The dedication is as follows :—

FAMILIARIBUS SUIS
NUGARUM SERIARUM SCRIPTOR.

From VERSES ON RELIGIOUS SUBJECTS

GUARDIAN ANGEL

MY oldest friend, mine from the hour
    When first I drew my breath;
My faithful friend, that shall be
    mine,
    Unfailing till my death;

Thou hast been ever at my side;
    My Maker to thy trust
Consigned my soul, what time He framed
    The infant child of dust.

No beating heart in holy prayer,
    No faith, informed aright,
Gave me to Joseph's tutelage,
    Or Michael's conquering might.

Nor patron Saint, nor Mary's love,
    The dearest and the best,
Has known my being, as thou hast known,
    And blest as thou hast blest.

Thou wast my sponsor at the font;
  And thou, each budding year,
Didst whisper elements of truth
  Into my childish ear.

And when, ere boyhood yet was gone,
  My rebel spirit fell,
Oh! thou didst see, and shudder too,
  Yet bear each deed of Hell.

And then in turn, when judgments came,
  And scared me back again,
Thy quick soft breath was near to soothe
  And hallow every pain.

Oh! who of all thy toils and cares
  Can tell the tale complete,
To place me under Mary's smile,
  And Peter's royal feet!

And thou wilt hang about my bed,
  When life is ebbing low;
Of doubt, impatience, and of gloom,
  The jealous sleepless foe.

Mine, when I stand before the Judge;
  And mine, if spared to stay
Within the golden furnace, till
  My sin is burned away.

And mine, O Brother of my soul,
  When my release shall come;
Thy gentle arms shall lift me then,
  Thy wings shall waft me home.

TEMPTATION

HOLY Lord, who with the Children Three
    Didst walk the piercing flame,
Help, in those trial-hours, which, save to Thee,
    I dare not name;
Nor let these quivering eyes and sickening heart
Crumble to dust beneath the Tempter's dart.

Thou, who didst once Thy life from Mary's breast
    Renew from day to day,
O might her smile, severely sweet, but rest
    On this frail clay!
Till I am Thine with my whole soul; and fear,
Not feel a secret joy, that Hell is near.

MODESTY

Sacramentum regis abscondere bonum est; opera autem Dei revelare honorificum.

[These verses are paraphrased from St. Bede. St. Ethelwald was the successor of St. Cuthbert at Farne.]

BETWEEN two comrades dear,
    Zealous and true as they,
Thou, prudent Ethelwald, didst bear
    In that high home the sway.

A man, who ne'er, 'tis said,
    Would of his graces tell,
Or with what arms he triumphed
    Over the Dragon fell.

So down to us hath come
    A memorable word,
Which in unguarded season from
    His blessed lips was heard.

It chanced, that, as the Saint
    Drank in with faithful ear
Of Angel tones the whispers faint,
    Thus spoke a brother dear:

"Oh, why so many a pause,
    Thwarting thy words' full stream,
Till her dark line Oblivion draws
    Across the broken theme?"

He answered: "Till thou seal
    To sounds of Earth thine ear,
Sweet friend, be sure thou ne'er shalt feel
    Angelic voices near."

But then the hermit blest
    A sudden change came o'er;
He shudders, sobs, and smites his breast,
    Is mute, then speaks once more:

"Oh, by the Name Most High,
    What I have now let fall,
Hush till I lay me down to die,
    And go the way of all!"

Thus did a Saint in fear
    His gifts celestial hide;
Thus did an Angel standing near
    Proclaim them far and wide.

PURGATORY

Nec possum in monte salvari, ne moriar; est civitas hæc juxta, ad quam possum fugere, et salvabor in eâ.

WEEP not for me, when I am gone,
    Nor spend thy faithful breath
In murmurs at the spot or hour
    Of all-enfolding death;

Nor waste in idle praise thy love
    On deeds of head or hand,
Which live within the living Book,
    Or else are writ in sand;

But let it be thy best of prayers,
    That I may find the grace
To reach the holy house of toll,
    The frontier penance-place,—

To reach that golden palace bright,
    Where souls elect abide,
Waiting their certain call to Heaven,
    With angels at their side;

Where hate, nor pride, nor fear torments
    The transitory guest,
But in the willing agony
    He plunges, and is blest.

And as the fainting patriarch gained
　　His needful halt mid-way,
And then refreshed pursued his path,
　　Where up the mount it lay,

So pray, that, rescued from the storm
　　Of Heaven's eternal ire,
I may lie down, then rise again,
　　Safe, and yet saved by fire.

HYMNS

MATINS—SUNDAY *

Primo die, quo Trinitas.

TO-DAY the Blessed Three in One
    Began the earth and skies;
To-day Death's Conqueror, God the Son,
    Did from the grave arise;
We too will wake, and, in despite
Of sloth and languor, all unite,
As Psalmists bid, through the dim night,
    Waiting with wistful eyes.

So may He hear, and heed each vow
    And prayer to Him addrest;
And grant an instant cleansing now,
    A future glorious rest.
So may He plentifully shower,
On all who hymn His love and power,
In this most still and sacred hour,
    His sweetest gifts and best.

---

* These Hymns are all translations from the Roman Breviary, except the last, which is a Commune Episcoporum.

Father of purity and light !
  Thy presence if we win,
'Twill shield us from the deeds of night,
  The burning darts of sin ;
Lest aught defiled or dissolute
Relax our bodies or imbrute,
And fires eternal be the fruit
  Of fire now lit within.

Fix in our hearts, Redeemer dear,
  The ever-gushing spring
Of grace to cleanse, of life to cheer
  Souls sick and sorrowing.
Thee, bounteous Father, we entreat,
And Only Son, awful and sweet,
And life-creating Paraclete,
  The everlasting King.

MATINS—MONDAY

Somno refectis artubus.

SLEEP has refreshed our limbs, we spring
    From off our bed, and rise;
Lord, on Thy suppliants, while they sing,
    Look with a Father's eyes.

Be Thou the first on every tongue,
    The first in every heart;
That all our doings all day long,
    Holiest! from Thee may start.

Cleanse Thou the gloom, and bid the light
    Its healing beams renew;
The sins, which have crept in with night,
    With night shall vanish too.

Our bosoms, Lord, unburthen Thou,
    Let nothing there offend;
That those who hymn Thy praises now
    May hymn them to the end.

Grant this, O Father, Only Son,
    And Spirit, God of grace,
To whom all worship shall be done
    In every time and place.

MATINS—TUESDAY

Consors Paterni luminis.

GOD from God, and Light from Light,
    Who art Thyself the day,
Our chants shall break the clouds of night ;
    Be with us while we pray.

Chase Thou the gloom that haunts the mind,
    The thronging shades of hell,
The sloth and drowsiness that bind
    The senses with a spell.

Lord, to their sins indulgent be,
    Who, in this hour forlorn,
By faith in what they do not see,
    With songs prevent the morn.

Grant this, O Father, etc.

MATINS—WEDNESDAY

Rerum Creator optime.

WHO madest all and dost control,
    Lord, with Thy touch divine,
Cast out the slumbers of the soul,
    The rest that is not Thine.

Look down, Eternal Holiness,
    And wash the sins away,
Of those, who, rising to confess,
    Outstrip the lingering day.

Our hearts and hands by night, O Lord,
    We lift them in our need;
As holy Psalmists give the word,
    And holy Paul the deed.

Each sin to Thee of years gone by,
    Each hidden stain lies bare;
We shrink not from Thine awful eye,
    But pray that Thou wouldst spare.

Grant this, O Father, etc.

MATINS—THURSDAY

Nox atra rerum contegit.

ALL tender lights, all hues divine
    The night has swept away ;
Shine on us, Lord, and we shall
    shine
    Bright in an inward day.

The spots of guilt, sin's wages base,
    Searcher of hearts, we own ;
Wash us and robe us in Thy grace,
    Who didst for sins atone.

The sluggard soul, that bears their mark,
    Shrinks in its silent lair,
Or gropes amid its chambers dark
    For Thee, who art not there.

Redeemer ! send Thy piercing rays,
    That we may bear to be
Set in the light of Thy pure gaze,
    And yet rejoice in Thee.

Grant this, O Father, etc.

MATINS—FRIDAY

Tu Trinitatis Unitas.

MAY the dread Three in One, who sways
   All with His sovereign might,
Accept us for this hymn of praise,
   His watchers in the night.

For in the night, when all is still
   We spurn our bed and rise,
To find the balm for ghostly ill
   His bounteous hand supplies.

If e'er by night our envious foe
   With guilt our souls would stain,
May the deep streams of mercy flow,
   And make us white again;

That so with bodies braced and bright,
   And hearts awake within,
All fresh and keen may burn our light,
   Undimm'd, unsoiled by sin.

Shine on Thine own, Redeemer sweet!
   Thy radiance increate
Through the long day shall keep our feet
   In their pure morning state.

Grant this, O Father, etc.

MATINS—SATURDAY

Summæ Parens clementiæ.

FATHER of mercies infinite,
   Ruling all things that be,
Who, shrouded in the depth or height,
   Art One, and yet art Three;

Accept our chants, accept our tears,
   A mingled stream we pour;
Such stream the laden bosom cheers,
   To taste Thy sweetness more.

Purge Thou with fire the o'ercharged mind,
   Its sores and wounds profound;
And with the watcher's girdle bind
   The limbs which sloth has bound.

That they who with their chants by night
   Before Thy presence come,
All may be filled with strength and light
   From their eternal home.

Grant this, O Father, etc.

LAUDS—SUNDAY

Æterne rerum conditor.

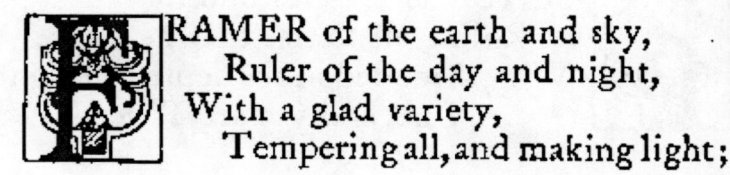

FRAMER of the earth and sky,
    Ruler of the day and night,
With a glad variety,
    Tempering all, and making light;

Gleams upon our dark path flinging,
    Cutting short each night begun,
Hark! Thy herald-cock is singing,
    Hark! he chides the lingering sun.

And the morning star replies,
    And unlocks the imprisoned day;
And the godless bandit flies
    From his haunt and from his prey.

Shrill it sounds, the storm relenting
    Soothes the weary seaman's ears;
Once it wrought a great repenting,
    In that flood of Peter's tears.

Rouse we; let the blithesome cry
    Of that bird our hearts awaken;
Chide the slumberers as they lie,
    And convince the sin-o'ertaken.

Hope and health are in his train,
    To the fearful and the ailing;
Murder sheathes his blade profane,
    Faith revives when faith was failing.

Jesu, Master! when we sin,
    Turn on us Thy healing face;
It will melt the offence within
    Into penitential grace:

Beam on our bewildered mind,
    Till its dreamy shadows flee;
Stones cry out where Thou hast shined,
    Jesu! musical with Thee.

To the Father and the Son,
    And the Spirit, who in Heaven
Ever witness, Three and One,
    Praise on Earth be ever given.

LAUDS—MONDAY

Splendor Paternæ gloriæ.

F the Father Effluence bright,
Out of Light evolving light,
Light from Light, unfailing Ray,
Day creative of the day:

Truest Sun, upon us stream
With Thy calm perpetual beam,
In the Spirit's still sunshine
Making sense and thought divine.

Seek we too the Father's face
Father of almighty grace,
And of majesty excelling,
Who can purge our tainted dwelling;

Who can aid us, who can break
Teeth of envious foes, and make
Hours of loss and pain succeed,
Guiding safe each duteous deed,

And infusing self-control,
Fragrant chastity of soul,
Faith's keen flame to soar on high,
Incorrupt simplicity.

Christ Himself for food be given,
Faith become the cup of Heaven,
Out of which the joy is quaff'd
Of the Spirit's sobering draught.

With that joy replenished,
Morn shall glow with modest red,
Noon with beaming faith be bright,
Eve be soft without twilight.

It has dawned ;—upon our way,
Father in Thy Word, this day,
In Thy Father Word Divine,
From Thy cloudy pillar shine.

To the Father, and the Son,
And the Spirit, Three and One,
As of old, and as in Heaven,
Now and here be glory given.

LAUDS—TUESDAY

Ales diei nuntius.

DAY'S herald bird
    At length is heard,
  Telling its morning torch is lit,
    And small and still
    Christ's accents thrill,
Within the heart rekindling it.

    Away, He cries,
    With languid eyes,
And sickly slumbers profitless!
    I am at hand,
    As watchers stand,
In awe, and truth, and holiness.

    He will appear
    The hearts to cheer
Of suppliants pale and abstinent;
    Who cannot sleep
    Because they weep
With holy grief and violent.

    Keep us awake,
    The fetters break,
Jesu! which night has forged for us;

Yea, melt the night
To sinless light,
Till all is bright and glorious.

To Father, Son,
And Spirit, One,
To the Most Holy Trinity,
All praise be given,
In Earth and Heaven,
Now, as of old, and endlessly.

LAUDS—WEDNESDAY

Nox et tenebræ et nubila.

HAUNTING gloom and flitting shades,
    Ghastly shapes, away!
Christ is rising, and pervades
    Highest Heaven with day.

His bright spear the dazzled night
    Chases and pursues;
Earth wakes up, and glows with light
    Of a thousand hues.

Thee, O Christ, and Thee alone,
    With a single mind,
We with chant and plaint would own:
    To Thy flock be kind.

Much it needs Thy light divine,
    Spot and stain to clean;
Light of Angels, on us shine
    With Thy face serene.

To the Father, and the Son,
    And the Holy Ghost,
Here be glory, as is done
    By the angelic host.

LAUDS—THURSDAY

Lux ecce surgit aurea.

SEE, the golden dawn is glowing
While the paly shades are going,
Which have led us far and long,
In a labyrinth of wrong.

May it bring us peace serene ;
May it cleanse, as it is clean ;
Plain and clear our words be spoke,
And our thoughts without a cloak ;

So the day's account, shall stand,
Guileless tongue and holy land,
Stedfast eyes and unbeguiled,
Flesh as of a little child.

There is One who from above
Watches how the still hours move
Of our day of service done,
From the dawn to setting sun.

To the Father, and the Son,
And the Spirit, Three and One,
As of old, and as in Heaven,
Now and here be glory given.

LAUDS—FRIDAY

Æterna cœli gloria.

GLORY of the eternal Heaven,
    Blessed Hope to mortals given,
    Of the Almighty Only Son,
    And the Virgin's Holy One ;
Raise us, Lord, and we shall rise
    In a sober mood,
And a zeal, which glorifies
    Thee from gratitude.

Now the day-star, keenly glancing,
Tells us of the Sun's advancing ;
While the unhealthy shades decline,
Rise within us, Light Divine !
Rise, and, risen, go not hence,
    Stay, and make us bright,
Streaming through each cleansèd sense,
    On the outward night.

Then the root of faith shall spread
In the heart new fashionèd ;
Gladsome hope shall spring above,
And shall bear the fruit of love.
To the Father, and the Son,
    And the Holy Ghost,
Here be glory, as is done
    By th' Angelic host.

LAUDS—SATURDAY

Aurora jam spargit polum.

THE dawn is sprinkled o'er the sky,
    The day steals softly on ;
    Its darts are scattered far and nigh,
    And all that fraudful is, shall fly
    Before the brightening sun ;
Spectres of ill, that stalk at will,
    And forms of guilt that fright,
And hideous sin, that ventures in
    Under the cloak of night.

And of our crimes the tale complete,
    Which bows us in Thy sight,
Up to the latest, they shall fleet,
Out-told by our full numbers sweet,
    And melted by the light.
To Father, Son, and Spirit, One,
    Whom we adore and love,
Be given all praise now and always,
    Here as in Heaven above.

VESPERS—MONDAY

Immense cœli conditor.

LORD of unbounded space,
   Who, lest the sky and main
Should mix, and heaven should lose
   its place,
   Didst the rude waters chain;

Parting the moist and rare,
   That rills on earth might flow
To soothe the angry flame, whene'er
   It ravens from below;

Pour on us of Thy grace
   The everlasting spring;
Lest our frail steps renew the trace
   Of the ancient wandering.

May faith in lustre grow,
   And rear her star in heaven,
Paling all sparks of earth below,
   Unquenched by damps of even.

Grant it, O Father, Son,
   And Holy Spirit of grace,
To whom be glory, Three in One,
   In every time and place.

VESPERS—TUESDAY

Telluris alme conditor.

ALL-BOUNTIFUL Creator, who,
    When Thou didst mould the world, didst drain
The waters from the mass, that so
    Earth might immovable remain ;

That its dull clods it might transmute
    To golden flowers in vale or wood,
To juice of thirst-allaying fruit,
    And grateful herbage spread for food ;

Wash Thou our smarting wounds and hot,
    In the cool freshness of Thy grace ;
Till tears start forth the past to blot,
    And cleanse and calm Thy holy place ;

Till we obey Thy full behest,
    Shun the world's tainted touch and breath,
Joy in what highest is and best,
    And gain a spell to baffle death.

Grant it, O Father, Only Son,
    And Holy Spirit, God of Grace ;
To whom all glory, Three in One,
    Be given in every time and place.

VESPERS—WEDNESDAY

Cœli Deus sanctissime.

O LORD, who, throned in the holy
    height,
  Through plains of ether didst
    diffuse
    The dazzling beams of light,
    In soft transparent hues;

Who didst, on the fourth day, in heaven
  Light the fierce cresset of the sun,
    And the meek moon at even,
    And stars that wildly run;

That they might mark and arbitrate
  'Twixt alternating night and day,
    And tend the train sedate
    Of months upon their way;

Clear, Lord, the brooding night within,
  And clean these hearts for Thy abode,
    Unlock the spell of sin,
    Crumble its giant load.

Grant it, O Father, Only Son,
  And Holy Spirit, God of Grace,
    To whom all praise be done
    In every time and place.

VESPERS—THURSDAY

Magnæ Deus potentiæ.

GOD, who hast given
      the sea and the sky
To fish and to bird
      for a dwelling to keep,
Both sons of the waters,
      one low and one high,
Ambitious of heaven,
      yet sunk in the deep;

Save, Lord, Thy servants,
      whom Thou hast new made
In a laver of blood,
      lest they trespass and die;
Lest pride should elate,
      or sin should degrade,
And they stumble on earth,
      or be dizzied on high.

    To the Father and Son
    And the Spirit be done,
    Now and always,
    Glory and praise.

VESPERS—FRIDAY

Hominis superne conditor.

WHOM all obey,—
Maker of man! who from Thy height
Badest the dull earth bring to light
All creeping things, and the fierce might
    Of beasts of prey.

And the huge make
Of wild or gentler animal,
Springing from nothing at Thy call,
To serve in their due time, and all
    For sinners' sake;

Shield us from ill!
Come it by passion's sudden stress,
Lurk in our mind's habitual dress,
Or through our actions seek to press
    Upon our will.

Vouchsafe the prize
Of sacred joy's perpetual mood,
And service-seeking gratitude,
And love to quell each strife or feud,
    If it arise.

Grant it, O Lord!
To whom, the Father, Only Son,
And Holy Spirit, Three in One,
In heaven and earth all praise be done,
With one accord.

VESPERS—SATURDAY

Jam sol recedit igneus.

THE red sun is gone,
    Thou Light of the heart,
Blessed Three, Holy One,
To Thy servants a sun
    Everlasting impart.

There were Lauds in the morn;
    Here are Vespers at even.
Oh, may we adorn
Thy Temple new born
    With our voices in Heaven.

To the Father be praise,
    And praise to the Son
And the Spirit always,
While the infinite days
    Of eternity run.

ADVENT—VESPERS

Creator alme siderum.

CREATOR of the starry pole,
    Saviour of all who live,
And light of every faithful soul,
    Jesu, these prayers receive.

Who sooner than our foe malign
    Should triumph, from above
Didst come, to be the medicine
    Of a sick world, in love ;

And the deep wounds to cleanse and cure
    Of a whole race, didst go,
Pure Victim, from a Virgin pure,
    The bitter Cross unto.

Who hast a Name, and hast a Power,
    The height and depth to sway,
And angels bow, and devils cower,
    In transport or dismay ;

Thou too shalt be our Judge at length ;
    Lord, in Thy grace bestow
Thy weapons of celestial strength,
    And snatch us from the foe.

Honour and glory, power and praise,
To Father, and to Son,
And Holy Ghost, be paid always,
The Eternal Three in One.

ADVENT—MATINS

Verbum supernum prodiens.

SUPERNAL Word, proceeding from
   The Eternal Father's breast,
And in the end of ages come,
   To aid a world distrest;

Enlighten, Lord, and set on fire
   Our spirits with Thy love,
That, dead to earth, they may aspire
   And live to joys above.

That, when the judgment-seat on high
   Shall fix the sinner's doom,
And to the just a glad voice cry,
   Come to your destined home;

Safe from the black and yawning lake
   Of restless, endless pain,
We may the face of God partake,
   The bliss of heaven attain.

To God the Father, God the Son,
   And Holy Ghost, to Thee,
As heretofore, when time is done,
   Unending glory be.

ADVENT—LAUDS

En clara vox redarguit.

HARK, a joyful voice is thrilling,
    And each dim and winding way
Of the ancient Temple filling ;
    Dreams, depart ! for it is day.

Christ is coming !—from thy bed,
    Earth-bound soul, awake and spring,—
With the sun new-risen to shed
    Health on human suffering.

Lo ! to grant a pardon free,
    Comes a willing Lamb from Heaven ;
Sad and tearful, hasten we,
    One and all, to be forgiven.

Once again He comes in light,
    Girding earth with fear and woe ;
Lord ! be Thou our loving Might,
    From our guilt and ghostly foe.

To the Father, and the Son,
    And the Spirit, who in Heaven
Ever witness, Three and One,
    Praise on earth be ever given.

ON THE FEAST OF A CONFESSOR BISHOP

THOU, of shepherds Prince and Head
    Now on a Bishop's festal-day
Thy flock to many a shrine have sped
        Their vows to pay.

He to the high and dreadful throne
    Urged by no false inspirings, prest,
Nor on hot daring of his own,
        But Thy behest.

And so, that soldier good and tried,
    From the full horn of heavenly grace,
Thy Spirit did anoint, to guide
        Thy ransomed race.

And he becomes a father true,
    Spending and spent, when troubles fall,
A pattern and a servant too,
        All things to all.

His pleading sets the sinner free,
    He soothes the sick, he lifts the low,
Powerful in word, deep teacher, he
        To quell the foe.

Grant us, O Christ, his prayers above,
And grace below, to sing Thy praise,
The Father's power, the Spirit's love,
Here and always.

SONGS

CANDLEMAS

THE angel-lights of Christmas morn,
   Which shot across the sky,
Away they pass at Candlemas,
   They sparkle and they die.

Comfort of earth is brief at best,
   Although it be divine ;
Like funeral lights for Christmas gone
   Old Simeon's tapers shine.

And then for eight long weeks and more,
   We wait in twilight grey,
Till the tall candle sheds a beam
   On Holy Saturday.

We wait along the penance-tide
   Of solemn fast and prayer ;
While song is hushed, and lights grow dim
   In the sin-laden air.

And while the sword in Mary's soul
   Is driven home, we hide
In our own hearts, and count the wounds
   Of passion and of pride.

And still, though Candlemas be spent
And Alleluias o'er,
Mary is music in our need,
And Jesus light in store.

THE PILGRIM QUEEN

THERE sat a Lady
    all on the ground,
Rays of the morning
    circled her round,
Save thee, and hail to thee,
    Gracious and Fair,
In the chill twilight
    what wouldst thou there?

"Here I sit desolate,"
    sweetly said she,
"Though I'm a Queen,
    and my name is Marie:
Robbers have rifled
    my garden and store,
Foes they have stolen
    my heir from my bower.

"They said they could keep Him
    far better than I,
In a palace all His,
    planted deep and rais'd high.
'Twas a palace of ice,
    hard and cold as were they,
And when summer came,
    it all melted away.

"Next would they barter Him,
  Him the Supreme,
For the spice of the desert,
  and gold of the stream ;
And me they bid wander
  in weeds and alone,
In this green merry land
  which once was my own."

I looked on that Lady,
  and out from her eyes
Came the deep glowing blue
  of Italy's skies ;
And she raised up her head
  And she smiled, as a Queen
On the day of her crowning,
  so bland and serene.

"A moment," she said,
  "and the dead shall revive ;
The giants are failing,
  the saints are alive ;
I am coming to rescue
  my home and my reign,
And Peter and Philip
  are close in my train."

THE MONTH OF MARY

GREEN are the leaves, and sweet the
    flowers,
  And rich the hues of May;
  We see them in the gardens round,
  And market-paniers gay:
And e'en among our streets, and lanes,
  And alleys, we descry,
By fitful gleams, the fair sunshine,
  The blue transparent sky.

Chorus.

O Mother maid, be thou our aid,
  Now in the opening year;
Lest sights of earth to sin give birth,
  And bring the tempter near.

Green is the grass, but wait awhile,
  'Twill grow, and then will wither;
The flowrets, brightly as they smile,
  Shall perish altogether:
The merry sun, you sure would say,
  It ne'er could set in gloom;
But earth's best joys have all an end,
  And sin, a heavy doom.

Chorus.

But Mother maid, thou dost not fade ;
   With stars above thy brow,
And the pale moon beneath thy feet,
   For ever throned art thou.

The green green grass, the glittering grove,
   The Heaven's majestic dome,
They image forth a tenderer bower,
   A more refulgent home ;
They tell us of that Paradise
   Of everlasting rest,
And that high Tree, all flowers and fruit,
   The sweetest, yet the best.

Chorus.

O Mary, pure and beautiful,
   Thou art the Queen of May ;
Our garlands wear about thy hair,
   And they will ne'er decay.

MARY, THE QUEEN OF THE SEASONS

(For an inclement May)

ALL is divine
  which the Highest has made,
Thro' the days that He wrought,
  till the day when He stayed;
Above and below,
  within and around,
From the centre of space,
  to its uttermost bound.

In beauty surpassing
  the Universe smiled,
On the morn of its birth,
  like an innocent child.
Or like the rich bloom
  of some gorgeous flower;
And the Father rejoiced
  in the work of His power.

Yet worlds brighter still,
  and a brighter than those,
And a brighter again,
  He had made, had He chose;

And you never could name
    that conceivable best,
To exhaust the resources
    the Maker possessed.

But I know of one work
    of His Infinite Hand,
Which special and singular
    ever must stand;
So perfect, so pure,
    and of gifts such a store,
That even Omnipotence
    cannot do more.

The freshness of May,
    and the sweetness of June,
And the fire of July
    in its passionate noon,
Munificent August,
    September serene,
Are together no match
    for my glorious Queen.

O Mary, all months
    and all days are thine own,
In thee lasts their joyousness,
    when they are gone;
And we give to thee May,
    not because it is best,
But because it comes first,
    and is pledge of the rest.

PETER AND PHILIP

IN the far north our lot is cast,
    Where faithful hearts are few ;
Still are we Philip's children dear,
    And Peter's soldiers true.

Founder and Sire ! to mighty Rome,
    Beneath St. Peter's shade,
Early thy vow of loyal love
    And ministry was paid.

The ample porch, and threshold high,
    Of Peter was thy home ;
The world's apostle he, and thou
    Apostle of his Rome.

And first in the old catacombs,
    In galleries long and deep,
Where martyr Popes had ruled the flock,
    And slept their glorious sleep,

Through the still night in silent prayer,
    Thou tarriedst, till there came,
Down on thy breast, new lit for thee,
    The Pentecostal flame.

Then in that heart-consuming love,
   Thou, through the city wide,
Didst wile the noble and the young
   From Babel's pomp and pride;

And, gathering them within thy cell,
   Unveil the lustre bright,
And beauty of thy inner soul,
   And gain them by the sight.

And thus to Rome, for Peter's faith
   Far known, thou didst impart
A rule of life, and works of love,
   And discipline of heart.

And the apostle, on the hill
   Facing the imperial town,
First gazed upon his fair domain,
   Then on the cross lay down,

So thou, from out the streets of Rome,
   Didst turn thy failing eye
Unto that mount of martyrdom,*
   Take leave of it, and die.

---

* On the day of his death, Philip, "at the beginning of his Mass, remained for some time looking fixedly at the hill of St. Onofrio, which was visible from the chapel, just as if he saw some great vision. On coming to the Gloria in Excelsis, he began to sing, which was a very unusual thing for him, and he sang the whole of it with the greatest joy and devotion," etc.—" Bacci's Life."

THE REGULAR SAINTS AND PHILIP

THE holy Monks, conceal'd from men,
   In midnight choir, or studious cell,
In sultry field, or wintry glen,
   The holy Monks,—I love them well.

The Friars too, the zealous band
   Of Francis and of Dominic,
They gather, and they take their stand
   Where foes are fierce, or souls are sick.

And then the unwearied Company,
   Which bears the name and sacred might,
The Knights of Jesus, they defy
   The fiend, full eager for the fight.

Yet there is one I more affect
   Than Jesuit, Hermit, Monk, or Friar,
'Tis an old man of sweet aspect,
   I love him more, I more admire.

I know him by his head of snow,
   His ready smile, his keen full eye,
His words which kindle as they flow ;
   Save he be rapt in ecstasy.

He lifts his hands, there issues forth
    A fragrance virginal and rare,
And now he ventures to our North,
    Where hearts are frozen as the air.

He comes, by grace of his address,
    By the sweet music of his face,
And his low tones of tenderness,
    To melt a noble, stubborn race.

O sainted Philip, Father dear,
    Look on thy little ones, that we
Thy loveliness may copy here,
    And in the eternal Kingdom see.

MARY AND PHILIP

THIS is the Saint of sweetness and
    compassion,
    Cheerful in penance, and in precept
    winning,
Beckoning and luring in a holy fashion
            Souls that are sinning.

This is the Saint, who, when the bad world
    vaunteth
Her many coloured wares and magic treasures,
Outbids her, and her victim disenchanteth
            With heavenly pleasures.

This is the Saint, with whom our hearts, like
    Moses,
Find o'er the waste that Tree, so bright and
    beaming,
Till 'neath her shade the sobered soul reposes,
            After its dreaming.

And then he shakes the boughs where it is
    lying,
Nor of their fruit are those sweet branches chary,
Mary the tree, Jesus the fruit undying—
            Jesus and Mary;

Jesu and Mary, Philip, and high Heaven,
Angels, of God the glorious reflexion,
To you be praise, to us from you be given
        Peace and protection.

JESUS AND PHILIP

PHILIP, on thee the glowing ray
    Of heaven came down upon thy prayer,
To melt thy heart and burn away
    All that of earthly dross was there.

Thy soul became as purest glass
    Through which the Brightness Increate
In undimmed majesty might pass,
    Transparent and illuminate.

And so, on Philip when we gaze,
    We see the image of his Lord;
The Saint dissolves amid the blaze
    Which circles round the Living Word.

The Meek, the Wise, none else is here,
    Dispensing light to men below;
His awful accents fill the ear,
    Now keen as fire, now soft as snow.

As snow, those inward pleadings fall,
    As soft, as bright, as pure, as cool,
With gentle weight and gradual,
    And sink into the feverish soul.

The Sinless One, He comes to seek,
    The dreary heart, the spirit lone,
Tender of natures proud or weak,
    Not less than if they were His own.

He takes and scans the sinner o'er,
    Handling His scholars one by one,
Weighing what they can bear, before
    He gives the penance to be done.

Jesu, to Philip's sons reveal
    That gentlest wisdom from above,
To spread compassion o'er their zeal,
    And mingle patience with their love.

THE HOLY TRINITY

THE one true Faith, the ancient Creed,
    Martyrs for it were fain to fight and
      bleed ;
    The holy Sign, our awful spell,
It is the Cross, triumphant over Hell ;
The Cross, the Creed, the Faith, O triply blest,
They sanctify our brow, and lips, and breast ;
The Cross, the Creed, the Faith, O triply blest,
Are on our brow, and lips, and breast.

The Church of God, the world-wide name,
Found in all lands, yet everywhere the same ;
Love with its thrilling unison
Knows how to knit ten thousand hearts in one.
Behold a triple bond where'er we rove,
'Tis one, 'tis Catholic, 'tis strong in love ;
O triply blest, 'tis ours, where'er we rove,
One, Catholic, and strong in love.

God's Mother dear, sweet lily flower,
And Saints on high, creations of His power ;
While to and fro the Church is driven,
Angels descend and rivet her to heaven ;
The warring Church below, the Church on high,
A golden chain unites the earth and sky ;
Angels, the Church below, the Church on high,
O triply blest, to us are nigh.

The eternal Sire, the gracious Son,
And the dread Spirit, the Heavenly Three in
    One;
On earth, the fair, the wondrous Child,
Joseph the meek, the Mother undefiled;
Three are in heaven above, on earth are three,
Bright images of heaven in their degree;
Three are in heaven above, on earth are Three,
O blest, and triply blest are we!

From
CALLISTA
[1856]

CALLISTA, / A SKETCH OF THE THIRD CENTURY. /

> Love thy God and love Him only,
> And thy breast will ne'er be lonely.
> In that one great spirit meet
> All things mighty, grave, and sweet.
> Vainly strives the soul to mingle
> With a being of our kind ;
> Vainly hearts with hearts are twined ;
> For the deepest still is single.
> An impalpable resistance
> Holds like natures still at distance.
> Mortal ! love that Holy One,
> Or dwell for aye alone.
> DE VERE.

London : / Burns and Lambert, 17, Portman Street. /
Cologne : J. P. Bachem. / 1856. /

THE two earlier songs, "Where are the Islands of the Blest ?" and "I wander by that river's brink," only the former of which Newman reprinted in his "Verses on Various Occasions," have little in common with the remaining contents of this volume. Still less has the fragmentary "Juba's Song." But the last, in especial, is here printed as representative of Newman's appreciation of and power of employing the old ballad form, where additional emphasis was gained by repetitions in which minute changes occurred. This song of Juba is the one thing preserved to us which gives a clue to what the development of Newman's muse might have been had he employed it upon secular subjects.

From CALLISTA

SONG

WHERE are the Islands of the Blest?
    They stud the Ægean Sea;
And where the deep Elysian rest?
    It haunts the vale where Peneus strong
Pours his incessant stream along,
While craggy ridge and mountain bare
Cut keenly through the liquid air,
And in their own pure tints arrayed,
Scorn earth's green robes which change and fade,
And stand in beauty undecayed,
    Guards of the bold and free.

For what is Afric, but the home
    Of burning Phlegethon?
What the low beach and silent gloom,
    And chilling mists of that dull river,
    Along whose bank the thin ghosts shiver,—

The thin wan ghosts that once were men,—
But Tauris, isle of moor and fen,
Or dimly traced by seamen's ken,
　　The pale-cliff'd Albion.

SONG

I WANDER by that river's brink
   Which circles Pluto's drear domain;
I feel the chill night-breeze, and think
   Of joys which ne'er shall be again.

I count the weeds that fringe the shore,
   Each sluggish wave that rolls and rolls;
I hear the ever-splashing oar
   Of Charon, ferryman of souls.

HYMN

THE number of Thine own complete,
    Sum up and make an end;
Sift clean the chaff, and house the wheat,—
    And then, O Lord, descend.

Descend, and solve by that descent,
    This mystery of life;
Where good and ill, together blent,
    Wage an undying strife.

For rivers twain are gushing still,
    And pour a mingled flood;
Good in the very depths of ill,
    Ill in the heart of good.

The last are first,—the first are last,—
    As angel eyes behold:
These from the sheep-cote sternly cast,—
    Those welcomed to the fold.

No Christian home, no pastor's eye,
    No preacher's vocal zeal,
Moved Thy dear Martyr to defy
    The prison and the wheel.

Forth from the heathen ranks she stept,
  The forfeit throne to claim
Of Christian souls who had not kept
  Their birthright and their name.

Grace formed her out of sinful dust ;
  She knelt, a soul defiled ;
She rose in all the faith, and trust,
  And sweetness of a child.

And in the freshness of that love
  She preached, by word and deed,—
The mysteries of the world above,—
  Her new-found, glorious creed.

And running, in a little hour,
  Of life the course complete,
She reached the Throne of endless power,
  And sits at Jesu's feet.

Her spirit there, her body here,
  Make one the earth and sky ;
We use her name,—we touch her bier :—
  We know her God is nigh.

JUBA'S SONG

THE little black moor is the chap for me,
When the night is dark, and the earth is free,
Under the limbs of the broad yew-tree.

'Twas Father Cham that planted that yew,
And he fed it fat with the bloody dew
Of a score of brats, as his lineage grew.

Footing and flaunting it all the night,
Each lock flings fire, each heel strikes light;
No lamps need they whose breath is bright.

* * * * *

Gurta the witch would have part in the jest;
'Tho' lame as a gull, by his highness possessed,
She shouldered her crutch, and danced with the rest.

Sporting and snorting, deep in the night,
Their beards flashing fire, and their hoofs striking light,
And their tails whisking round in the heat of their flight.

* * * * *

Sporting and snorting in shades of the night,
His ears pricking up, and his hoofs striking light,
And his tail whisking round in the speed of his flight.

* * * * *

Gurta the witch was out with the rest;
'Tho' lame as a gull, by his highness possessed,
She shouldered her crutch, and danced with the best.

She stamped and she twirled in the shade of the yew,
Till her gossips and chums of the city danced too ;
They never are slack when there's mischief to do.

She danced and she coaxed, but he was no fool ;
He'd be his own master, he'd not be her tool ;
Not the little black moor should send him to school.

* * * * *

She wheedled and coaxed, but he was no fool ;
He'd be his own master, he'd not be her tool ;
Not the little black moor should send him to school.

She foamed and she cursed—'twas the same
 thing to him ;
She laid well her trap ; but he carried his
 whim :—
The priest scuffled off, safe in life and in limb.

  * * * * *

She beckoned the moon, and the moon came
 down ;
The green earth shrivelled beneath her frown ;
But a man's strong will can keep his own.

  * * * * *

From
HYMNS FOR THE USE OF THE BIRMINGHAM ORATORY
[1857]

Hymns / for the Use of / the / Birmingham Oratory. /

Dublin : / Printed by John F. Fowler, / 3, Crow Street, Dame Street. / 1857. /

From HYMNS FOR THE USE OF THE BIRMINGHAM ORATORY

ST. PHILIP NERI

THIS is the Saint of gentleness and kindness,
    Cheerful in penance, and in precept winning;
Patiently healing of their pride and blindness,
        Souls that are sinning.

This is the Saint, who, when the world allures us,
    Cries her false wares, and opes her magic coffers,
Points to a better city, and secures us
        With richer offers.

Love is his bond, he knows no other fetter,
    Asks not our all, but takes whate'er we spare him,
Willing to draw us on from good to better,
        As we can bear him.

When he comes near to teach us and to bless us,
  Prayer is so sweet, that hours are but a minute;
Mirth is so pure, though freely it possess us,
        Sin is not in it.

Thus he conducts by holy paths and pleasant,
  Innocent souls, and sinful souls forgiven,
Towards the bright palace where our God is present,
        Throned in high heaven.

[This poem, although apparently a revised version of the "Mary and Philip" in "Verses on Religious Subjects," diverges so widely from it as to be essentially a different poem, and contains phrases so exquisite that it has been decided to reprint both in the present volume.]

PURGATORY

HELP, Lord, the souls which Thou hast made,
  The souls to Thee so dear,
In prison, for the debt unpaid
  Of sins committed here.

Those holy souls, they suffer on,
  Resigned in heart and will,
Until Thy high behest is done,
  And justice has its fill.

For daily falls, for pardoned crime,
  They joy to undergo
The shadow of Thy Cross sublime,
  The remnant of Thy woe.

Help, Lord, the souls which Thou hast made,
  The souls to Thee so dear,
In prison, for the debt unpaid
  Of sins committed here.

O by their patience of delay,
  Their hope amid their pain,
Their sacred zeal to burn away
  Disfigurement and stain,

O by their fire of love, not less
   In keenness than the flame,
O by their very helplessness,
   O by Thy own great Name,

Sweet Jesu, help, sweet Jesu, aid,
   The souls to Thee so dear,
In prison, for the debt unpaid
   Of sins committed here.

INDEX

	PAGE
All-bountiful Creator, who	305
All is divine	323
All tender lights, all hues divine	291
And would'st thou reach, rash scholar mine.	197
Are these the tracks of some unearthly Friend	156
As viewing sin, e'en in its faintest trace	269
As, when the hand some mimic form would paint	270
Athens and letters followed on my stage	261
A year and more has fled.	71
Banish'd the House of sacred rest	135
Between two comrades dear	282
Bide thou thy time	232
Bloom, beloved Flower	122
Cease, Stranger, cease those piercing notes	168
Chill blows the wind; the sun's enfeebled power	45
Christ bade His followers take the sword	180
Christ's Church was holiest in her youthful days	226
Christ only, of God's messengers to man	236
Come, Holy Ghost, who ever One	250
Could I hit on a theme	125
Creator of the starry pole	311
Day's herald bird	298
Dear Frank, this morn has ushered in	83
Dear Louisa, why	116

INDEX

	PAGE
Dear sainted Friends, I call not you	172
Death was full urgent with thee, Sister dear	96
Deep in his meditative bower	192
Did we but see	155
Do not their souls, who 'neath the Altar wait	243
Each trial has its weight ; which, whoso bears	203
Ere yet I left home's youthful shrine	132
Faint not, and fret not, for threatened woe	201
Fair Cousin, thy page	109
Far sadder musing on the traveller falls	237
Father of Lights, by whom each day	253
Father of mercies infinite	293
Fierce was the whirlwind of my storm-tossed mind	263
Framer of the earth and sky	294
France ! I will think of thee as what thou wast	218
" Give any boon for peace "	188
Glory of the eternal Heaven	302
Green are the leaves, and sweet the flowers	321
Hark, a joyful voice is thrilling	314
Haunting gloom and flitting shades	300
Help, Lord, the souls which Thou hast made	349
Hid are the saints of God	112
How can I keep my Christmas feast	134
How didst thou start, Thou Holy Baptist, bid	184
How long, O Lord of grace	222
How shall a child of God fulfil	223
I am a harp of many chords, and each	90
I am a tree, whose spring is o'er	79
I am rooted in the wall	91
I bear upon my brow the sign	136

INDEX

	PAGE
I bow at Jesu's name	143
I dreamed that, with a passionate complaint	179
I have been honoured and obeyed	146
I lost, O Lord, the use of yesterday	265
I rise and yield my clasped hands to Thee	266
I sat beneath an olive's branches grey	171
I saw thee once, and nought discerned	178
I wander by that river's brink	339
If e'er I fall beneath Thy rod	149
In childhood, when with eager eyes	94
In service o'er the Mystic Feast I stand	268
In the far North our lot is cast	325
In times of old, ere Learning's dawning beam	60
Ladies, well I deem, delight	105
Latest born of Jesse's race	176
Lead, Kindly Light, amid the encircling gloom	151
Let others sing thy heathen praise	204
Let the sun summon all his beams to hold	56
Let us arise, and watch by night	247
Light of the anxious heart	256
Lord, in this dust Thy sovereign voice	114
Lord of unbounded space	304
"Man goeth forth" with reckless trust	87
Man is permitted much	186
Many the guileless years the Patriarch spent	175
Martyr of Christ, thy fight is won	257
May the dread Three in One, who sways	292
Memory gifts, with the early year	118
Mid Balak's magic fires	212
Mortal! if e'er thy spirits faint	148
Moses, the patriot fierce, became	147
My breath is spent; Menalcas, check your pace!	39
My Father's hope! my childhood's dream	241
My home is now a thousand mile away	133

INDEX

	PAGE
My oldest friend, mine from the hour	279
My sister, on a day so dear	67
My smile is bright, my glance is free	142
Now is the Autumn of the Tree of Life	224
Now that the daylight dies away	254
Now that the dreary cold of winter flies	50
O aged Saint ! far off I heard	191
O comrade bold of toil and pain	235
O Father, list a sinner's call	138
O God from God, and Light from Light	289
O God, of Thy soldiers	258
O God, unchangeable and true	252
O God, the Lord of place and time	251
O God, who hast given	307
O heart of fire ! misjudged by wilful man	145
O Holiest Truth ! how have I lied to Thee	267
O Holy Lord, who with the Children Three	281
O Lord and Christ	215
O Lord ! when sin's close-marshalled line	190
O Lord, who thron'd in the holy height	306
Oh ! miserable power	141
O Mother Church of Rome	238
O piteous race	213
Oh, prophet, tell me not of peace	137
O purest semblance of the Eternal Son	162
Oh rail not at our brethren of the North	216
O say not thou art left of God	153
O specious sin	242
O that Thou wouldest rend the breadth of sky	164
O that thy creed were sound	239
O Thou, of shepherds Prince and Head	315
O ye who seek the Lord	255
Of the Father Effluence bright	296
Once, as I brooded o'er my guilty state	139
Once cast with men of language strange	219

INDEX

	PAGE
Paler have grown the shades of night	248
Peace-loving man, of humble heart and true	207
Philip, on thee the glowing ray	331
Poor wanderers, ye are sore distrest	210
Prune thou thy words, the thoughts control	183
Say, hast thou track'd a traveller's round	170
Say, who is he in deserts seen	231
Secure in his prophetic strength	194
See the golden dawn is glowing	301
She is not lost ;—still in our sight	99
Sleep has refresh'd our limbs, we spring	288
Some one whisper'd yesterday	275
Supernal Word, proceeding from	313
The Angel-lights of Christmas morn	317
The ark of God has hidden strength	227
The better portion didst thou choose, Great Heart	150
The coachman was seated, the ribbons in hand	102
The dawn is sprinkled o'er the sky	303
"The Fathers are in dust, yet live to God"	160
The holy Monks, conceal'd from men	327
The little black Moor	342
The Muse has sway in the truant mind	75
The number of Thine own complete	340
The one true Faith, the ancient Creed	333
The red sun is gone	310
The star of morn to night succeeds	249
The Sun has risen o'er Belleville's lengthen'd height	3
The time has been, it seemed a precept plain	195
The world has cycles in its course, when all	229
There is not on the earth a soul so base	161
There is one only bond	220
There sat a Lady	319
There strayed awhile, amid the woods of Dart	127

INDEX

	PAGE
They are at rest	173
They do but grope in learning's pedant round	166
This the Saint of gentleness and kindness	347
This is the Saint of sweetness and compassion	329
Thou to wax fierce	181
Thrice bless'd are they, who feel their loneliness	167
Thy words are good, and freely given	182
Time was, I shrank from what was right	189
'Tis long, dear Annie, since we met	123
To-day the Blessed Three in One	286
Two brothers freely cast their lot	154
Two sinners have been grace-endued	164
Tyre of the West, and glorying in the name	230
Unwearied God, before whose face	185
Wake, Mother dear	233
We are not children of a guilty sire	211
Weep, Mother mine	221
Weep not for me	111
Weep not for me, when I am gone	284
What time my heart unfolded its fresh leaves	140
When first earth's rulers welcomed home	225
When first God stirred me, and the Church's word	198
When Heaven sends sorrow	157
When I am sad, I say	240
When I look back upon my former race	158
When I sink down in gloom or fear	152
When I would search the truths that in me burn	209
When mirth is full and free	228
When royal Truth, released from mortal throes	199
Whence is this awe, by stillness spread	163
Whene'er across this sinful flesh of mine	144
Whene'er goes forth Thy dread command	165
Whene'er I seek the Holy Altar's rail	159
When shall our northern church	205
Where are the Islands of the Blest?	337

INDEX

	PAGE
Where'er I roam in this fair English land	131
While life's young dawnings o'er the meads diffuse	62
While Moses on the mountain lay	174
Who madest all and dost control	290
Whom all obey	308
Why loiterest within Simon's walls	234
Why, wedded to the Lord, still yearns my heart	169
"Woe's me!" the peaceful prophet cried	193
Ye cannot halve the Gospel of God's grace	217

THE END

Under the same Editorship.

THE CHURCH OF THE FATHERS. By JOHN HENRY NEWMAN (afterwards Cardinal). A reprint of the first edition. Crown 8vo. 3s. 6d. net.

THE SACRED TREASURY
Edited by FREDERIC CHAPMAN
Pott 8vo. (6 × 3¾ inches).
Bound in Cloth . . Price 2/- net.
Bound in Leather . Price 2/6 net.

THE POEMS OF JOHN HENRY NEWMAN
(afterwards Cardinal). With Portrait

Known the world over by his exquisitely beautiful "Lead, kindly light," Newman's standing as a poet is not at all generally recognised. Yet his verse had as much to do with the success of the Oxford movement as had " The Christian Year" of his friend Keble. He first collected it in 1868, and but few additions were subsequently made. The present volume contains, besides a number of early poems now first brought together, of the utmost interest as throwing light on Newman's family life and early influences, a long poem in two cantos, entitled "St. Bartholomew's Eve," written during his first years at Oxford, in collaboration with his friend, J. W. Bowden, and of such extreme rarity that only two or three copies are known to exist. With one or two unimportant exceptions, the contents of the 1868 volume are also here included.

DIVINE CONSIDERATIONS. By JOHN VALDESSO.
The English Translation of Nicholas Ferrar. With George Herbert's Prefatory Epistle and a Portrait

Juan de Valdes, the author of the "Hundred and Ten Divine Considerations," was one of the most notable of the Spanish Reformers of the sixteenth century. The correspondent of Erasmus, the twin brother of the secretary of the Emperor Charles V., and for a time the chamberlain of a pope, his exalted connections alone probably saved him from persecution on account of his opinions, and, as it was, he had to leave his native land to ensure his safety. His writings were condemned, and the greater part of them so effectually suppressed that some of them remain to this day introuvable, whilst others have only come to light during the past fifty years. The present volume attracted the attention of the famous Nicholas Ferrar during his travels in Italy, and from an Italian version he made an English translation, which he submitted for the approval of his friend George Herbert, just as Herbert handed to Ferrar the manuscript of " The Temple," to suppress or print as he thought fit. Ferrar's translation was published at Oxford in 1638, and a distorted version of it appeared at Cambridge in 1646, but this is the first time that an edition of it, as Ferrar left it, has been prepared since the original publication at Oxford. Ferrar is perhaps best known to the modern reader from the prominence given to the description of his community at Little Gidding in the romance " John Inglesant."

THE HUNDRED BEST POEMS OF JOHN AND CHARLES WESLEY. With Portraits

If John and Charles Wesley had not been the sons of a poet and poets themselves, it is hardly too much to say that the spread of Wesleyan Methodism could never have been as world-wide as it has. Their hymns were even more influential than their sermons, and in them the dead evangelists yet speak wherever the English language prevails. Such universal favourites as " Jesu, Lover of my soul," and " Hark! how all the welkin rings" (generally perverted into "Hark! the herald angels sing"), however, though they may have kindled a love of verse in households where poetry was quite unknown, do not prepare one to learn that the complete poetical works of the brothers extend to thirteen volumes of about five hundred pages each. From this immense mass of verse it has been the editor's endeavour to select one hundred poems, which, judged purely by poetical standards, may legitimately be described as " The Hundred Best Poems of John and Charles Wesley."

THE SPIRIT OF LOVE. By WILLIAM LAW, Author of the " Serious Call." With Portrait

William Law had the misfortune through the extraordinary popularity of one of his works, the famous "Serious Call to a Devout and Holy Life," to find all his other writings thrown into comparative obscurity. Yet from time to time there have been editors to call attention to one or other of his beautiful religious treatises. The temper of his mind, which trended towards mysticism, was probably further urged in that direction from the circumstance that conscience forced him into the ranks of the non-jurors. He was for long a kind of private chaplain to the aunt of Gibbon the historian, who in some sort was probably himself indebted to him. The treatise here reprinted is amongst the most interesting and beneficent of his writings, filled with a piety that does not pall, and free from rancour, as its title, " The Spirit of Love," befits. But Law could on occasion show himself a fighting parson as his controversy with Hoadly (the celebrated Bangor controversy) shows; and his reply to Mandeville's "Fable of the Bees" proved to his opponents that they had a skilled controversialist to defend themselves against. Law, however, is of most value to us nowadays in his capacity of gentle teacher and soother " when sleep comes to close each difficult day," and it is certain that many will gladly place this edition of " The Spirit of Love" beside their " De Imitatione," and their " Holy Living and Holy Dying."

JOHN LANE, THE BODLEY HEAD, VIGO STREET, LONDON, W.

HF 5381 .M568 1990

Mogano, M.

How to win pr...

Y0-CKN-708

DATE DUE

JAN 0 6 1997			
JAN 0 6 1997			

DEMCO 38-297

NEW ENGLAND INSTITUTE
OF TECHNOLOGY
LEARNING RESOURCES CENTER

Other Titles in the Better Business Series

How to Start and Run Your Own Business, 7th edition, 1989, M.Mogano

How to Start and Run Your Own Shop, 2nd edition, 1988, P.Levene

How to Give a Successful Presentation, 1988, I.Richards

The Shopkeeper's Handbook, 1989, P.Levene

How to Get a Better Job, 1989, M.Mogano

The Husband and Wife Business Partnership: What the Law Says, 1989, D. and M. Owles

How to Use a Computer to Improve Your Business, 1989, I.Richards

Forthcoming titles

Independent Taxation for the Husband and Wife, 1990, D. and M. Owles

How to Run a Better Business, 1991, M. Mogano

Better Business Series

How to Win PROMOTION

Mike Mogano

NEW ENGLAND INSTITUTE
OF TECHNOLOGY
LEARNING RESOURCES CENTER

Graham & Trotman
A member of the Kluwer Academic Publishers Group
LONDON/DORDRECHT/BOSTON

Graham and Trotman Ltd
Sterling House
66 Wilton Road
London SW1V 1DE
UK

Kluwer Academic Publishers
101 Philip Drive
Assinippi Park
Norwell, MA 02061
USA

ISBN 1 85333 381 6 (Paperback)
ISBN 1 85333 088 4 (Series)
© M. Mogano, 1990
First published in 1990

British Library Cataloguing in Publication Data
Mogano, Mike
  How to win promotion.
  1. Business firms. Personnel. Promotion
  I. Title II. Series
  658.3142

ISBN 1-85333-381-6

Library of Congress CIP data is available from the publisher.

This publication is protected by International Copyright Law. All rights reserved. No part of this publication may be reproduced, stored in a retrieval system, or transmitted in any form or by any means, electronic, mechanical, photocopying, recording or otherwise, without the prior permission of the publishers.

Typeset in Garamond by Selectmove Ltd
Printed and bound by Billing & Sons Ltd, Worcester

Contents

	PREFACE	vii
Chapter 1	TAKING STOCK OF YOURSELF	1
	Are You in the Right Company? • Getting to Know Yourself • Knowing Your Limitations • The Quality of Life • Out In the Open • A Job or a Career? • What Have You Got Now? • Be Yourself • Summing Up •	
Chapter 2	ARE YOU PROPERLY QUALIFIED?	10
	Full Time Study • Part Time Study • Correspondence Courses • The Open University • The Open Business School • Teaching Yourself • Adding a Language • Other Avenues •	
Chapter 3	A STRUCTURED CAREER APPROACH	23
	Setting Objectives • Mind Over Matter • Clearing the Way • Do You Fit? • Is The Time Right? • Are You Ready Technically? • Discussing Your Desires • Dealing with Setbacks • Especially for Women •	
Chapter 4	HOW WELL DO YOU KNOW YOUR EMPLOYER?	34
	Company Policy • The Market Place • The People • Administration • Controls • Finances •	
Chapter 5	EXPLOITING YOUR ABILITIES	46
	Lifestyles • Project Your Personality • Getting Yourself Organized • Creating Initiatives • Taking Decisions • Improving The System • Learning To Negotiate • Purchasing Power • Dealing With Problems • Opportunities For Women •	
Chapter 6	RELATIONSHIPS WITH SUPERIORS	57
	Formal Relationships • Get To Know Your Boss • Know The Organization • The	

Political Game • Promotion Patterns • Staying Informed • Socializing • Grading Systems • Appraising Performance • Promotion Interviews • Keeping Contacts •

Chapter 7   **MANAGING OTHER PEOPLE**   69
Determining Your Responsibilities • Setting Objectives • Reviewing Performance • Be Tolerant Of Others • Earning Respect • Effective Management • Be A Real Leader • Keeping In Touch • Keeping Up Morale • Motivating Others • The Art Of Delegation • Managing Difficulties •

Chapter 8   **COMMUNICATING WITH OTHERS**   83
How Important Is It? • Channels of Communication • Avoiding Bad Communication • The Magic Of Technology • Face To Face • Using The Telephone • Meetings, Meetings... • Writing Reports • Consultations • Presentations • Going To Press • Better Reading • Communicating Abroad •

Chapter 9   **MARKETING SKILLS**   98
Developing A Plan • A Competitive Edge • Knowing Your Customers • Market Research • Public Relations • Promotional Activities • Advertising • Distribution Channels • Monitoring Progress •

Chapter 10   **BEATING YOUR TARGETS**   108
Understanding Budgets • Types Of Budgets • Flexible Budgets • 'Uncontrollable' Factors • Defining Your Accountabilities • Setting Objectives • Information Systems • Assessing Performance • Assessing Yourself • Making Sure Of Success •

Chapter 11   **FIT FOR THE JOB**   118
A Healthy Body • Health Clubs • Check Your Body • You Are What You Eat • ...and Drink • Avoiding The Weed • Dealing with Stress • On The Road • A Good Night's Sleep • A Rounded Life • Positive Thinking

FURTHER READING   129

Preface

This book is aimed at anyone who wants to get on in the world.

Life is to be enjoyed, but enjoyment can be improved if, on the one hand you are satisfied with life, and on the other possess sufficient funds to make it possible! Moving up the promotion ladder is the only method I know of achieving both these ends!

It provides you with the satisfaction of knowing you are doing your job well and, at the same time, putting a few extra coppers into your pay packet.

Gaining (or rather winning) promotion is not a matter of luck and, in today's fast-moving world, you certainly do not have to wait to fill dead men's shoes. Managers in all occupations are reaching that goal at a far more tender age than in times gone by.

Employers, though, remain selective and seek to promote those who will most benefit the company. The game is thus still competitive.

The winners will be those who best understand the game. The way to do that is to make a detailed study of the rules and that is what this book sets out to do – to provide you with the rules of the promotion game and how to win it.

The rules are not exclusive to the United Kingdom and overseas readers are able to make the same moves by merely adjusting to the conditions existing in their own country.

Throughout the book the use of the male terms 'he', 'him' and so on are used purely for consistency and should always be construed to include equally the female version. Indeed, women may even have a slight advantage in that many major employers follow a policy of ensuring at least equal representation in the higher ranks!

I wish you every success.

Mike Mogano

Solihull
May, 1990.

To Betty Wilde, an early source of inspiration

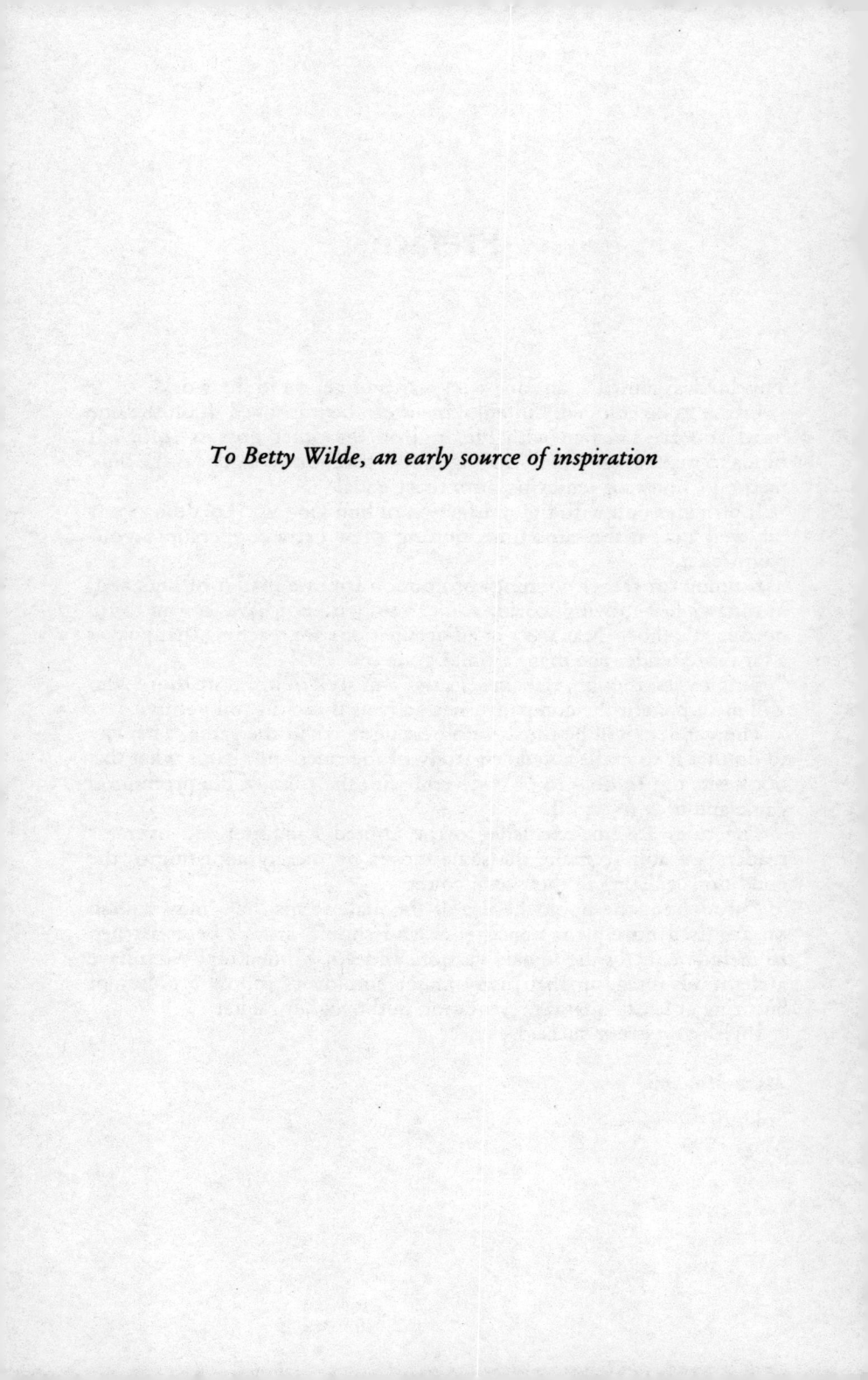

CHAPTER 1

Taking Stock of Yourself

One of the most exciting things that can happen to you is to gain promotion at work.

You are overjoyed. Colleagues are, generally, pleased for you. And you can't wait to get home to pass the news to equally delighted family and friends.

Promotion normally means more money, more responsibility, better status and – perhaps most important of all – the opportunity to get your teeth into what is often virtually a new job. It probably brings with it supervisory duties, a greater degree of delegation and heightened job satisfaction. All of these are likely to result in a better standard of living, a more satisfied mind – and, quite likely, a healthier body. What more could you ask for?

So how do you go about achieving this seventh heaven? Isn't it just luck, you might ask; a question of dead men's shoes or the boss's fancy?

Nothing could be further from the truth. In our increasingly competitive society, employers generally give a great deal of thought to the people they believe should move up the ladder. Larger concerns, especially, devote much time to manpower planning, often looking five or ten years ahead to make certain they have enough staff of the right calibre, age and experience to fill the posts they envisage being created.

What we will attempt to do in this book is to show you the way towards significantly improving your own chances of being promoted within your own organization. Getting a better job elsewhere is more specifically covered in *How To Get a Better Job* by the same author.

Aiming for promotion is a science, and thus can be learned. You will be shown what you need to know and do to bring your talents more noticeably to the attention of your employer. For talents you undoubtedly have in the very fact that you seriously desire promotion; the lacklustre will never consider it, or they treat it so lightly that their objective is never achieved.

Success cannot, of course, be guaranteed. But diligence, and a determination to win, will, without doubt, give you the edge over your working colleagues – and that is the first step towards being promoted.

Are You in the Right Company?

This is a question to ask yourself before you proceed any further.

If you are part of a two-man concern, and the other half is your employer, your chances of promotion must be slim, to say the least. He *may* decide to retire, and hand the business to you, but you are clearly not the type of person who will wait that long!

Similarly, if you work for a very small family firm where grandson John, or cousin Stephen, are obviously being groomed for better things, and there is a tradition not to elevate non-family employees, you will again become frustrated.

However, working for a large company whose policy is to promote from within may also not prove to be the answer if its management style is not one with which you could live comfortably. Or perhaps the sector in which you operate presents no attractions whatsoever in the longer term.

Any of these reasons could mitigate against the possibility of promotion. If *you* are unhappy in your present environment, it is likely to show. And that will be sufficient for your employer to exclude your name from his deliberations if a vacancy at a higher grade occurs.

So, firstly, be happy with your surroundings. You may not be perfectly satisfied with your present position (indeed, we are assuming this to be the case), but improve your chances by making certain you are working for an employer you can live with, in an industry which excites you. That way, your enthusiasm will show.

A sea-change may, therefore, be necessary before you embark upon your objective. Do not be put off, though, by the need for this. Every castle must be built on solid foundations; starting off on sand will only prove disastrous.

We will assume you have reached the point where upgrading with your present company is the challenge that excites you. Before you proceed any further, you have someone to meet – the real YOU!

Getting to Know Yourself

Later on we will be looking at how you can assess your own strengths and weaknesses. Before you can do that, though, you must know your real self.

Take a look, therefore, at the following qualities.

Temperament

What kind of attitude do you possess? Are you easy-going by nature, prepared to accept the status quo and somewhat annoyed when changes cloud the horizon? Or are you eager for new challenges, always ready to adapt and accept improvements?

Leadership

We will be taking a very detailed look at this necessary attribute later on, but at this stage you must be prepared to be extremely honest with yourself to find out to what degree you possess the qualities of a leader.

Have you a preference for taking orders, or for giving them? Do you find it frustrating to have to accept instructions from others when you feel that, left alone, efficiency would result if your own ideas were followed? Are you comfortable in dealing with subordinates, or is every awkward instruction creating tension in your breast? Do you feel you could deal with unsavoury decision-making, such as giving notice to a colleague? Or would such ideas be undermined by your allowing your heart to overrule your head?

Honest answers to these questions – and honest they must be, for the one person you cannot fool is yourself – will begin to help clarify your degree of leadership. Do not worry at this stage if some aspects concern you; providing you believe you can deal competently with decision-making, true leadership will come with further experience. Even Genghis Khan took a few years to learn the art fully!

Willpower

Can you achieve goals whatever the opposition? Can you weave your way through the defence, keeping the objective clearly in sight without allowing minor crises to upset you?

Past personal experiences should come readily to mind, pinpointing your success (or otherwise) in reaching previously set targets. 'Stickability' is going to be vital if you're determined to make that better job.

Confidence

This is another essential ingredient. Confidence is something which shines through to others and, to be ahead of the field, you are going to need it.

All of this might appear as if you need to be super-human, but this is not the case. Just take a look around you, at your fellow workers, both in your own organization and in others. Look at those in a supervisory position; are they really very different from yourself? Could you not fill some of their shoes? That is precisely what you are setting out to do – and there is no reason at all why you should not succeed!

Knowing Your Limitations

In Chapter 3, when you begin to set yourself clear objectives, you will have to be very honest with yourself and link up what you want to achieve with what you also know are your limitations.

These may, of course, be few although in real life most of us would be prepared to admit – at least to our own inner thoughts – that horizons really do exist for us. There can only be one Prime Minister (at a time, anyway!), perhaps half a dozen Admirals, a limited number of millionaires – and only one boss of your own company!

Your present qualifications may, possibly, inhibit certain lines of promotion, although you can do something about this, and we look at this aspect in Chapter 2.

Experience can only come with years and, quite possibly, youth may currently be against you. But this does not, of course, prevent you from making that next grade – and that is our current objective.

Another factor that needs deliberation at this stage is whether or not you are ready to uproot yourself and move to another part of the country, or indeed across the world. Companies are becoming increasingly multi-national, and the advent of 1992 will call for categories of staff willing to move around Europe almost at the drop of a bowler. However keen you are it is still generally an unnerving experience. There is never a right time to sell your house, despite what friends will tell you! In a buoyant market you may have little trouble in selling, but you cannot afford to be out of the market place for too long as prices rise, whilst if the market is flat it can take months of frustration finding a buyer.

At a time when you have gained promotion, the last thing you want on your mind is the often unknown cost and certain hassle of having to sell your house. There are, fortunately, a number of very efficient relocation companies, although they generally act on behalf of businesses rather than individuals; see if your employers will take them on board to ease you and your family through a house move.

A specialist firm which offers individuals advice on moving home is National Starpoint, based at Alexandra House, Sandon Road, Stafford. National Starpoint is run by Jeremy and Jennifer Eadie who set up in business when their own house move fell through and they realized that there had to be hundreds of families in similar, often desperate, situations.

They will sort out everything connected with a move for you, from advising regional house prices to the telephone number and surgery opening hours of the local doctor, which can prove to be important to someone with a young family. They have produced a great number of 'local guides' which cover everything from the time it will take you to get to work, with a whole range of alternative routes, to the membership fees of the local golf club, the pick of the area's restaurants, theatres, and even the architectural flavour of the nearest towns. Picture postcards accompany the guides.

Moving could radically alter your lifestyle. But, unless you investigate fully the pros and cons beforehand, the alteration may not be to your liking. Only you – and your family – can decide. But do not dither, for it is imperative that you make up your mind at this stage whether or not you are truly mobile if your promotion wishes demand it.

All of these aspects, then, should be taken into account before you begin your campaign. Head up a sheet of paper with the categories listed above and, after due thought and consideration, jot down your true feelings on each of them. If any appear to present barriers, reconsider but do not waiver from what you know to be the truth. Honest answers now, and the ability to recognize these and stick to them, will make for an easier exercise as it develops.

The Quality of Life

Life is about work and play, and the latter may well suffer, at least for a time, as you work your way up the ladder rungs of success.

We must assume, at this stage, that you have the 'managerial streak' in you; a manager has been defined by Binder Hamlyn Management Consultants as someone who has:

- Accountability for the quantity, quality, timing and cost of a particular output of work which is greater than he can perform personally; he therefore has subordinates to whom he can delegate part of the work; and
- Authority over his subordinates (within the constraints of the policies of the organisation) to:
    Veto appointments;
    Assign work;
    Assess relative performance; and
    Remove from their roles those whose work does not meet agreed standards.

If this sounds like your present role – or the one you would like to fill – then we will further assume that you are on the way to promotion!

There will not, of course, be a 'nine to five' routine. Go-ahead employers are now looking for total commitment and it is only those prepared to give that little extra who will remain in line for promotion. So now is the time also to decide:

- How many hours am I prepared to commit each day, each week? Will occasional (or even frequent) evening and/or weekend working be tolerated?

- Will staying away at night present a problem? Or working overseas for short spells?
- How much pressure can I cope with? Does additional responsibility act as an adrenalin – or does it present problems associated with stress?
- Am I prepared to spend additional time studying? What impact might this have on family life?
- Am I prepared to give up some of the hours I currently spend socializing?

Answers to these questions will provide you with a guide as to the quality of life you are seeking and whether or not it is likely to accord with your promotion hopes. They are vital to your decision-making and there is no point in trying to fool yourself with dishonest answers.

Out in the Open

As anyone involved in wars knows, a task is more easily achieved if people pull together.

A problem shared is a problem halved, and this applies as much to the desire to be promoted as to passing the driving test or any other examination. You will benefit from talking – and listening – to others, be they family, friends, or workmates.

Almost without exception you are likely to receive encouragement, sympathy, advice – or a mixture of all three. Listen carefully to what others' reactions are; many may have already experienced what you are currently going through and, by encouraging them to talk, you will become the recipient of free advice. Do not ignore any comments (even the frivolous ones!), for after a while they are likely to form a pattern which should prove a useful guide in the planning of your campaign.

Bounce ideas off those you know you can rely upon to take your desires seriously. You will be surprised how rewarding this experience can be, but do ask friends to be absolutely frank and not offer merely condescending and polite talk. If the same criticism of some aspect which you believed unimportant keeps recurring, it will need a re-think. Value the fact that this advice is costing you nothing at all!

A Job or a Career?

Employers are not generally the fools many of us take them for. Your superiors are unlikely to have achieved their status by just being there; they were, almost certainly, selected.

But why were they selected? Why not your colleague – or, indeed, you?

There are likely to have been a number of very valid reasons. One of these will no doubt have been their level of commitment. This is where, for each individual, a job differs from a career. Many, probably most, employees go to work in the morning, give their time diligently and return home at night. Thereafter their time is their own. These people, however, are in 'jobs' and not in a 'career', for that is where the subtle difference lies. A career man – or woman – is 'always' working, night and day. Work is taken home, either in the briefcase or in the mind. It is worked on over and over again, whether in the car, in bed or even the bathroom!

This is the effect of stress, although it is not necessarily harmful. As long as the 'carrier' can switch off whenever he pleases, then his mind, and his body, will be perfectly content. Used correctly, stress can be converted into positive energy and directed towards achieving your goals.

Have no doubt, though, that if you are intent on progression within your company, you must be career-orientated. If you are a 'job person' this will be noted and you are unlikely to be selected for that next promotion. Employers want go-getters – so join the club!

What Have You Got Now?

One thing to be certain about before you enter the promotion stakes is that, in some way or another, you will have something better than you have now. The only sure way of ensuring this is to know what you have got now – so sit down and take a cold, hard look at your present post.

Be thorough. Take account of any side benefits you currently enjoy which, in your search for pastures new, you might otherwise overlook (although generally within the same organisation these are unlikely to deteriorate).

Security will be an important feature to measure. As a 'run of the mill' employee (if, indeed, that is what you now consider yourself), your present job may be a lot more secure than the senior positions within the company where, for instance, a 'hire and fire' doctrine may exist. Performance management schemes may dictate certain accomplishments must be met to ensure job continuity; even Public Company chairmen are not entirely safe!

As we have already seen, the number of working hours will almost certainly increase as you step up the ladder, although, in the early days at least, you may not feel yourself fully recompensed. Full rewards tend to come later in life, after several years at the helm – or at least somewhere near it.

Responsibility will increase, but then that must be one of your aims, as must a higher level of authority and delegation. All of these things will come with greater seniority and must not be shirked.

As well as defining your present situation, it is as well to get to know the real YOU. Try the 'interview technique' – sit down and imagine you are being asked a series of questions by an interviewer. Actually ask yourself the questions (it is better done in private!) and begin by trying the following headings:

Practical: Are you the sort of person who approaches a task in a pragmatic manner, eager to plod on until a solution appears? Will you worry at a problem until it is resolved?

Creative: Do you favour the artistic approach? Is your solution to problems based more upon ideas than hard facts, however outlandish they may appear at the time? Are you always trying to change things?

Organized: Do you know where everything is? Are you methodical in your everyday life, returning items to where they 'belong'? Do you insist that your working environment is neat and tidy with a place for everything? Do you maintain a careful diary of your movements?

People: Are you good at motivating others? Are you content in the company of others when working? Does delegation come easily? Do people listen to your views and can you influence them in times of necessity? Do you find yourself caring how others think and feel? Are you a natural mixer?

Verbal: Are your thoughts and ideas expressed in a clear and concise manner? Are your written reports equally meaningful? Are you at ease in negotiating and communicating with others? Do you welcome a strong sense of autonomy?

Numeric: Are you quick with figures? Do you utilize them to the full when promoting your arguments, either verbally or as part of reports?

Straight answers to each of these questions (along with a few of your own) will help to 'categorize' you, although do not worry if some answers appear to conflict with others. None of us fits exactly into a neat little box.

What you will begin to get, however, is a feel for the sort of person you are. And, to enjoy promotion and the additional responsibilities which go with it, you are likely to need at least some of the above characteristics. We cannot be more specific than this at this stage, for the essential elements will depend very much upon the type of work you are carrying out. This is an exercise for you.

One method of conducting this is to take a close look at your immediate superior and list those ingredients of success which you believe he should have; he may not, of course, in your view, possess them at present! Clearly if a wide gap exists between your own view of yourself and the sort of person your superior needs to be, then you may need to return to the drawing-board. If a re-think confirms your earlier view, perhaps promotion would prove to be a disaster and you should re-read the section above entitled 'Are You in the Right Company?'

On the assumption, however, that everything fits, then your chances of success appear to have improved!

Be Yourself

During much of this self-assessment exercise you may have felt that you were beginning to appear a square peg in a round hole. Do not despair!

One of the most difficult tasks of all is to try to take an inward look at ourselves; it can prove very confusing. Human nature rarely allows us to be entirely honest with our inner self and it is a rare person indeed who sees himself as others see him.

At the same time, in character assessments, we can often be quite ruthless with ourselves and exaggerate minor faults to convince ourselves that we are being perfectly honest. This can prove quite demeaning and demoralizing, turning us into near-wrecks. This method of approach must be avoided at all costs. Start with the belief that no-one is perfect, and that even we have faults, and you should remain sane!

At the same time employers are not seeking automatons but straightforward human beings with the ability to do a job well and who have a commitment towards a common goal. Perfectionists do not exist and, if they did, they could not hide their faults for ever!

So be yourself, warts and all. What really matters is that you believe you are capable of doing a better job in your present organization than you are doing at present – no more is currently asked of you.

Summing Up

By now you should have a clearer idea of:

- Your objectives;
- Your inner self;
- Your capabilities; and
- Your limitations.

What about your personal strengths and weaknesses? These will be surveyed in Chapter 5. There will be a need to build upon strengths, and correct weaknesses, both quite achievable targets if you set your mind to them.

What we must now look at, however, is whether or not you are suitably qualified to take that upward step . . .

CHAPTER 2

Are You Properly Qualified?

In so many instances an element of luck exists and being in the right place at the right time has, for many people, proved to be the start of a fresh challenge in their career.

Large organizations, especially, restructure their staffing pyramids at regular intervals, creating new opportunities for employees who had, until then, considered themselves unpromotable or at the peak of their careers. With little warning they are thrust into rejigged responsibilities, providing them with renewed impetus and the opportunity to exploit previously untapped potential.

This, of course, is the ideal, although it is not as uncommon as you might imagine. Keep your eye open, therefore, particularly if you work for one of the major companies in the country, for likely reorganizational changes. Spot an opening, if you are able, and make a structured pitch for it. Do not be afraid, for instance, to make an approach to an appropriate superior at the earliest possible moment to express your interest in a particular position, making it clear why you believe you are the only one for the job.

Re-organization apart, though, you need to assess your present qualifications and ensure that these are not going to let you down in your candidature for promotion.

The term 'qualification' itself can be somewhat misleading, for – in certain careers – it can overlap with 'experience'. There can be a thin dividing line between the two and certainly someone with solid experience in a particular field could, in certain circumstances, be favoured ahead of a colleague well qualified but short in learning. The important thing for you to remember at this stage is that you can do very little about experience, but perhaps a lot about additional qualifications.

If you believe yourself lacking in experience, then make certain that you are currently gaining the right sort. If, in your view, your present job is not providing you with the necessary experience to move on to something higher, then either make this clear to your employer or, in the extreme, switch jobs. Hopefully, of course, he will listen to your plea, and, indeed, appreciate that he has on his books an employee keen to progress which, in the long run, can only be good for his organization.

ARE YOU PROPERLY QUALIFIED?

Take a good look around you at the people who are being promoted. Analyse each case and ask yourself why he or she has been chosen. Especially, enquire into their qualification level to add to your own store of knowledge for the future. Do not be shy of asking your colleague what qualifications he has if this is unknown to you; he will almost certainly welcome the interest and you may learn a lot more than you had hoped for.

Look, also, outside your own organization, at friends, neighbours, relations. Investigate their qualifications and, although in most cases they will not be relevant to your own career, try to establish a pattern of matching levels of certified knowledge to upward progression.

You will notice that qualifications will vary with different generations. The chairman of your company, for instance, may have no qualifications at all; he may either be a self-made entrepreneur or be of an age when, as a younger man, entry levels were less demanding.

All chartered accountants today, for example, must start with a University degree although many in practice began their careers without one. Qualifications for the teaching profession have moved up several pegs during the past ten years or so, whilst engineers, lawyers, veterinary surgeons and so on all require more demanding certificates of competence before embarking upon their professions.

Generally speaking, the younger you are the more demanding an employer is likely to be. So if you missed out on some of those scholastic examinations, particularly if this was a relatively recent phase, you will have to think about having another crack at them to reach your promotion goal.

We will assume that you are entirely dedicated to your cause (anything less could result in failure) but you will also have to consider how equally dedicated you are to improving your qualification base if this is going to prove necessary. Ask yourself:

- How much time will I be able to devote to study?
- Do I possess the necessary financial outlay, and am I prepared to forego a few luxuries?
- Am I also prepared to give up leisure pursuits?
- What is my family's view on all of this?

There are a variety of methods by which you can get yourself better qualified, including:

- Residential establishments
- Government or privately run colleges
- Correspondence courses
- Self-tuition

- Specialized courses and institutions

Let us take a closer look at them.

Full Time Study

Although we start with this method, it is probably the least likely to suit your particular circumstances, for most courses will entail a long period (anything from one to six years) off-the-job training and you would need to have an exceptionally understanding employer!

Nevertheless, it is worth considering, bearing in mind that, if your employer sees you as a long-term executive intent upon progressing rapidly through his organization, an 'investment' in your future is of similar advantage to him.

If a University degree is, therefore, within your grasp, firstly obtain the first-class brochure published by the Universities Central Council on Admissions, commonly referred to as 'UCCA'.

This body was established in 1961 by the universities themselves to solve some of the problems arising from the increased pressure of applicants for admissions. It is managed by a Council of Management on which all the universities in the United Kingdom, except the Open University, the University of Buckingham and Cranfield Institute of Technology, are represented. It controls and centralizes the admission to all universities represented, allowing candidates the freedom to make a responsible choice and at the same time allowing each university freedom to select its own students.

It does not provide academic advice such as which university to choose or entrance requirements but, once you have made up your mind on your favourites, it takes over. It can be found at P.O. Box 28, Cheltenham, Gloucestershire, GL 50 1HY.

Its handbook provides basic details of all courses at the 44 or so universities in the UK leading to a first degree or a first diploma. A first degree is normally a bachelor's degree, such as BA, B.Sc., or LLB, although in Scotland the MA is a first degree. A few M. Eng. courses are also covered.

Mature candidates are welcomed and should provide an account of their experience, employment history and any other relevant factors when applying, including reasons why, if they prefer, they want to study at a university. A separate brochure entitled 'Mature Students and Universities' is available, free of charge, from UCCA.

Your employer may possibly sponsor you; details of sponsorships available are published by the Manpower Services Commission. Grant details are available from DES Publications Despatch Centre, Government Buildings, Honey Pot Lane, Stanmore, Middlesex, HA7 1AZ or, for Scottish students, from the Scottish Education Department, Awards Branch, Haymarket House, Clifton Terrace, Edinburgh, EH12 5DT.

ARE YOU PROPERLY QUALIFIED?

Hobsons Publishing PLC, Bateman St., Cambridge, CB2 1LZ publish a book specifically on sandwich courses if you are able to combine or alternate study with industrial or professional training. It is better to speak to the University of your choice before writing to UCCA.

Choice of subject is up to you but remember that you need to plan at least twelve months ahead for entry to most universities.

In addition to the universities are the hundreds of Polytechnics and Colleges catering for full-time study dotted up and down the country and, in this case, the body to write to for details is the Council for National Academic Awards (CNAA) at 344–354 Gray's Inn Rd., London, WC1X 8BP; a special booklet for older students is available.

Most CNAA courses follow the standard pattern of three years' full-time study but many are sandwich courses combining academic study with supervised work experience. There are also, of course, part-time courses.

Awards available are:

- Bachelor of Arts (BA);
- Bachelor of Science (B.Sc.);
- Bachelor of Education (B.Ed.); or
- Diploma of Higher Education (Dip.H.E.).

You will normally qualify for a mandatory grant for a full-time course, unless you have previously pursued a course of higher education, or if you cannot fulfil certain residential requirements, or you are attending certain privately funded colleges. Make enquiries at an early stage of your local education authority.

Finally, consider the possibility of gaining a Master's Degree in Business Administration or MBA.

This is normally a one-year course of study run by the country's top management colleges such as Ashridge and the City University Business School in London. It is especially suitable for people who have gained both general and specific experience in a working environment and who are then keen to progress into the higher echelons of management.

Tuition is intense and the volume of required reading, research and course work particularly arduous. Leadership skills head a host of managerial techniques taught and there is little doubt that a potential employee boasting an MBA qualification is taken very seriously.

Part Time Study

Opportunities remain unlimited for anyone wishing to expand their knowledge. A few hours a week dedicated to the specialist subject of your choice allows you the freedom to participate in new areas, opening up fresh horizons and enabling you to go for that promotion goal.

Hundreds of colleges await you and the sheer number of possible courses becomes a daunting prospect in itself. You must avoid, though, chasing down inopportune avenues.

Begin, not with the college prospectus, but with your defined list of objectives. Browsing through a myriad of topics will deflect your positive thinking and put you in danger of electing for an attractive course in landscape painting instead of one to further your career!

Scour your local area to find out what different colleges have to offer and look not just at traditional teaching methods but at some of the new ones which make full use of modern technology, including home videos and personalised tutorial packs.

Get hold of *The Open Book*, a guide to Open College courses published by The Open College, Suite 470, St. James's Buildings, Oxford St., Manchester M1 6FQ. Claiming to be the fastest growing training establishment in Europe, the Open College makes use of existing educational establishments to provide people with new skills and abilities, and is encouraged by the Government.

Open Learning methods are used, giving you the opportunity to choose when, where and how to study. You proceed at your own pace and at a time and place that suits you best. Appropriate materials are provided and it is then up to you to decide how you want to do the work; ideal for someone in full-time employment. A national network of Open Access Centres exist where you can obtain help and advice and join a college; a 'hotline' on 0235–555444 (in Scotland 041–334–3141) is available to tell you your nearest Access Centre.

Course material is interesting, practical and yours to keep for ever. It includes:

- Workbooks
- Resource books
- Practical kits
- Audio tapes
- Video tapes
- Computer software
- Assignment books

Alongside the practical work are Channel 4 programmes, generally transmitted at lunch times.

Some universities now offer Open Studies programmes and although many of the courses are leisure related, keep your eye open for specialist subjects especially aimed at those wishing to further their careers. Classes are held at centres of education and elsewhere within the vicinity of the organizing university.

Several management colleges specialize in career development, amongst them Cranfield School of Management, Cranfield, Bedford, MK43 0AL, which has a depth of experience in the subject and caters for managers' needs at various stages of development. Its specialized courses include the Young Manager's Programme, Management Development Programme, General Management for Specialists and a Programme for Senior Managers.

Henley is another Management College offering sound, practical experience of the business environment both on a residential basis and through the Distance Learning concept; speak to them at Greenlands, Henley-on-Thames, Oxon. RG9 3AU. Other similar institutions with long histories of teaching management techniques include: Manchester Business School, Booth St. West, Manchester, M15 6PB; Ashridge Management College, Berkhamsted, Hertfordshire, HP4 1NS; and Insead, 77305 Fontainbleau Cedex, France.

Other colleges offer specialist tuition in subjects ranging from engineering to computer studies, through accountancy, secretarial skills, etc., and most good libraries will track down suitable directories for you. Most are run on a commercial basis and thus charge fees, so before enrolling with a college not known to you, make as many enquiries as you can within their sphere of knowledge to ensure they are legitimate; there are a few around which are not all that they claim to be. It is imperative that the piece of paper with which you finish up is universally recognized.

Correspondence Courses

Whilst these are a perfectly suitable medium for thousands of students eager to learn, they do not suit everyone. Before you embark on this course, therefore, think carefully through the implications of not being able to put questions directly to a tutor.

Questions can, of course, be sent through the post but by the time you receive the answer, others will have no doubt sprung to mind! Some colleges include an annual seminar for face-to-face sessions but these cannot equal the ready availability of a specialist who is able to provide on-the-spot information.

Some students find they cannot cope with correspondence style tuition; others, though, have found it very effective, giving them the flexibility to study precisely when they choose. Try to define your own category before you sign on!

Obtain a list of those colleges accredited for correspondence by the Council for the Accreditation of Correspondence Colleges (CACC), 27 Marylebone Road, London, NW1 5JS, which was established in 1969 as an independent body with the co-operation of the Secretary of State for Education and Science who nominates experienced educationalists for the Council. Standards are set for all aspects of postal tuition and a college is not given accredited status unless it conforms with these standards; regular checks are made.

There are only about 40 colleges in the UK entitled to CACC status,

but between them they offer a wide variety of topics covering both general and specific subjects. Three examples are:
- The Rapid Results College, Tuition House, 27/37 St. George's Rd., London, SW19 4DS, which offers professional examinations in Accountancy, Banking, Computing, Finance, Management, Marketing, Transport etc. as well as basic educational courses, a law degree and police promotion examinations.
- Transworld Education College, 8 Elliot Place, Clydeway Centre, Glasgow, G3 8EF, which specializes in providing courses to enable you to obtain a better job. Building, Electronics, Personnel Management, Agriculture, Engineering and Business Management are just a few examples:
- National Extension College, 18 Brooklands Avenue, Cambridge, CB2 2HN, is an educational charity with 25 years of experience of providing a high quality comprehensive service to correspondence students and was established to provide second chance education for adults. Its 300 or so tutors are active in universities, colleges and schools and there are flexi-study links with local colleges.

The Open University

Tens of thousands of people can testify to the fact that their lives have been changed, often quite dramatically, by the use of this particular teaching medium.

Clearly, it is going to prove especially suitable for you in the achievement of your goal of promotion since, although it will obviously take up a lot of your time, you can study almost whenever you please. Indeed, with a video recorder available, you can set your own study patterns without interference.

Studying at home still requires a mountain of willpower, and, probably, the support of family and friends. Planning your own studies around other activities will not prove easy but the outcome can be very rewarding.

The Open University was founded by Royal Charter in 1969 with the aim of providing educational opportunities for adults who prefer, or are only able, to study in their own homes and in their own time. It uses a multi-media approach to teaching, including the use of television, video, audio cassettes, correspondence and face-to-face tuition, and has been judged one of the most important innovations ever in the British educational system.

It uses thirteen regional centres to provide nationwide coverage and over 250 study centres exist for the use of students. Over 70,000 people have already gained full degrees by this method.

A superb opportunity exists for you to further your chances of securing promotion through a whole range of courses with this objective specifically in mind. The courses vary in length and include areas such as computing, engineering, management, health and the social services. Some lead to an academic qualification whilst others provide updating, but all are specialized and relevant to professionals and have been designed primarily for those who have had practical experience in a given field and who wish to develop or broaden their skills or understanding to a higher level.

The amount of previous experience or knowledge required will vary from course to course, although many assume none at all. Be careful, though, to ensure that you can cope with a particular course before enrolling.

You will have a choice of some 130 courses, with the intention of gaining 'half credits' or 'full credits' until you have enough to qualify for the Bachelor of Arts degree. This is likely to take you between three and six years to complete and perhaps a little longer for a BA (Honours) degree where eight full credits are needed as opposed to six. The degree can be either arts or science based and is recognized as being equivalent in every way to a full degree from any other British university.

The time necessary can be reduced if you are granted 'advanced standing' in recognition of successful previous study at higher educational level. And if you already hold a degree, the Open University offers the opportunity to take a taught or research based higher degree.

Each course lasts, normally, from February until October and, for a full credit course, you may be spending up to 14 hours each week studying.

You can see that it's a big step and it will cost you money. Fees can, however, be paid in instalments and your local education authority may agree to help. Employers, also, are sometimes keen to assist with finance, especially if they see you moving up in their company.

The regional centres are happy to talk things over with you before you commit yourself and your nearest centre can be found by contacting the Open University at P.O. Box 71, Milton Keynes, MK7 6AG.

The Open Business School

This is part of the Open University and one of the largest providers of management education in the country, offering a wide range of distance taught short courses covering every aspect of management.

It was set up in 1983 since when over 18,000 registrations have been received from managers in all sectors of industry and commerce. In addition, some 2,500 companies and organizations have shown their confidence in the School by sponsoring participants. One of these is the British Institute of Management (BIM) which makes a number of bursaries available each year on 'The Effective Manager' course. Details are obtainable from the BIM, Management House, Cottingham Road, Corby, Northamptonshire, NN17 1TT.

Because of its popularity the School has since established its own School of Management as a full faculty of the University able to offer students increased opportunities in management education and research, including an MBA degree.

Fees are modest, and the courses are flexible enough to form part of company training programmes or be enhanced by in-house sessions.

No formal entrance qualifications are called for and anyone living in the UK (or, indeed, in Belgium, Luxembourg, the Republic of Ireland or at a B.F.P.O. address in Europe) aged over 18 can apply to The Open University address above.

Courses vary in length between 8 and 30 weeks, with some three to five hours of weekly study necessary, although 'The Effective Manager' course takes a little longer. Study time can include attending tutorials and completing written assignments. Multi-media tuition is provided in a similar way to that used by the Open University.

Several professional bodies have recognized certain of the courses provided as being eligible for part exemption from their examinations, including the Institute of Personnel Management and the Institute of Marketing. Make certain, first, that you understand eligibility before committing yourself to a particular course if your aim is to gain a professional qualification.

'Women into Management' is precisely what it says and is an eight-week course especially for women who want to enter, or return to, a management career.

The Open Business School is fully recognized by industry and commerce and boasts an impressive 'client' list which includes the BBC, British Airways, Courtaulds, Ferranti, GEC, ICI, Royal Insurance, Texaco, United Kingdom Atomic Energy Authority and many others.

Teaching Yourself

For those with superior willpower, and the energy and time to devote to it, there is always the 'self-help' method of tuition by using freely available text books and other learning material, thereby saving on some of the costs incurred using a third party.

Your local library, particularly the larger ones, should prove a ready source and, with a carefully planned programme over a clearly defined period, you should be able to raise your qualification level to a desired standard.

This method may take you longer than the traditional correspondence course but may suit your temperament. Seek out the recommended reading books and, alongside these, study past examination papers usually obtainable from the relevant professional body. Check out employment requirements at the start to avoid disappointment.

Television and radio programmes, such as those aimed at Open University students, can help although they will probably have to be backed up by written material.

This method is not highly recommended and is only suitable for those with the determination to succeed, following a period of cautious research, and is unsuitable for anyone requiring regular prompting and encouragement.

Adding a Language

Will an additional language assist you in your goal of gaining promotion? Before answering this question, it might be advisable to take a long rather than a short term view.

The promotion you are immediately seeking may have little relevance to languages but remember, in the longer term, one of the most marketable commodities in employment is the fluent use of a language other than your native one. And it is not as difficult as you might imagine to gain this expertise.

It will, of course, take a little time – it is considered that 300 to 400 hours of study are required to get you to intermediate level – but the satisfaction to be gained is immeasurable. For future job searching, it will almost certainly ease the path.

The Europeans and the Japanese, in particular, have led the way in providing their export ambassadors with the ability to speak in English and, if we are to compete successfully, we must follow that lead.

If you have a basic, even school-day, knowledge of French or German, then start with that. You may be able to cut out a lot of the initial tutorials and even surprise yourself at how quickly you can progress. Some people, of course, are more adept at learning a new language than others but until you try you will not really know. Do not be put off by early difficulties; set yourself a realistic timetable by which you are able to read and speak basic sentences and then take further progress a step at a time.

Visiting the country of your choice and listening to, as well as speaking, that language will move your learning on by leaps and bounds. The accents and intonations of the French language, for instance, can only be heard authentically in France.

For the basics, though, choose your method of study very carefully. Many early attendees of night classes at local colleges find themselves frustrated after two or three sessions simply because the teaching level is either too basic or too advanced for them. If you intend to adopt this method, seek out the tutor before you book yourself in to find out precisely whether he is dealing with 'absolute beginners', those with a little knowledge or those already near-fluent and wishing to improve themselves further.

Language schools, either residential or on a distance learning basis, are worth considering. However, beware of some of their claims. To speak Spanish from a standing start in just 3 1/2 weeks, as some claim, is going to take an awful lot of willpower!

Many, however, allow you to test the water for a week or two, guaranteeing your money back if you are not fully satisfied. Before you get too enthusiastic, be satisfied that you are the sort of person who can study by the correspondence method.

Forget, incidentally, the boring methods by which you may have learned basic French or German at school; today's language schools are far more sophisticated and tuned in to the very latest methods of communication, including use of the subconscious coupled with background music to speed along your learning process!

The BBC through both radio and television, offer useful language courses alongside specialist books and cassettes which can be purchased beforehand. Videos are available from their World Service division on a 'money back guarantee' basis; write to DMP Organization (UK) Ltd., 1 Rhosili Road, Brackmills, Northampton, NN4 0JE.

Language courses commonly available include:

- Chinese
- Turkish
- Spanish
- Italian
- German
- Russian
- French.

Other Avenues

Consider joining the British Institute of Management (BIM), based at Management House, Parker St., London, WC2B 5PT, which acts as a central body for the country's managers. Since its foundation in 1947 it has devoted itself exclusively to the development of the art and science of management.

As well as being a powerhouse of information, the BIM also runs conferences, courses and seminars at regular intervals throughout the year in London and many other centres. A Careers Advisory Service is available to members, manned by experienced counsellors and with access to information on courses, placement agencies, vocational guidance centres and other sources of advice on career changes and development. The advice service is free to members although a charge is levied for each counselling interview.

Management House also contains one of the largest management libraries in the world with over 70,000 books, journals, pamphlets and company documents available for reference and borrowing.

Enquire also of the British Association for Commercial and Industrial Education (BACIE), 16 Park Crescent, London, W1N 4AP, a voluntary non-political charity founded in 1919 and operating in the fields of vocational education and training.

BACIE is a member of the Manpower Services Commission's voluntary registration scheme for the training of trainers and consequently maintains a Review Group which keeps an eye on this important aspect of education. Courses and workshops are designed on a modular basis to ensure maximum flexibility for those taking part, and courses may be taken at almost any time of the year. Although mainly a corporate membership organization, individuals are welcome to join and make use of the full membership services, including discounts on courses and free use of BACIE's comprehensive information service and library. Courses are both residential and non-residential and are being constantly updated to meet the needs of industry and commerce. Aims for each are clearly set out as guidelines and an indication is provided as to the sort of people who would best gain from the sessions.

Arm yourself with a copy of *Your Guide to our Employment, Training and Enterprise Programmes* published by the Department of Employment and obtainable from any Job Centre. It will guide you through the morass of assistance available from government sources and also provides details of counselling and advice centres.

Several commercial training schools encourage trainees to use interactive video as a teaching method; for instance, Interactive Information Systems Ltd. (Telephone 071–278–3731) has developed what is known as the Talent System. It is used by such major employers as the Bank of England, IBM, the Halifax Building Society, British Airways, Shell and Access. Courses include 'Finance for Non-Financial Managers', 'Understanding the Basics of Marketing' and 'Managing Time as a Scarce Resource'. See if you can talk your employer into making use of it.

Women seeking promotion into management, as well as being catered for by the Open Business School (see above), have a wide choice of specialized courses, such as the 2-day one run by Management Technology Education, Suite 4, 48 Upper Berkeley St., London, W1H 7PN entitled 'Women in Management'. This course, amongst other objectives, aims to identify ways in which some of the traditional constraints facing women in management can be successfully overcome.

All of these methods of equipping yourself for a job higher up the ladder will naturally vary from country to country and overseas readers should make enquiries of their local Chamber of Commerce, library, government sources and professional bodies. All are there to help.

Let's move on to how you should structure your approach to the goal you have set yourself . . .

CHAPTER 3

A Structured Career Approach

Some decisions can produce instant realization. Desiring an ice-cream in an ice-cream parlour, for instance, can quickly bring about a satisfactory end result providing you are in possession of the necessary currency. Deciding to change your motor car may take a little longer to fruition. The market place must be weighed up, alternatives sought, finance perhaps arranged and you will readily accept from the start that the whole process will take time.

Gaining – or, more correctly, *winning* promotion will certainly take longer. If you are to tackle the task with determination – as you must – a clearly defined process in a logical manner must be adhered to. Wartime battles are not generally won on the day itself; the path to success has been carefully planned beforehand.

So how do you plan?

You will already have undertaken the basics, as outlined in the previous two chapters, and we will thus assume that you have taken stock of your own strengths and weaknesses, and begun measures to equip yourself with the necessary qualifications if a few shortfalls had become clear during your self-investigation.

Now you must:

- Get to know the company you work for as thoroughly as you can;
- Begin to exploit your own talents so that they are drawn to the attention of those who matter;
- Manage your relationships with those above and below you to get as many people as possible on your side;
- Communicate effectively;
- Recognize the importance of the marketing function in any successful enterprise and play your full part in developing this discipline;
- Measure up to, and indeed better, your superior's expectations of you, whether these are defined by performance levels or not; and, finally
- Keep yourself fully fit in mind and body for the job in hand.

The remaining chapters will prepare you for these tasks, but before that you will benefit from an analysis of the present situation as it affects you.

Setting Objectives

Desires are generally more easily achieved if they are quantified. Uncertainty as to whether you would prefer an ice-cream or a sandwich will probably leave you feeling dissatisfied (and, possibly, hungry!); making a firm decision is more likely to lead to satisfaction!

Determine, therefore, in a clear manner what your objectives are, preferably in the short, medium and longer term and couple with these your desired levels of reward and responsibility. Your plans might look like this:

- *First Level*: Within nine months secure a supervisory position at my present workbase, earning £3,000 more than my current salary;
- *Second Level*: Within five years obtain a managerial post either at my present workbase or at another of the company's UK bases with responsibilities for development within the manufacturing sector earning a package worth at least £25,000 at current prices;
- *Third Level*: Within ten years become eligible for a senior executive position either at home or abroad with divisional responsibility earning £35,000 p.a. plus normal perks.

We have thus defined specific desires within set timescales and preferred remuneration packages. Reality may prove to be very different but that does not matter at this stage; the objectives are *today's* and can be flexed at any time in the future according to your own wishes.

What is imperative at this time is that you remain realistic and not float away into cloud cuckoo land. By all means set your sights testingly high but do not expect the Chairman's job next week!

You will see from the above example that you are expecting to remain with your present employers and this is not a bad basis to use at this time. In practice, if you are a high-flyer, you will probably (although by no means certainly) switch employers during your working life. For now, however, we are aiming only at the *next* job and, if that is to be the promotion you wish, we are assuming that it will be with your present employers.

Mind Over Matter

As well as the *hard* assets you have gained at this stage in your life, there is another asset – less tangible but far more powerful – which you should learn to bring into play to achieve your goal. The hard assets are the qualifications for which you have striven, the experience you have acquired and the tangible benefits gained from knowing friends and colleagues along the way. But you also have the ability to tap into another source of inspiration and encouragement which, in certain respects, far outweighs the tangible advantages so far acquired. This is your own mind and, properly directed, it can assist you in your quest.

The application of psychology to a myriad of problem areas is well recognized in our modern world. Equally accepted is the fact that, where this can be applied by the individual seeking the solution, the resolution of that problem is considerably eased. 'Heal thyself' was the biblical interpretation and is every bit as valid today.

This is not to say that the task is an easy one. It does call for a strong will and a methodical application of the necessary principles. Given your determination to achieve your goal, though, it should prove less difficult than in other circumstances.

This book does not aim to train you in the art of mind over matter, but some understanding of its underlying applications will not go amiss. Further study is recommended, either through books specializing in the subject or attending one of many courses on the subject now available; a selection are referred to later.

Success is achieved through:

- Clearly identifying your goal, so that there is no doubt about where you wish to get to;
- Equally identifying the paths needing to be trodden to reach that goal;
- Defining possible obstacles and how these might be overcome; and, most importantly
- Believing in yourself and your capabilities.

Unless you are able to convince yourself as to the realism and achievability of what you are setting out to do, then the journey will be a wasted one. For this reason alone, it will be worth your while spending some time on this aspect of your task.

Your employer, certainly if he is one of the majors, may already be taking advantage of one of the many man management institutions now offering courses and seminars aimed at improving people's perceptions of their own abilities. If you have not been selected to attend, do not hesitate to put yourself forward; as has been pointed out earlier, most forward-thinking employers are delighted with workers who show signs of self-advancement.

Time Management International runs assertiveness courses, normally over a two-day period, where ambitions are assessed, analysed and redirected if necessary. Positive thinking is encouraged and managers are asked to detail their attributes and are in turn taught as to how these can leapfrog them up the ladder of success.

At Man Management similar techniques are used, and attendees encouraged to go for minor successes at a time rather than attempting a gigantic leap up the ladder.

Single day courses are held at Structured Training plc's management base, where participants are encouraged to get to know themselves better and then to build success upon that knowledge.

Training videos are available from Video Arts which has been in the field of management encouragement for many years and is used by leading corporates from all sectors of industry and commerce. It was started by comedy actor John Cleese and others who were early pioneers in the identifying of management disciplines which could be built upon, both to improve individual job satisfaction and company profits.

All of these courses currently cost about £200 a day, or a little less on longer courses, but you may consider the investment worthwhile when measured against your expectations of higher financial rewards in your new job!

Clearing the Way

It is said that 'ask a busy man if you want something doing' is a truism. It is for the very reason that a busy man – or woman – has to organize his life in such a structured way that he is able succesfully to carry out so many duties.

Others, less busy, do not have the same pressing demands upon their time and thus are more likely to fall down when something additional is asked of them.

You, of course, are going to be very busy. Busy at organizing that goal of promotion which you seek, and this will undoubtedly take a great deal of your otherwise spare time. For this reason you need to sweep away all other important demands, leaving the way clear to give full concentration to the task in hand.

What might these other demands consist of? They could relate to other aspects of your work, family commitments, community duties or merely items of self-interest such as sports and hobbies. During your promotion campaign, the decks must be cleared of any such extraneous demands.

Take family ties, for instance. This is probably not the time to be starting a family, considering a move of house or even settling children into new schools. If your spouse is working, then he or she would be well advised not to be considering something new in the line of work for the time being. Any one of these items is stressful and the resultant impact will undoubtedly put you off your major priority.

Captaining the local cricket team, or commencing lessons in photography are other issues best avoided whilst you have the main task in hand. There are exceptions, of course, and you may be the very strong-willed type able to cope with dual priorities, particularly if one is related to an outside interest, but unless you are quite certain that this is the case, then do not risk it.

Work issues require careful consideration. They may just be the spur you need to gain recognition, such as developing a new project or test marketing a fresh service. In these cases, it may be possible to tie in your promotional desires with achieving something a little 'over the top', thereby gaining admiration from your superiors.

In general, however, aim at leaving your mind entirely uncluttered to concentrate on the one goal. That way you are much more likely to find the net.

Do You Fit?

Job descriptions are becoming the norm. It used to be the case that, when someone was employed, they were taken on as either a 'carpenter' or a 'secretary'. Employers today, and again especially the larger ones, are much more likely to present you with a full description of all your duties.

For them it encapsulates your responsibilities and levels of authority; for you it helps to identify more precisely the areas of expected achievement, something for you to gauge your performance against.

It is to be hoped that you are already working to a detailed job description and are thus used to the ways in which these are drawn up. If not, it is a subject worthy of further study for in time you are likely to meet this method of job categorization. Let us look briefly at what a job description might look like:

Regional Manager:

- Responsibility to Board for marketing function in region;
- Responsibility for preparation and achievement of annual marketing plan;
- Contribution to Head Office on new product development and competitor activity;

- Development of new outlets and review of current sites;
- Regional personnel training function and identification of future managers;
- Advertising budget and publicity expenditure.

This is a simplified version of, normally, a more complex brief, but provides you with an example of the type of responsibilities likely to be encompassed in the job description of a fairly senior employee.

What is suggested here, however, is not a look at your present job but the one which you covet. The one you are aiming to be promoted into.

Take a large, blank piece of paper and complete it with headings applicable to the job you have in mind. Try to cover every responsibility likely to be in the hands of the incumbent and then develop these headings into greater detail, pinpointing day-to-day activities as you see them, coupled with any strategic roles you are able to identify. Consider each managerial function likely to be involved and estimate, if you are uncertain, the job holder's role in each of these.

To whom is he responsible? Who are his subordinates? Does he have an area, regional or head office function? Does he have responsibilities outside his everyday activities? Is he responsible for budgeting, or is he merely provided with expenditure and/or income levels?

These, and other, questions demand answers. You may be in the fortunate position of being able to discuss these with your superior, especially if your ambitions are known and accepted; he, in turn, may of course also be ambitious!

When you have completed your task – take a couple of weeks or so over it, for inevitably items will fly into your mind at odd moments once you concentrate upon it – tidy up the list into some format of a job description, and now the real work begins.

Self-analysis is once again called for in testing yourself on each and every point to measure your acceptability or otherwise; do not fool yourself on this exercise. It is very unlikely that your present attributes will match up in every respect to those apparently required, for otherwise you are practically in the job already! Gaps of knowledge, experience or personality are likely to emerge and it is upon these that you must now concentrate.

Do not be afraid of shortcomings. Look upon them as opportunities rather than threats and begin now to calculate what is needed to overcome them. Add willpower to your answers and you are half-way there!

Is the Time Right?

The precise timing as to when you might expect promotion is easy to gauge when it's a case of 'dead men's shoes'; if you have to wait until your immediate superior either dies or retires, then at least the latter may be calculable.

This, however, is far too long for you to wait. You will be better occupied looking at your own organization rather than merely the people who work within it.

In times of rapid development, diversification and expansion, jobs are more likely to be created than simply filled. So take a close look at your company and gauge where the opportunities are likely to arise.

Are sales rising dramatically? Then almost certainly additional sales people will be needed along with those who manufacture the items, if this is the case. Administrative, financial and personnel functions will also grow to handle the increasing workload, and there will be opportunities for promotion in each of these areas.

Is a new depot to be opened? Is the Head Office function being decentralized? Are additional specialists being taken on? Is the firm expanding overseas?

Any one of these developments may create opportunities for you. Most companies are happier promoting from within, as opposed to bearing the heavy costs of advertising for personnel and the inevitable difficulties of choosing the right people. Even if they operate a 'devil you know' principle, it might work in your favour!

Try and estimate anyone who might move on who is already ahead of you; if you can work out a satisfactory progression chart involving your own preferment you may finish up doing both your employer and yourself favours!

If none of this seems feasible, do not be downhearted. If you work for a relatively small concern, it may prove very difficult to calculate any sort of job progression but this must not put you off your cause. Many a secretary has been promoted into a marketing or administrative function, only to prove he or she can readily cope with the added levels of responsibility. In a smaller company, you are that much nearer the boss and thus his ear; use it to your advantage.

Are You Ready Technically?

Probably the fastest moving ingredient in any business today is its reliance upon technology. There were those who, only a few years ago, scorned the advance of computers and who advocated their demise within a decade. Instead we have witnessed their growth beyond everyone's expectations and hardly a week passes without the announcement of some further enhancement to their capabilities.

Alongside your own growth of knowledge, therefore, you must maintain an equal sense of the advances being made in the world of technology.

Computer usage is no longer confined to the secretarial, administrative and technical functions of a business. Management information systems have been developed in order to provide senior executives with up-to-date knowledge, as well as to pass confidential information throughout an organization in a secured manner. Individual passwords are available and access to the systems in use can be tailored to include limited numbers of personnel.

Managers need to understand, use and adapt computer systems to keep themselves briefed as to how their organization is performing and, more importantly, to monitor changes in order to measure their effectiveness. There is little point in introducing new products or services within a company unless detailed records of their sales are available to allow appropriate management to fine tune any necessary adjustments to react to changing trends in the market place.

Information technology is thus a vital component in every manger's tool-box, and he must be aware of the latest developments to keep himself not just abreast, but ahead of, his competitors. You may already be well down this road and in a position to keep yourself informed of what is on offer. If you are not, though, it is something to be ignored only at your peril.

Several useful information technology magazines are readily available in the bookstalls and study of these will pay dividends; better still, if you are not computer-literate, buy yourself one of the relatively cheap Personal Computers (PCs) now on the market and bury yourself in a handbook. It may open up new fields you had not thought possible!

All manner of communications are undergoing a revolution and we already have available, for instance, electronic mail (or 'E-mail'), allowing letters and memoranda to be communicated from computer screen to screen without the necessity of conversion to print.

The use of fibre optics in the telecommunications field is enabling far greater use to be made of telephone lines, and facsimile (or 'fax') machines are now commonplace, even in moving vehicles. Laser printers are taking over from the more noisy matrix or daisy-wheel varieties, and satellites are being used to bounce messages across the world in fractions of a second.

Voice acceptable machinery is now technically possible, thus bypassing the necessity to transfer messages firstly to paper and then by post.

Unless it is your particular discipline, you do not need to become a computer boffin, but in today's fast-moving world of business, you certainly must keep abreast of modern communication technology if you are seeking higher levels of employment.

Discussing Your Desires

As part of your game-plan, it may be necessary to talk over your wishes with one of your superiors. Handling interviews generally is covered in more detail when you reach Chapter 8, but in the meantime we will take a brief look at how this particular face-to-face should be conducted.

Planning must be your watchword. It would be fatalistic merely to button-hole your intended subject in a corridor on the spur of a moment and pour out your heartfelt longings for promotion. To gauge his reaction, simply put yourself in his place and imagine what *you* might feel in those circumstances!

The following is a suggested plan of campaign:

- Determine precisely to whom you should speak. This may be your immediate superior (although probably not if it is his job you are after!), another of your superior colleagues or someone in a personnel function.

- Consider whether your wishes will be better served by firstly writing to that person, outlining your case and then following this with a request for a chat, or merely seeking an interview from the start. Much will depend upon your preferred line of attack, coupled with the likely empathy of the party you are approaching, but generally the more formal line, i.e. writing first, helps to emphasize the determination of your intentions.

- If you decide to write, keep it reasonably brief (say no more than 1 page of personalized size notepaper), factual and to the point. The emphasis should be upon your *desire* to be promoted, for you can outline the *reasons* more fully when you meet. Emotion should not feature in any shape or form.

- The interview should be requested, as far as is possible, in an entirely confidential environment and, in appropriate circumstances, be 'off the record'. If, of course, you are seeing the Personnel Manager and your wish is an open secret, then the reverse will be the case and your interview properly recorded.

Plan what you are going to say beforehand and keep your opening gambit as brief as possible. Allow the other party to ask as many questions as he sees fit but make certain you are equipped for the answers. The questions likely to be asked are not difficult to guess and will naturally include your reasons for seeking a change, your qualifications for the higher post and, probably, your longer term ambitions.

Listen very carefully to what the other person has to say and, especially, note any advice given. Do not be afraid of going into the meeting with a notepad and jotting down any specific recommendations; this will again show how determined you are to achieve your goal.

Dealing with Setbacks

'If at first you don't succeed, try, try, try again – then quit – you can't go on for ever' may have been acceptable to its author W.C. Fields, but it certainly will not do for you!

Accept from the outset that you are as human as the rest of us and that no-one can be consistently successful. There are, therefore, likely to be setbacks along the way and you must learn to live with them.

But living with them and despairing, as opposed to living with them and learning from them and picking yourself up again, are as different as chalk and cheese. Take a cold, backward look at what went wrong, analyse it, add it to your store of knowledge, and move forward again with an even greater amount of determination. A positive attitude is clearly called for and by now you should be getting used to this.

Setbacks come in all forms. They may be linked directly to your working situation, such as missing out on a hoped-for promotion, receiving a disappointing personnel report or, at worst, finding yourself completely out of a job through redundancy or the liquidation of your employers. Devastating though any one of these might appear at the time, it is important that you view such 'disasters' as only minor hiccups on your road to success.

Many an employee, for instance, finding himself out of work through no consequence of his own has, in time, discovered it to be a blessing in disguise when measured against a more attractive alternative which presents itself. The pressing need to canvass the working arena can spotlight opportunities previously unconsidered, necessity truly being the mother of invention – or, in this case, innovation.

Personal setbacks well away from the working environment may also temporarily stall your drive towards success. Serious illness within the family, even death, will of course have an impact upon your challenge, but even these in time will heal and any stumbling should, hopefully, prove only temporary.

So, remember again, we are all human and none of us is in a position fully to control every aspect of our lives. With the goal you have set yourself, your task must be firstly to accept and secondly to overcome any pitfalls you meet along the way.

Especially for Women

Whilst this entire book is aimed equally at both men and women seeking promotion, it will not go amiss to emphasize the improving opportunities which now exist for women throughout commerce and industry, if only to counter the often repeated suggestion that their chances of success are fewer.

You have only to look at the fields of accountancy, law and even the construction industry, for instance, to see how clearly women are proving their equality with men in the advancement to the top of these professions.

A recent survey revealed that more women than ever are landing top jobs in industry, coupled with the fact that their pay is rising faster than that of men.

The report, instigated by the British Institute of Management and Remuneration Economics, showed that nearly eight in every one hundred top jobs were held by women, up from less than seven a year earlier. And women get there earlier, too; average age was quoted at 37 compared with 43 for their male counterpart.

Female directors did even better, reaching that position at an average age of 39 against 47 for men.

There is a clear message there for ambitious ladies, so go to it!

But, male or female, there is another facet of your campaign planning to mount to increase your chances of success. That is to get to know the company you currently work for very much better ... let's see how you go about it.

CHAPTER 4

How Well Do You Know Your Employer?

By now you should know yourself a little better. You will have analysed your own character, along with your strengths and weaknesses. You are in a good position to know whether or not you are ready to slot into that next job.

But you are only one side of the story. A successful job partnership, just like a successful marriage, must have two parties. Your employer is the other party.

To create that success, you must understand one another. Your employer will try to do that through the medium of its personnel department and regular reviews of your performance. For your part, it is essential that you fully understand the nature of the body for whom you work.

This might appear a mind-bending exercise, especially if you work for one of the giants, but by breaking it into segments it can become very much easier. Even if your job is with a smaller concern, the segments equally apply; the task of analysis merely becomes simpler, with the one exception that you may not have available as much detailed financial information that would be open to public view with a company quoted on the Stock Exchange.

The suggested split is as follows:

- *Company Policy*: What is the culture? What is the public image of your employer? Are there rules to be obeyed? How much planning is done?

- *The Market Place*: How big is it? Where is it located? What is the competition? What products and services are provided? How effective is the marketing? Is the business keeping pace with new technology?

- *The People*: What is the organizational structure? Who manages the company? Who makes the real decisions? What promotion patterns exist? How good is training? What are employee relations like?

- *Administration*: How is the company organized? How effective

are communications? What systems operate? Is an Organization and Methods approach used?
- *Controls*: Is planning properly used? What budgetary controls exist? How is information monitored?
- *Finances*: What does the Balance Sheet look like? How strong are the underlying assets? Is the business profitable?

Let us examine each of these in turn.

Company Policy

Every business must have a policy – only the more forward-looking ones actually define it.

The policy is a statement of a company's major objectives, along with the ways and means of achieving them. Such objectives may, for instance, revolve around achieving a greater market share or developing a new product. Other objectives may include reaching a certain size in terms of annual turnover or, say, expanding to the extent that a clearly defined market territory is saturated.

Policy should remain a movable feast, for inevitably external conditions change. These may relate to political, economic or legislative factors and a business must stay poised to take advantage of new opportunities or meet any threats posed.

Along with knowing your company's policy, you should also be aware of its culture. This is not easy to define, but think of it as equivalent to the personality of an individual and you will then begin to understand why the merger of two businesses does not always work out; there is a clash of culture.

Corporate culture shows through in the working environment of a business, in its methods of operating, in its management structure and in such less tangible signs as whether or not an air of optimism and opportunity pervades or are all new ideas trampled upon in favour of yesterday's successes.

If you are not comfortable with the culture you have identified, you will find it difficult to move along the ladder of progression. Signs of a healthy and forward-looking culture include:

- New products and services regularly coming on stream;
- High awareness of customer needs;
- Employee enthusiasm;
- Open management; and
- Flexibility in decision-making.

Know the public image of your company. Is it high profile, such as Coca-Cola, or does it keep itself to itself? Either approach may, of course, prove successful, but it is your job to understand the reasons behind such decisions.

Most companies also have 'rules' which must be followed by those anticipating success within the organization. These rules include both the written rules available to all employees and, invariably, a few unwritten ones as well.

Think of them more as conventions and you won't go far wrong, but do not try to counter them, at least until you are in the Managing Director's chair!

How well does your company plan ahead? Does it operate a one, five or ten year plan? Does it have a plan at all? Are major projects thoroughly evaluated, proposed products researched and market tested? All of these questions demand answers and are of undoubted interest to the dedicated, long-term employee. Proper planning points to better prospects.

The Market Place

Every business is situated somewhere or other within its own market. It may be – in the case of brands such as Cadbury's, General Motors, House of Frazer and so on – the leader, or one of its leaders, or it may be in the pack with dozens, hundreds or even thousands of others seeking a share.

The business may predominate in a certain sector due to its historical strengths but at the same time may be emerging into new fields to establish a wider product base; Plessey is such an example – it has long been a major electronic company, but more recently has entered the aerospace arena.

Try to determine where your company sits. Is it a national, or even international, name, known to all within the industry, or is it struggling for familiarity in a highly competitive environment? Or does it stand somewhere in-between? Your reason for establishing this information, of course, is to take a view on your company's future and the part you wish to play in this.

It is also useful to know whether or not your company can boast a 'competitive advantage' for, if it can do so, it should be able to sustain such advantage over its competitors whilst market conditions remain the same, thus safeguarding its profitability. A competitive advantage is where a business is especially successful in one of the following major areas:

- Production of its goods;
- Marketing those goods;
- Distributing them;
- Developing them to meet consumer needs; or
- Researching and designing new goods.

Although we have referred specifically to goods, service industries can have similar competitive advantages, to include in-house expertise in creating rather than producing their products, and delivery systems as opposed to distribution networks to get them to their customers.

Know where your company is geographically located in its market, i.e. does it serve local needs only, or has it the ability to cover the UK, or even a global, market place? What precisely are its products or services and are these constantly reviewed to meet changing conditions?

One thing you should certainly know about your company, in your quest for promotion, is exact details of its various locations, for these may play an important part in your future career. Are there bases around the country, or overseas, where you may find yourself working in due course? A good grasp of these at this early stage will help when that magic day arrives posting you to one of them; if you have done your homework properly, you will already know much of what is in store for you at your new location.

Is your company growing steadily or remaining static? Is its management aware of developing market trends or does it tend to lag behind in matching competitors' products? What proportion of its market place does it command and is this a falling or rising percentage?

Find out as much as you can about the company's pricing policies, for these tend to indicate its level of aggressiveness and strength *vis-à-vis* its competitors.

A product or service can be offered to the consumer at either:

- The basic cost to produce it, plus an 'acceptable' margin for profit; or
- A price which the supplier believes the consumer will accept, where the cost bears little relation to the sought-after figure.

What might be acceptable, of course, in terms of an added profit margin can vary considerably. Something of a particularly high quality may command a premium; alternatively, a company may adopt a policy to recover a minimum percentage by way of return on the capital it employs or upon the cost base.

If market conditions restrict what a company may add, then the going will be a little tougher than where the end user is prepared to pay well over what the basic cost might be. Where is *your* business situated – and what are its prospects?

Does it, indeed, have a well thought-out marketing plan? We will be looking at marketing in much greater detail in Chapter 9, although you should at this stage begin to obtain a feel for your company's own strength (or perhaps weakness) in this area.

Many businesses founder despite being built upon good products simply because the owners overlook the importance of marketing. Marketing, incidentally, is far more than the mere selling of goods or services; it is the identification of your customers' needs and the creation of an efficient delivery system to get those items to them at an acceptable profit to the business. All highly successful concerns rely on expert marketing; is yours one of them?

Another common cause of corporate collapse is the failure to invest sufficiently in new technology to maintain at least parity with competitors. How does your company fare? Does one of the management have a responsibility for monitoring technological advances and trends? Is sufficient capital set aside to purchase the necessary plant and machinery? How much research is undertaken? Answers to these questions will help you to assess your company's ability to recognize changes and meet the requirements which they demand.

Lastly, in the market place, take a look at how the business deals with the competition. Does it meet it head on, continually amending prices to maintain market share, or does it instead track competitive movements, keeping itself ready to adapt policies as necessary?

Competitors – or likely competitors – should never be ignored. Business life is a hard one and they are there to grab your customers at the first opportunity of weakness on your part. Make certain the company you work for is on top of the heap.

The People

Every business is merely a collection of people of all shapes, sizes, sexes and capabilities, and whilst their shape, size or sex is unlikely to have any impact upon the whole, the sum of their capabilities will determine the level of their success. So, in looking at your particular business you must weigh up the capabilities of its people, as well as study its policy and its organization.

Do you know who the directors are? If it is a major or public concern, you should at least know their names and, hopefully, a little about their background and how long they have been in the job. If they are constantly changing, find out why. Who are the senior managers, and what are their responsibilities? What is your own chain of command?

A business with a tidy, compact structure is likely to do better than one with a less clear, loose arrangement where employees are uncertain as to their lines of communication and responsibility. Clear definitions should exist as to reporting lines and everyone should know who is his immediate 'boss'.

Non-executive directors or officers may exist who play a part in guiding the strategy of a company but who do not have a day-to-day responsibility. It is important that there is not undue interference from such individuals, or clashes are likely to occur with executive members of management, i.e. those responsible for actually running the business. Try to determine whether lines of responsibility are clear in your company.

Ideally, an organization chart should exist which makes it plain to all who are involved who is responsible for what and where his reporting lines lie. Who, for instance, deals with purchases of smaller capital items for the business – is it the Purchasing Manager, the Finance Director, the Office Manager, or does everything have to be referred to 'someone on high'?

Determine, also, who really wields power in your company. Are decisions taken by individuals or committees, and how long does this decision-making process take?

Are people allowed to change things, or does everything have to stay the same? Is there a Suggestions Scheme, often a good indication of a well-run business?

Of course, if you work for a subsidiary of a larger corporation the position may be very different. But there should still be positive decision-makers on board, at least for the more mundane, day-to-day matters. It's a bad sign if permission in triplicate has to go up the line for every little item.

All but the smallest business should have someone delegated to fulfil the personnel function, but the way in which this is operated is invariably a good guide as to whether or not the business itself is a healthy one.

The giants, for instance, will have specialist departments offering guidance and assistance in all aspects of personnel, from maternity leave to help with retirement. Welfare of employees should be high on their priority list, to include the development and training (both internally and outside the business) of all individuals showing promise.

A well structured promotion policy should thus exist, with properly maintained records and each employee having a clear idea of his potential. Regular interviews would form part of this discipline, with advice being offered by superiors where performance is not up to scratch. Is this how things operate where you work?

Another indicator of a company's seriousness in evaluating its workers is its attitude towards staff training, which can take many forms:

- Induction training – being told about the business and its rules and regulations;
- On the job training;
- Internal courses;
- External training, especially of the management stream;
- Conferences, seminars, etc.

Do all of these exist, in some shape or form, and are they truly effective? Do people feel fully trained, or is it just lip-service in operation? A defined programme for each employee should be in place, although this ideal probably exists only in the very large concerns in the UK.

Check on your employer's attitude towards Trade Unions, if one is appropriate in your profession. Whilst the more enlightened fully open their doors to employee representative bodies, it would be wrong to condemn those who prefer to operate without them, for worker are often either better paid, or benefit from additional 'perks', in such companies. What is important, however, is whether or not those in charge recognize the basic rights of individuals, either through accepted union channels or on a one-to-one basis. Employers must at least be seen to be fair to make the grade here.

Administration

How well organized and administered is the business for which you work? In the same manner in which certain individuals tightly control their everyday lives, whilst others panic from crisis to crisis, so there are wide differences between corporate organizations.

Those better organized have systems in place to give them an early warning of troubles ahead, be they likely shortages of personnel, changes in market trends or any of the thousand or more other internal and external factors which affect the health of business life.

A properly structured organization can usually be spotted from the following ingredients:

- There is a clear route through which orders are channelled and recorded;
- Key activities are highlighted;
- Individual employees know their precise duties and relationships with others;
- All resources, human, financial and otherwise are properly directed;
- Systems are in place to monitor results of the activities undertaken; and
- External events likely to have an impact on the business are noted at an early stage.

It is important to recognize that the administration exists to serve the core elements of a business and not the other way around. Some of the large companies in this country, and notably certain of our public concerns, remain guilty of being run to serve their own internal rules rather than identifying and meeting the needs of their customers.

Take a close look at the systems in operation in your company and observe how efficient, or otherwise, they are. Are they creaking at the seams – or regularly updated? Are they user-friendly, or do operatives have no confidence in them? Does duplication exist, as is so often the case?

Do not be too downhearted, of course, if you do not have too much faith in the systems currently in place. If you are seeking to move up the ladder in your organization, then, as you do so, you should have increasing opportunities to change old habits. It could pay you, therefore, to spend a little time in devising more efficient systems in readiness for your next promotion. Current management too often has little time to better systems which it knows are far from perfect and could welcome your input at an appropriate stage. Bide your time and make your move when it is most likely to do you some good!

You may have to be tactful, of course, if your company employs an Organization and Methods section and some prior consultation with them, if necessary, may be wise.

Commonly known as 'O and M', this is the name given to any conscious attempt to improve the organization, simplify and improve the methods, and generally create and maintain an efficient administrative machine. It was first used by the Civil Service during the 1940s but has been adopted, in many different guises, by industry and commerce since then.

A specialist in the subject, or more often a team, will examine very closely all the 'administrative routes' an order, for instance, when received has to follow. Forms will be studied, jobs timed and an analysis follows to see whether or not a better method can be found of doing the job.

If these specialists are already employed in your company, are they carrying out an effective job themselves? If they do not exist, should they?

Fast communication methods are vital to any expanding business and for this reason we devote an entire section – Chapter 8 – to this subject.

In the meantime, begin to study the ways and means by which your organization communicates, both internally and with the outside world. Later on, we will together try to assess how good it is at it.

One other way you can gauge the probable efficiency of your own business is by looking at the degree of delegation.

By definition, delegation is the transferring to others of the responsibility for the performance of a specific task or the making of decisions in a general or specific area of activity, thus freeing the delegator to carry out more senior duties. It would thus be wrong for a company to expect its higher paid personnel to be making relatively minor decisions, and more disastrous for juniors actually to be running the business – but it happens!

It is impossible to lay down clear rules as to what decisions should or should not be delegated to others. A sensible view has to be taken and you might now care to consider whether you, for instance, could delegate more, or whether you believe insufficient authority is delegated to you from above. A good balance already in existence points to a well-run business.

Controls

Every good organization should be in control of itself. It will achieve this ideal through targeting, or budgeting, its expectations for any given period (often a year at a time) and following this up with monitoring actual achievements against these expectations.

Many smaller businesses operate without the strictures of budgeting although, increasingly, its benefits are being recognized. The main benefits of budgeting include:

- It sets the objectives of each department;
- It provides a means of measuring success, not only of the company's performance but of those individuals responsible for that part of the budget;
- It should help to highlight major features, such as material costs or advertising expenditure;
- Departmental budgets, when added together, provide a yardstick for the performance of the business as a whole; and
- Problems come to light much earlier than in the absence of a budget.

Budgets may be split into sub-budgets, either to control expenditure or monitor income. Methods of formulating the original figures vary greatly and the subject is studied in greater detail in Chapter 10, but if your company is not using some form of control, you should ask yourself why.

Any business which is not at least measuring its *actual* performance on a regular basis is heading for trouble, and again many differing methods of achieving this end exist.

The important point is that such systems are operating and on a topical basis. Some businesses do not really know how they are doing until production of the annual accounts, often six months or more after the financial year end. Clearly, this is a disastrous way for any employer to be 'looking after' his affairs.

Ideally, management accounting information systems should be in place to provide the directors or owners with a guide as to the level of results the previous month. These figures should become available certainly before the end of the following month. How do yours compare?

Finances

Some people can read a Balance Sheet of a business in the same way that others read a novel. Millionaires thrive on it, but it can take years of practice. What we will attempt here is to show you the sort of things you can learn about the company you work for simply by studying its annual accounts.

This assumes, of course, that they are readily available. If the company is a public one, then they certainly should be (and their absence could be a warning sign) within a few months of the financial year end. As an employee, you may be handed a copy; if you are also a shareholder, then you will certainly be sent one.

Balance Sheets and Profit and Loss Accounts are, however, freely available to the public for every private or public limited company, once they have been lodged with Companies House in Cardiff. Your accountant, stock broker or bank manager should be able to obtain a copy for you, and this is recommended if you are not entitled to one by virtue of any other reason. Once understood, they may tell you a lot of which you were previously unaware.

Accounts of partnerships and sole traders are not, incidentally, available to anyone other than the owner or owners, unless you are a tax officer!

Look at the Balance Sheet first. At what date has it been measured? Clearly, the more recent the better and you should be wary if the figures are, say, almost twelve months old, for the picture may have changed, for better or worse, since then. Balance Sheet figures are at a point in time, in other words all the assets (what the business owns) and liabilities (what it owes) are valued on one precise day. You can see, therefore, that the difference between the two (hopefully more assets than liabilities!) is the net value of the business.

This figure is only as good as the bases of valuation used, and for this reason an auditor has to certify that the view is a true and fair one. Occasionally an auditor is not entirely happy with the situation and will, therefore, 'qualify' a set of accounts, giving his reason for doing so.

Assets may include:

- Freehold or leasehold land and buildings;
- Plant, machinery, vehicles, etc;
- Materials, stocks, finished goods;
- Debtors (monies owing to the business), cash; and
- Investments.

Liabilities could comprise:

- Creditors (monies which the business owes to others);
- Taxation;
- Bank overdrafts and loans, etc.

You will also see an item entitled 'Capital and Reserves' which provides a breakdown of the difference between total assets and total liabilities and is thus the net value of the business to which we referred earlier.

This item may be in the form of shares, a reserve (or surplus) in the valuation of land and buildings and, usually, the total of profits accumulated since the business was formed.

Let us look next at the Profit and Loss Account which, as opposed to the Balance Sheet being on one day only, is the result of, normally, a year's trading, reflecting the difference between total income and total expenditure, and hopefully resulting in a profit!

Do not be too deterred, though, if you see that a loss has been made for the period, for companies, just like individuals, experience times when they spend more than they earn. What is more important is, firstly, that an acceptable explanation is provided for the loss and, secondly, that profits are normally made.

You will probably see reference to both 'Gross Profit' and 'Net Profit' and, for our purposes, you need only concentrate upon the latter. The line 'Profit on Ordinary Activities before taxation' is generally the most important piece of information and the one which will tell you how profitable, or otherwise, the business by which you are employed is.

You can, if you want to take this a stage further, calculate what percentage this figure is of total sales and, possibly, compare this with earlier years if you have the figures available to you. Many other comparisons, using ratio analysis, are possible, but you are advised to study other publications if your interest is further aroused.

So far we have talked only about assets, liabilities and profit. What we have not mentioned is the lifeblood of every business – cash.

And this, regrettably, is where the annual accounts are of no help whatsoever. They may tell you what was in the bank on a certain day several months ago, but this is rather like measuring the level of a river in the summer when you are ready to fish in the winter, or vice versa. A company's cash holdings will vary daily and only the proprietors (or finance director, as the case may be) will have access to that daily information.

Cash is, however, essential and shortage of cash is the one thing that will bring a business to its knees. This is not to say that lack of liquidity is the *cause*, for poor management is far more likely.

Whatever you read into the accounts, therefore, remember that a little knowledge can be a dangerous thing and that good management is the key to any successful business. If, looking around, you are convinced that you are working in this kind of environment, then you are more likely to seek advancement in that organization.

Let us now see how you now go about influencing others through your own particular skills . . .

CHAPTER 5

Exploiting Your Abilities

Let us start with some basic assumptions:
- You are ambitious;
- You have thought seriously about your future career;
- You are sufficiently qualified and/or experienced (or are taking steps to be so) to move on to something more demanding; and
- You are raring to go. . . .

You know all this – but do your employers?

There is something known as the 'centre of the world syndrome' which highlights the fact that, whilst many of us believe others know all about us, this is invariably untrue. An example in business is the man who sets himself up to manufacture something new, sits back and waits for customers to make their way to his door, and subsequently fails because he has not properly advertised his wares.

Do not let this happen to you. It certainly may not be necessary to shout from the rooftops that you covet your boss's job, but some in-house manoeuvering and lobbying may be necessary to get your message across to those who matter. Do you know who those people are? It may be merely the personnel officer, but equally it could be one of the general management who influences promotions in your organization. It may even be half a dozen or more people, in which case your task becomes a little more difficult, but far from impossible given the right tactics. These should include presenting both yourself and your work in first-class order at all times. How you go about this includes the following.

Lifestyles

Keeping fit in body and mind is left to Chapter 11 to provide more detail, but let us take a look here at how you live and how you present yourself externally at work.

You may say that what you do outside your place of work has little bearing on promotion, but this is far from true. If you are reaching out for branches further up the commercial or industrial tree, you will be mixing with different classes of people and be expected to converse knowledgeably on a number of basic subjects.

If your lifestyle, therefore, consists of staying at home every evening

EXPLOITING YOUR ABILITIES

curled up with a novel, this is unlikely to broaden your mind sufficiently to cope with your new surroundings.

Make sure, therefore, that you are worldly-wise by regularly reading intelligent newspapers and magazines, watching informative rather than 'soap' television and generally conversing with your peers on topics of the day. Study managerial publications and books, and widen the horizons of your mind as far as you are able.

Take an interest in local and national politics (but preferably do not take sides too vociferously!) and play a part in organizations such as the Round Table, amateur dramatics, charitable bodies or specific interest societies. Take your turn as treasurer, secretary or chairman, however hesitant at first you might be, for such positions are usually far from onerous and can instil confidence once tackled.

Watch your eating and drinking habits, for garlic or alcoholic breath may turn your superior off far stronger than any lack of experience or qualifications on your part!

And, naturally, dress the part. Looking good these days need not cost a fortune; neatness and cleanliness are the cornerstones of good fashion. This golden rule must apply each and every day; the one time that you forget to clean your shoes will be the one time your boss notices.

Project Your Personality

Some people will tell you that you cannot change, that each and every one of us is born with in-built characteristics that stay with us throughout our lives. This is gobbledegook.

It is true that our genes are passed on to us by our parents, but that is not to say that we are unable to mould our make-up to suit our environment. Character building is alive and well. 'Natural' shyness can be overcome, public speaking can be learned and personalities 'rounded'.

You will, during Chapter 1, already have analysed your own strengths and weaknesses and, if you have not done so by now, it is important to consider ways and means to improve, or better still overcome, the latter. Do not take 'no' for an answer; treat this as your biggest challenge so far and be determined to succeed.

What you mustn't be, of course, is 'pushy' and over-confident. You are aiming at a blend of your natural personality, honed at the edges to soften any abrasive tendencies, and the (apparently natural) confidence associated with any potential leader.

This may not prove as difficult as you thought. Look back at the assumptions we made at the beginning of this Chapter, add the obvious dash of intelligence which you have in seeking a better deal for yourself and you are three parts there. You are left with identifying those areas needing some polish and ensuring that others see you as someone confident enough to tackle greater responsibilities.

You may need a large tin of polish, but that should not deter you. If, for instance, you tend to fly off the handle rather more quickly than is desirable (a quite common feature, especially amongst the young!), then adopt a measure of stifling this in favour of more considered comment. Teach your brain to engage gear before your mouth does so by using key words in such situations. 'Promotion' could be an appropriate one whenever you would otherwise have caused an outburst. Whisper it to yourself, through gritted teeth if necessary, giving yourself that vital fraction of a second in which to remember your cause and either control your response or shut up!

If, on the other hand, your problem is a general lack of response, especially when in multiple company, look for a slight pause in the conversation and offer your views. This should at least attract either agreement or disagreement, thus maintaining your place in the discussion. You may have to force yourself in the early days until you reach the stage where your intervention becomes quite natural to you; then you have succeeded!

Confidence comes with knowledge. Look at Patrick Moore talking about the stars, or Paul Daniels on magic, and you will see that this is so. Their immersion in the subject is so well based that they are able, at the drop of a public dinner, to comment confidently for as long as you wish on their special topic. Ask either of them to speak, say, on the breeding of silk-worms and they will (probably!) appear as unconfident as you or me.

So know your subject. Make a list of those that apply to your particular occupation and become, if not an expert, at least comfortably knowledgeable enough to conduct a conversation and inject fresh ideas into the topic. This is, clearly, not an overnight exercise and will require careful planning. It will be worth it.

Do not ever be afraid of asserting your own views. Providing your opinion is backed by sufficient depth of study, take the lead in stating your case. If it is taken up by colleagues, you have won the day – if counter-arguments prove sufficient to swamp it, accept gracefully and move on to the next item. Do not harbour grudges – you will not win every case.

Getting Yourself Organized

Time is the most precious limited resource available to us – do not waste a moment of it.

Anyone anxious to get on in their organization will, generally, be 'working' practically all of their waking day. Important tasks to be completed are likely to enter their minds the minute they wake up, remain there whether travelling, eating or merely doing 'nothing', and remain there, unless completed, until they fall asleep at night.

There is absolutely nothing to fear if this is the case; it is a quite normal pattern for any conscientious executive. It is NOT the sign of a workaholic; that is someone who is 'physically' involved in work almost every waking minute and who is unable to 'turn off'.

And therein lies the key – you MUST learn to switch off. Whether it is called for due to demands by family or friends, or desirable because you want to watch a television programme (or, indeed, get some sleep!), it is imperative that you are able to control the mode your brain is in. Practice will bring perfection but if you find it especially difficult, set specific times when you will not consider a particular working task. If a forthcoming meeting is worrying you, for instance, write down the problem and the way you intend to tackle it but, if it calls for further thought, discipline yourself not to think about it until, say, 7 p.m. or some other 'convenient' time.

Organizing your working day is also a matter of discipline. Parkinson's Law knows no barriers and will, if untreated, ensure that work expands to fill the time available.

Priorities should be determined each day. Maintain a list of jobs to be carried out and delete them as they are completed. Either daily or weekly, depending upon the type of job you are doing, re-write the list, with the most urgent at the head. If certain tasks must be completed that day, write them in red ink.

Estimate the length of time each task will take to ensure that deadlines can be met. Delegate whenever possible; although subordinates may not carry out a duty to your entire satisfaction, they can at least complete the basic research and, in any event, delegation forms part of their training. They will never learn if not given the opportunity.

Remember to allow 'buffer time' for tasks not originally scheduled. Experience suggests that as much as 40% of a working day can be absorbed by unplanned, spontaneous and social activities.

Longer term planning, of course, is also essential and it may be necessary to look as far as twelve months ahead, especially if you are involved in a budgeting process. List also, therefore, those more important strategical tasks which must be completed over the next six or twelve months, ask yourself how long each will take to complete and plan accordingly.

If something calls for deliberate thought over an extended period, take advantage of those otherwise wasted periods, such as driving to work, travelling by train or even sitting in the bath!

If you are involved in organizing any kind of function, from a business luncheon to a week's conference, then plan it down to the last detail. Take advice from others more experienced, if available, and sit down with all those participating to run through the 'programme' and iron out any possible disasters. Either set up a 'dry run' or work through the event from the day before to the day after. Consider:

- Is overnight accommodation required?
- Do all the participants know how to reach the venue?
- Should copies of meeting material be made available beforehand?
- Are name badges required?
- Are all overhead projectors, etc. in place and working?
- Are all catering arrangements in hand?
- Will notepaper and pencils be required?

If you are having to visit someone, ensure that you know the way, precisely where you are going, and allow a margin in the travelling time. Meetings and agendas are dealt with in Chapter 8.

Creating Initiatives

One of the most potent methods of getting yourself remembered in any organization is to create and see through a successful initiative. Regrettably, this applies also to unsuccessful strategies if put into place but, apart from not overlooking this, we will not dwell on it!

We have already seen that one of the signs of a forward-looking company is its readiness to take on board regular doses of innovative ideas. These ideas almost entirely emanate from employees – why shouldn't you be one of them?

Try, as far as possible, to stand back from the business and look at what it is trying to achieve, be it additional volume, market share, improved profitability or whatever. Completely forget how it is already aiming for that ideal and concentrate, instead, on how YOU would achieve the same end. What products and services would you be providing? How would you structure the company? Where would you base it and its distribution network?

Answers to these, and similar, questions should contribute towards the creation of entirely new ideas. Many will be unworkable, given the current establishment and culture of the organization, but, equally, a few may survive the test. It is upon these that you may be able to base your initiatives.

They must obviously be thought through for practical application, cost constraints and their implication on the whole, although it is not your task to detail the minutiae; there will be other brains available for that. But they must be clearly defined, written down and humanly achievable.

Always discuss new possibilities with a colleague first; he may well come up with a snag which you had overlooked. Two heads are definitely better than one in this situation.

Once you are convinced that an innovative idea is worth pursuing further, take a look at its practicality from all angles. Who will put it into force? How will it fit into the present systems? What might it cost? What resources are needed? How much profit will it generate? Does it fit the company culture?

If, after assessing its viability as far as you are able, you remain convinced that the business would benefit from your initiative, prepare a draft paper outlining the advantages and any possible downsides and, again, ask a working colleague to take a close look at it.

If he goes along with your idea, then is the time to approach your boss. Ask him, if he agrees, if you can see the project through. Then, if your baby is successful, you will be associated with its benefits and be on the way to promotion.

Taking Decisions

One way of revealing your own self-confidence is to be a decision-maker.

Obviously, your decisions are going to have to be – in the main – the right ones. But do not be afraid of making them in the first place. A common feature of staff who do not progress to any extent in an organization is the fact that they are afraid of making decisions, always leaving the final 'Yes' or 'No' to others.

But do make sure that the decisions you are taking lie within your current authority; you will certainly not be thanked for a decision taken which rightly belongs to others. There will be occasions, of course, when you will be faced with doing so, such as absences of superiors due to holidays, sickness and so on, but these are likely to be rare.

Never, never take impulsive decisions. This is not to say that sometimes they are called for in a very short space of time but that should not prevent you from giving the facts every consideration, even if this process takes a matter of seconds. Bigger decisions may have to be left for a few hours, days or even weeks whilst essential research goes on.

Decisions always have to be in the interests of the company and its shareholders or owners, as opposed to the interests of any one individual. This may at times produce difficult, even harsh, choices, but commercial judgement must overrule.

Collect as much information as you can in the time available concerning the problem prior to coming to your decision. Consult colleagues as necessary and put in hand any digging or delving into statistical information needed to guide you to the right answer. By all means use your instinct but do not allow the available facts to override it. Try not to come to a decision prior to receiving all the relevant information; if you are not careful, you may select only those facts which support your original view.

Sometimes the decision-making process should be left to others working for you. Good delegation is another sign of effective management and you must not be forced into making all the decisions in your section; if you are one of a team, ensure that others are playing a part as well.

If the decision is outside your authority but you have been asked for a view, prepare all the necessary facts, point to both the advantages and disadvantages of each choice, summarize and make your own recommendation, giving your reasons. In time, you may find that the decisions become yours!

Improving the System

A good way of getting noticed is to suggest some method of improving the current system.

This may vary from a minor improvement to an administrative routine to wholesale changes in the way your company runs, say, its distribution systems. We are considering here something less major than a new initiative, discussed above, but something which, over a period, may save thousands of pounds and for which again, you, will be remembered.

Much, however, of what was advised under 'Creating Initiatives' also applies.

Take a close look at the present system. Try to analyse why things are done that way, investigate means by which they might be improved and talk your ideas over with workmates. Do not be put off if many of your 'improvements' are quickly knocked on the head for reasons of, say, less efficiency, cost or the fact that they have already been tested. Persevere and you will win through.

Look at some of the basic routines at first. Are all the forms which are completed really necessary? Could some be amalgamated, or even dispensed with? Is there duplication in the recording system? Does it take an undue amount of time to transmit information from one point to another? How much is technology, such as computerization, in use and is it the most efficient available?

All this will take time, but have patience. There is no need, of course, to do all this 'daydreaming' at work; lying in bed at night may produce the effective alternative you are seeking and may even send you soundly to sleep afterwards!

Remember that all systems should help to serve the company's objectives and not the other way round. They are only there as part of the process to produce the goods or services on offer; any redundant systems should be abandoned.

EXPLOITING YOUR ABILITIES

If you have worked for your present company for a short time only, you are in an envious position to spot improvements. We all, after a while, tend to take for granted the status quo, be it filling in a document which no-one looks at, or really needs, to not noticing that the office wallpaper is faded and needs replacing! Try to stand back and view the current systems with an outsider's eye. Question everything, and something may emerge which no-one else has spotted before.

Learning To Negotiate

One of the major facets of management which you will have to add to your armoury in your determination to win promotion is the art of negotiation.

You may be used to it already, or it may be entirely new to you. Whichever is the case, though, you can never have too much practice.

You may have tried it without knowing. Certainly if you have been on holiday to any of the Mediterranean or Eastern resorts, you will no doubt have haggled over the price of a souvenir; this is no less than negotiating. It is merely the art of bargaining to arrive at a mutually satisfactory end result.

There have to be a few essential elements present, however. Each party must genuinely want to reach a solution and there has to be a solution that can be reached. It does not really matter how far apart the two parties are at the beginning. As long as each party is prepared to bend a little and listen to the other's arguments, then a result is achievable. That result, whilst not the ideal in either's view, should be at least satisfactory to both parties involved.

There are a few golden rules to observe if your negotiating is to proceed smoothly:

- Keep calm under all circumstances. Annoyance is a clear sign of weakness which the other party will take advantage of.
- Do not tell lies. You will almost certainly be caught out and may have to back down to a position worse than would otherwise have been the case.
- Remain polite. Being cynical of your opponent may strengthen his resolve to gain the advantage.
- Do listen to the opposing arguments and recognize those which arouse your sympathy; give a little.
- Avoid going down side avenues; stick to the main issues.
- Prepare well.

The last is the most important, for a badly prepared negotiator will almost certainly lose a few points. Prepare your strongest arguments, with facts or figures to back them up, and list them in order of priority. Tick them off as that subject is covered during the negotiating process, but beware of firing all your big guns too early. Just as a field marshal would do, keep some strength for the final burst.

Estimate, also, what your opponent's strengths might be and have counter-arguments ready, as far as possible, for when these are raised. If necessary, seek a further meeting if points come forward demanding further research on your part; avoid appearing surprised but do not waffle. Counter-arguments on your part which later turn out to be spurious will only damage your case.

Purchasing Power

An effective means of showing others your ability can be yours if you have buying powers delegated to you by your company.

With the exception of labour costs, the buyer in most businesses is the largest spender, often accounting for well over 50% of a company's sales turnover in manufacturing or retailing situations.

When such large proportions are involved, minute percentage savings can represent significant sums of money, which are very likely to be drawn to the attention of the proprietors! If you are in this envious position, therefore, exploit it as far as possible in your own interests.

Effective buying can be enhanced by any of the following methods:

- Spread your suppliers so that you are never reliant upon any one of them. Equally, ensure that none of those suppliers are reliant solely on your own company's success.

- Regularly review suppliers and the prices they charge.

- Beware of constantly selecting the cheapest supplier; there will be cases where undercutting the market can only be achieved for a limited period and you will soon have to be looking around again.

- Build up a good, personal relationship with your suppliers.

- Maintain proper records of quantities and prices so that reference can always be made to past purchases if necessary.

- Monitor poor deliveries, discrepancies and items of inferior quality. Make certain that your suppliers understand that shoddy service will not be tolerated.

- Seek appropriate discounts for early payment or large quantities.

If the system already in use is super-efficient, then it may be somewhat difficult to improve upon it. But keep up your reviews and, if you can detect ways in which improvements could be instigated, bring these to the attention of your superior. Question everything and try to involve yourself in the production or selling processes to more fully understand the needs of the business.

By so doing, you may spot areas of duplication or inefficiency which might otherwise have gone undetected.

Dealing With Problems

Trouble-shooters win promotion, for they are recognized for their natural capabilities for resolving problems in favour of their employers. See if you can acquire the art.

Running a business involves risks, and risks create problems. They are, therefore, a quite natural component of company life and should not be treated as something out of the ordinary. Once you accept that:

(a) Every business has its problems;
(b) That these occur quite regularly; and
(c) All are resolvable;

then they will not come as a surprise, nor will you fear not finding solutions.

Liken it to climbing a mountain. This, naturally, has its risks and these in turn cause problems, some minor, some quite serious. Finding the next foothold may cause a temporary problem, quickly resolvable; breaking your leg in a crevasse is much more serious but a 'solution' still has to be found. Do you wait for assistance, or attempt to crawl to safety? A problem has to be resolved in either case.

Tackling problems must be carried out with clarity of thought and a careful weighing of the pros and cons. If necessary, list advantages and disadvantages of each solution, add a touch of 'gut' feeling and judge which appears to have the most going for it.

Never be afraid of talking problems over with others. Multiple heads are better than one and discussion is likely to bring out points which would otherwise have remained hidden. Frank talking about a problem quite often brings about its own solution quite naturally, without the need for difficult heart-searching for an answer.

Be certain that the true problem is recognized. Faulty goods coming off the end of a production line may be due just as much to unhappy workers as to a manufacturing difficulty. Much time could be wasted in applying answers to the wrong problem.

Diagnosis is thus essential before beginning to seek answers. Define the real difficulties and be certain where the root cause lies. If the problem is a human one, is it related to lack of experience, shortage of training or, more likely, one of attitude? If sales are below expectations, are the products or services the most appropriate for your market place as opposed to more marketing effort being required? If costs are rising at an unacceptable rate, could inefficiency be the underlying cause rather than uncontrolled expenditure?

Once properly diagnosed, the real problem can be tackled in a methodical manner.

Finding the solution, however, is not the end of the matter. It has to be implemented and the results monitored to ensure that the resolution is successful.

Go about problem identifying and resolving in this manner and your name will soon be noticed!

Opportunities For Women

Whilst all of the above obviously applies to both sexes, there is no doubt that women who exhibit managerial ability will be offered the ladder of promotion by eager employers, especially those committed to a set proportion of female executives.

Many positions traditionally held by men are becoming equally shared, especially in the fields of law, accountancy and similar professions.

One report has stated that the majority of the new jobs to be created in the mid-1990s will be filled by women, partly as a result of the falling-off in the numbers of school leavers. Wives in particular, after bringing up their families, are being attracted back to work, whilst creches are being established to woo the younger ones. One major bank has announced its intention to set up 300 such creches around the country in an effort to win back former staff with young families.

Overseas it has been found that British trained women do particularly well and in Japan, for instance, they are so rare that they have an automatic advantage, even if it is initially based on curiosity only!

Do not be afraid of asking your employers what their attitude is to women progressing up the ladder, for at least you will have brought your goal to their attention.

CHAPTER 6

Relationships With Superiors

Having the right connections is going to be important to you in your quest for promotion.

Influencing your superiors, therefore, must form part of your plan of campaign. But first, know which superiors you have to influence to make the impact you seek.

All of us have a boss but, in turn, so does our boss, especially in the larger organizations. Some companies make it quite clear to whom you are responsible; in others the structure may be more loose. Indeed, you may be part of what is commonly known as a 'matrix management' system, whereby there are all sorts of 'dotted line' responsibilities, both upwards and sideways.

Your immediate superior may, for instance, have authority for certain aspects of your work, whereas for others you have to report elsewhere. If you work in production, although the Works Manager may exercise prime authority, it is quite possible that the Quality Controller also has some say. Technical employees may have dual reporting lines perhaps through both manufacturing and marketing managers.

Identifying just who your real boss is may, therefore, take some guesswork, but it is worth the effort. Having done that, you then have to decide whether or not that is the most appropriate quarter in which to stake your claim! Quite possibly, influencing your immediate superior may prove ineffectual and you would be better advised to move one step up the seniority ladder to the next man. On the other hand, one of the directors (or even the Chairman!) or, possibly, the Personnel Officer is the right person to pull the strings for you.

Before you set off on your campaign, make certain you know who has the power to promote you.

Do not sneer at this 'Who you know, rather than what you know' impact on your likely prospects. The London Management Consultancy, MSL, interviewed 884 executives for a survey on promotion and found that the 'old school tie' was still one of the best passports to a better job. There is no doubt that the old boy network is still alive and well.

Over a third of those interviewed had landed improved jobs through internal promotion on the recommendation of colleagues, whilst ten per cent obtained their posts in the first place through personal contacts. And the further up the organization they were, the greater this type of influence had on their promotion; just under 50% of the top jobs in the survey had been filled by people already within the organization.

Thus personal contacts and internal promotion proved to be the two most likely ways of reaching higher posts. So do not ignore them!

Formal Relationships

Distinguish between the differing forms of relationships within your organization which may exist in one or more of the following four categories:

- *Direct relationships*. These exist between any employee and his immediate superior to whom he is responsible.
- *Specialist relationships*. These are those where the superior has responsibility for some specialist function, such as personnel matters, but no direct authority over the individual.
- *Lateral relationships*. As suggested, these exist where members of management relate to each other on a horizontal plane, none of them being responsible for the others. An example would be the relationship which exists between the Sales Manager and the Production Manager.
- *Staff relationships*. Where a senior member of management employs a Personal Assistant, the relationship between them is a personal one only and the junior of the two may not have any authority other than to issue the orders of his immediate boss.

It would be as well, if one does not already exist, to draw up an organization chart for your company, marking the different types of relationships as they appear to you. Keep it by you for a period, amend it according to experience and encircle the names of those members of management who might be able to influence your future career.

Get to Know Your Boss

Merely identifying those who may make your path easier is insufficient; just as important is finding out how each might be influenced.

You will know already, from experience of life itself, that some people are more impressed than others when you blow your own trumpet. Much will depend upon their own levels of experience and maturity. Tell a young manager that you have been down the Nile and he is likely to express further interest; tell the ageing Chairman and he will probably wonder why you are wasting his time!

Try, therefore, to weigh up the people you need to impress. Are they the sort to listen to your exploits and achievements, or do they prefer to gauge you by results? Do they appear to have the time to discuss your aspirations or are you better served simply by coming up with the right answers time and time again?

Some bosses prefer to have initiatives and decisions communicated to them by way of a paper; they like to have the time to digest your views, perhaps discuss them with others and, subsequently, to pass your paper back to you with their comments and action. Others favour the 'negotiating' approach whereby they like you to discuss your ideas with them and they can bat opinions backwards and forwards before reaching a decision. Some like paper, some hate it.

So get to know your man. Discovering his *modus operandi* may help to overcome his likely rejection of new ideas, for, as The Wyatt Company found when its consultants interviewed over 3,000 workers in British industry, only a third of bosses were willing to act on suggestions put to them by their subordinates. They were, apparently, stopped by class consciousness, a fear of making mistakes and the desire to protect their own positions.

You may need to be persistent, but do not make a nuisance of yourself. Recognize when it is no longer viable to press home your ideas – and beware of seeking confirmation from another superior. You are just as likely to end up antagonizing your most fruitful source of promotion.

If you find yourself with a new boss, spend some time studying his personality and wishes before you attempt to press home your thoughts and suggestions. In his early days he is unlikely to implement major changes for fear of upsetting his own position. It may take a little time for him to adapt before he becomes conducive to fresh thought.

In the meantime, though, keep a watchful eye on your own situation, for it could be in jeopardy. Assess whether your role is becoming more central to the company, or are you being moved to the fringe? A danger signal could be if the new chief talks to you far less than his predecessor.

The secret, therefore, is to study your superiors. Get to know what makes them tick and cultivate them accordingly.

Know the Organization

It is just as important to know the culture of your company as that of your immediate superior.

Hopefully, you will already have established that you are the kind of person likely to succeed in your organization. Most major concerns seek, and promote, a particular type of individual. Look at Marks and Spencer ladies, for example, or merchant banking executives. They are not, of course, all clones, but there are similarities of style, part of it induced by company training methods but, lurking underneath, a commonality of personality that suits the business.

If necessary, adapt your style to fit the bill. Be yourself, of course, but smooth the edges where you feel it is to your advantage.

Dress in the company style. This, again, does not preclude individuality, but if suits for ladies are in, do not buck the trend. Long hair for men may be frowned upon, and whilst you may prefer this, your quest for promotion must come first. When you are chairman, you can change the culture!

Working habits should be studied. Do people arrive quite early, preferring an extra hour at that end of the day to allow them time to catch early trains home? If so, try and follow a similar pattern yourself; avoid being the odd man out. Lunchtime habits may vary from working right through to spending an hour in a local pub; there is certainly no need for you slavishly to conform, but at least show that you are happy to fit in with such arrangements.

Watch how meetings are conducted. Make sure you are always on time, press home your points with courtesy and follow up any action delegated to you. More detailed conduct is covered in Chapter 8.

Listen to the company grapevine and keep in touch with people in the know. The boss's secretary is certainly in this category and it is quite likely that the secretaries in general will know more about what is happening than many of the senior managers!

Several organizations have adopted the principle of in-house advertising job vacancies. If one appeals to you, apply in the prescribed manner and by all means lobby those responsible within reason, but do not overplay your hand. Your record and experience will already be known and there is no real need for it to be re-emphasized. What you might do, however, is to declare how you would tackle the job and this could gain you a few points when in competition with others.

If vacancies are advertised externally also, you will have to pit your wits against these other applicants, but here you have the advantage. You already know the company well and, if you are well thought of, should head the queue.

The Political Game

Knowing the way your boss operates and knowing the organization are not enough. You also have to learn about the political game which is played in almost every firm and, in particular, the larger ones.

This has little to do with politics in the party sense, but bears close resemblance to the weapons and strategies our politicians use in Westminster. These include lobbying to support particular interests, withdrawing support when you wish to barter for an advantage, in-fighting and playing the deadly art of intrigue. There are no Queensberry rules in the workplace!

Lobbying takes place when one member of the management wishes to gain support for his policies. He will approach colleagues, on a very informal basis and invariably when socializing, to check out their views; if he has sufficient support he knows he can get his ideas through the system. Beware, therefore, of casual questioning, for you may find yourself offering an instant view which you may, on later reflection, not wish to confirm.

Withdrawing support is somewhat more subtle. It is a means by which you are able to bargain policies, agreeing to back those of colleagues on the understanding that similar encouragement is given to your own. Timing is all-important in these negotiations and playing of your aces must be carefully mapped out. Bridge players should do well!

In-fighting is another common aspect of office or factory politics. Workers take sides, offering support for those ideas most likely to benefit them personally. Rarely do the interests of the company enter the argument. People switch from side to side as counter-arguments are put forward until a clear imbalance is reached in favour of one view or the other.

Intrigue comes into play when employees keep their feelings to themselves, revealing their true colours only at the most opportune moment. This can be a deadly game, especially if you nail *your* colours to the wrong mast!

Corporate politics, in the same manner as the Parliamentary variety, is all about power and power-spotting. Do you know, for instance:

- Who are the real players in your company?
- Who do they, in turn, influence?
- What are the important issues?
- How are these decided, and by whom?
- Who should you therefore cultivate?

Stay tuned to the office grapevine. It is usually the most informative of all communication channels. When you are part of it, then you know you are on top!

Promotion Patterns

Every company has its own promotion policy. Some, like banks, favour in-house promotions, i.e. they grow their own executives. Others, especially industry, buy people in on a regular basis. Most businesses, however, go for a mix of the two.

Even if a job is advertised externally, applications are not debarred from other employees and, quite often, are actively encouraged. Your personnel manager will at least be able to provide to the engaging manager details of your qualifications, experience and track record which can easily be verified. Applicants coming out of the blue often exaggerate and their true abilities cannot really be known until they have been fully tested.

Speed of promotion varies from one employee to another, but most big companies nowadays try to identify their high-flyers early on. They are often put through a rigorous testing routine, which might include psychological interviews, and, if they pass with flying colours, they are marked down for rapid promotion.

This will be interspersed with periods of training, on both internal and business school courses, in an attempt to inject specialized knowledge in a condensed form.

Try to identify the types of training in your organization, which might include any or all of the following:

- *Induction training*. Intended to introduce the new entrant into the ways the company works. This might include programmed learning or distance learning.
- *On-the-job training*. As the name implies, experience is gained from sitting or standing next to a qualified employee for a set period, often moving from one to another to complete the knowledge pattern.
- *Supervisory training*. Suitable for potential junior line management and probably including some business school experience.
- *Management training*. A de-luxe version of the above aimed at developing further managerial and intellectual skills.
- *Courses, seminars, workshops, business games, etc*. To add to the knowledge gained from work experience.

See where you believe you should fit in and seek a nomination to available courses or periods of on-the-job training. Forward thinking employers welcome candidates who come forward; it often saves the personnel division the sometimes difficult task of identifying and selecting suitable course attendees!

Determine, also, likely patterns of promotion and attempt to slot into these according to your own perception of where you want to go. Do not be backward in coming forward!

Staying Informed

If you intend to get on successfully in your business, you must, above all, stay informed.

You must aim to know everything important that is going on around you which might affect your future plans. This will include details about the company itself, its policies, its general management, possible changes of direction, potential takeovers, as well as more mundane matters affecting employees in general.

You may be a party to some of this information, but not all of it. It's your task, however, to make certain that you are not left behind in the information stakes. Cultivate those people likely to be 'in the know' and, through constant brushing of their sleeves, you will not be kept in the dark.

You will soon learn that the more involved you are in company matters, the better informed you will become. If you go off alone every lunchtime, ignore all social activities and avoid being part of any of the natural 'cliques' which form in every company, you will quickly become disinformed.

The rule is not only to listen and to observe, but to contribute also. Your views, if well-founded, will be respected and in time you may find yourself becoming an originator of new thinking and policies. That's the time you will get noticed.

Adopt a strategy of making the right contacts and keeping them. After a while in your present position, you will have spotted those people worth listening to – and those with views extreme enough to be ignored! Keep a private list of who you should be making contact with and how often; check it once a month and, where there are gaps, make certain you fill them.

Determine why policy changes are made and what impact they will have upon the business. Will they at the same time have an impact upon your personal aspirations?

Discuss future plans regularly with colleagues. See if you can improve upon such plans. Do not take fresh policy for granted; if it appears to have flaws, say so. Dogmatism, of course, is not called for here and you must learn when to step gently back. But do not let that put you off contributing.

Create a network of contacts, both within and outside the organization – it is often surprising how much you can learn about your own company from outsiders! Read the trade press and, if possible, talk to buyers and suppliers. Company magazines, accounts, circulars and notice boards should all be assiduously studied.

Your ultimate aim is not only to be well informed, but to be the fount of all knowledge yourself!

Socializing

We touched upon your lifestyle in Chapter 5, but communicating your desire to move onward and upward can be achieved not only through professional commitment but by participating actively in the social life of your company.

But this will depend upon the type of activity and who else is there. Merely visiting the local pub every lunch-time or evening with immediate colleagues is unlikely to advance your cause. What is needed is a plan of campaign to make certain your socializing is both effective and enjoyable; it should not be done for duty alone.

Enquire over a period what extra-mural activities take place and who takes part. These might vary from club-type activities, through sports associations, committee work and charitable contributions, to contests, sponsorships and public relations items.

Decide, firstly, which arouse your interest. And only after that those which might advance your cause. To take up tennis, which you might hate, merely because the boss's wife plays is both foolhardy and dangerous. Your interest must be genuine, but that is not to say it cannot have a dual purpose!

Socializing opportunities may also exist between company employees and 'clients', who might take the form of customers, buyers or suppliers. Reciprocal hosting is the norm and you should ensure that you neither go 'over the top' nor exceed company policy on entertaining matters. Guidelines usually exist and these should be studied beforehand to avoid any unnecessary embarrassment.

Entertaining at home, whether colleagues or customers, can have its hazards and should be considered carefully before embarking on such a course. The major danger (apart from dropping the turkey on the floor!) is that conversation may become limited to the common denominator (i.e. work) and if your partner is not a party to this, it will degenerate into a one-sided affair. If you do entertain in this manner, therefore, be wary at all times of steering conversations towards subjects of interest to all parties present. Some early reference to the workplace is quite in order, but thereafter the event should become one in which everyone can participate.

Sort out your priorities on the socializing front – you can only fit in so much. Joining five clubs and committees may occupy each weekday evening but after a while will become tiresome. Instead of achieving your original aim, your work may well become adversely affected.

Take on only what stimulates you and in a quantity which you can easily handle.

Grading Systems

Understanding your company's method of grading different staff according to their level of responsibility is an important element in your getting on. If you fail to comprehend the methods used, how can you expect to climb the ladder?

Job grading is a means of assessing the value of a job to the particular organization; the company is then able to set appropriate levels of pay and perks. Taken into account are the following:

- Degree of responsibility and authority;
- Experience necessary to undertake the job;
- Formal qualifications desirable;
- The skills essential to fulfil the tasks which the job entails;
- Hours and conditions worked, etc.

Personnel managers usually take known and longer-established positions as 'base jobs' and these become standard grades. Less responsible jobs naturally become lower graded, whilst more senior posts carry higher grades. The whole system is subject to a great degree of personal input, usually by senior managers, and is thus not always entirely fair. It tends to be criticized in a lot of large companies, but finding a fairer, alternative method is not as easy as some people think!

Get to know how many grades operate in your business, as well as whether or not any of these are sub-divided, and the differing criteria for entering each. This information is normally readily available through the personnel function, since it is communicated to staff bodies and other representative associations.

After a while you should also be able to pinpoint who is in which grade, although there could be cases of individuals holding grades higher than their jobs entail, but not normally lower. This could be due to jobs being downgraded, or merely employees having been moved about during a restructure.

The grade itself is usually established by awarding a number of points to each facet of the job, sometimes weighting these by using a multiplier according to the importance of each. The figures are then added together and the grade determined according to a band of numbers set by the company. For example:

- Grade 1 – 27 to 31 points;
- Grade 2 – 32 to 40 points;
- Grade 3 – 41 to 52 points;
- Grade 4 – 53 to 65 points; and so on.

Look out, therefore, for jobs graded more highly than your own, identify the reasons, and make sure you qualify yourself for these if they appeal to you.

Appraising Performance

More and more employers are demanding greater performances from their workers and the trend is towards systems of measuring these on a regular basis. Results provide an indication of where higher rates of pay are justified – and who should be promoted.

All kinds of systems operate, from the very basic requiring a supervisor to assess whether or not a subordinate has performed well, to senior managers undergoing regular, often quarterly, reviews of their performance in a number of previously set areas. These appraisal interviews, lasting up to three hours at a time, can be quite intensive, but are intended to help both parties to reach required objectives.

The bigger concerns adopt sophisticated monitoring systems, such as those introduced by Hay Management Consultants, although many of them are open to criticism of lack of objectivity. Complaints include:

- Subjective views by hierarchical superiors are often necessary for appraisals to be completed;
- Resultant pay differentials, after fine performances by a few, can cause conflict and resentment;
- Working in teams becomes difficult if people have individual performance bases;
- If a large part of the performance element is linked to corporate performance, policy factors may be outside the control of certain individuals.

The old adage that you can't keep all of the people happy all of the time is certainly true of performance systems. Those who do well will be content, others unhappy.

Your task, firstly, is to understand the system. You can only beat it if you know it! When performance targets are first set, make certain that they are achievable – testing, but achievable. Devise action plans to bring them about and agree these with your superiors; any resource costs, involving people, premises or technology, should be agreed at the same time. You will not be able to do the job without the necessary tools.

Put the action plans into being as soon as possible and introduce monitoring systems to find out if they are working. It may be necessary to set up these systems before the period under review commences; new computer programs take time to establish themselves. Measure progress regularly and fine tune if it is needed.

Prepare yourself thoroughly for performance appraisal reviews. Run through your tasks and make a written note of how you have progressed with each. Keep these notes in the same order as your original objectives so that each can be clinically discussed at your interview. If you have fallen down anywhere, admit it but provide credible reasons for your failure. If any objectives are proving impossible, discuss ways and means by which they might be achieved or seek abandonment.

The whole area of performance management, especially if it is related to pay, is unscientific, but most companies do their best to make it work. Do not fight the system – join it and it may be to your benefit.

Promotion Interviews

Under this heading, we will look at any discussions you have with any of your superiors concerning your promotion wishes, whether or not a current vacancy occurs.

This might, therefore, range from an informal chat over a drink with your immediate boss to a full-blown personnel division interview where you are offered a better position.

The secret lies in planning every one of these sessions. You should have given prior thought to who you wish to tackle, the most appropriate location and how the conversation is likely to go.

Raising the question of your promotion over a casual drink can be unrewarding; your boss may not take you as seriously as you would like. It is much better to seek a quiet word when you feel he is at his most beneficial – five o'clock on a Friday is probably unwise! If you know him reasonably well, you should be aware when he is likely to have a few moments to spare. He is probably more amenable in his own surroundings, so stick to office locations where appropriate.

Run through what you are going to say beforehand. Attempt, as far as possible, to gauge his reactions and be ready to counter any likely arguments nullifying your upgrading. If things do begin to go against you, do not over-press your case. Ask for time to reconsider your position and tackle him again when you have repaired your case.

He will expect to learn why you should be considered above others perhaps equally eligible, and how you would handle the new job. Have your initiatives prepared and be ready to expound upon them. You probably have just a few moments to impress him!

Interviewing techniques are dealt with in greater detail in Chapter 8.

Keeping Contacts

Keep a record of all the people who could be useful to you. This should include not only senior colleagues, but customers and others with whom it will pay to keep in contact.

You are likely to meet people on training sessions, at conferences and seminars and other places where similarly minded workers make contact. They may not be able to assist your cause today, but if they are equally ambitious they are likely to get on and in time could become influential. Maintain contact on a regular basis and make certain you record any changes of address or employer.

Keep business cards in a safe place, preferably in one of the plastic or leather folders available on the market. When the folder is full, take out all the cards and re-file them in alphabetical order by either personal name or company. At the time of collecting each card, jot down on the back where and when you collided; however good your memory, you are bound to forget a few!

Maintain a business diary, recording times and places of meetings, conferences, etc. and, at the end of each year, store it where it can easily be retrieved. It is surprising how useful it can be to refer to a specific event if you are renewing contact with someone you met earlier.

Some of the most useful people to meet are those in allied trades or professions, so membership of trade bodies or federations is highly recommended. Go along to their meetings and, if you have the opportunity, serve on the committee. There is no better way to increase your circle of business acquaintances (or to become known yourself) by becoming secretary, treasurer or chairman of your local professional association.

Keep records, too, of favourite restaurants, theatres and other places of entertainment, so that you are prepared if you have to look after business guests with little warning beforehand. A selection of differently graded hotels can also prove a boon, especially if your boss asks you for such information!

Anything else likely to prove important in your quest for promotion should be carefully noted down for the day when it will come in useful.

Let us move on to how you can improve your chances further through the management of others . . .

CHAPTER 7

Managing Other People

In the smart organization, everyone has to be a manager.

They have to be especially good at doing something in order to achieve the organization's objectives. And this will almost certainly involve taking responsibility for money, people or projects – or all three – in other words, a managerial task.

Gone are the days when 'managers' issued orders, and others obeyed. Today, successful people work in teams, responsible for joint decisions, and delegation is far more widespread.

Employees who would in earlier times have merely followed instructions are now expected, and encouraged, to think more deeply about their tasks and apply themselves to them in the best way they see fit. Training is aimed at self-motivation. Customer care is more prevalent as competition increases and the need to attract and retain customers is recognized as a company's foremost aim.

People – like you – who take the initiative, whether or not delegated responsibility has been formalized, will prove to be tomorrow's winners, and get promoted. Always, of course, operate within the confines of your authority, but this should not deter you from offering solutions to problems, suggesting better ways of carrying out tasks, and imposing fresh thought upon your organization.

Determining Your Responsibilities

So that you are quite certain where your authority ends, and therefore where recommendation can begin, you should firstly establish your own lines of responsibility.

You may be responsible for one or more of the following functions of management:

- *Legislative*. This is the level at which policies are formulated and designed. In most companies this function will be carried out by a Board of Directors or, in smaller companies, by the Managing Director or perhaps a management team. Policies, generally, will be set for the longer term and not dramatically amended unless market conditions demand it, although flexibility must exist to enable minor changes to take place along the way.

- *Judicial*. Formulation is fine, but someone has to interpret the policies and this is usually the task of the Managing Director in the larger firm or line management elsewhere. Interpretation is a vital link in the chain towards fulfilment to avoid original objectives being missed and is generally handled at a senior level.
- *Executive*. Once interpreted, policies have to be implemented and this may be the task of varying levels of 'management' or, indeed, employees not generally considered to be in the management layer. This is, perhaps, where you fit in – or seek to enter.

Wherever you are currently in your organization, determine those areas for which you are responsible. These may already have been laid down quite clearly in a job description or accountability statement but, quite often, this is not the case and you should seek clarification.

It is important that you know when your responsibilities might be exceeded; beyond these, therefore, you must consider how best to approach superiors with new ideas and challenges. Look back at the last Chapter again for guidance.

Setting Objectives

If your work includes responsibility, or even partial responsibility, for others, then it is as important for them to be carrying out their functions properly as it is for you. They are, after all, a reflection of your leadership and, in your search for higher pastures, you will probably be judged as much by your team's performance as your own.

Set to this, therefore, with a determined will. Thorough preparation will pay dividends.

Firstly, determine for whom you are personally responsible and for which of their functions, if not all of them. If this is unclear in any way, clarify the position with your superior; preferably, obtain from him a written objective statement along with a note of those who are to report directly to you. Then make quite certain that these people are aware of their reporting lines; leave them under no illusion as to who will be giving them their instructions and guidance, and to whom they should report.

If there are several involved, call them together to explain your own duties and how the team can, by pulling together, achieve these to the benefit of all. Explain precisely what these benefits might be, which could include bonuses, other 'perks', merit rises, promotion – or, in tough circumstances, even the retention of their present jobs!

This meeting is best held in undisturbed surroundings and, preferably, well away from the normal place of work. Two-way discussion should be actively encouraged, for this will often lead to improved ways of achieving the objectives set. Seek participation, and co-operation, from everyone involved. Decisions need not be unanimous, but dissenting parties must be encouraged to toe the line and not cause factions within your group. Teams pulling ropes in different directions are likely to fall apart!

Once agreed on the way forward, write it down. Make sure this conforms with the outcome of the meeting and then let every participating member have a copy. It is a good idea, also, to obtain everyone's signature to this piece of paper so that there can be no arguing about it later.

All this, of course, is just part of good leadership which we will take a closer look at later in this Chapter.

Reviewing Performance

Merely agreeing how the team is going to achieve its objectives, and writing these methods down, is only part of the story. The other part is to regularly review how each individual is performing against his particular objectives.

These reviews, now common in most large organizations, form an essential part of an employee's development and are important to gain ongoing commitment and engender motivation.

Their regularity will depend upon the company's policies and, sometimes, vary as to the seniority of the individual involved. Whilst, historically, they were often annual events, forward looking companies now insist on their taking place quarterly as a minimum. Sales orientated bodies sometimes review salesmen's performances monthly, or even weekly, with a view to correcting adverse figures before they recur.

Reviews help to identify, *inter alia*:

- Progress, or otherwise, to date;
- Excellent or very poor performers at an early stage;
- What is required to correct poor performances;
- Any training requirements;
- Statistical data for reward systems;
- Promotion prospects; and
- Target adjustments, or setting, for the following period.

These appraisal interviews are especially important for the employee under scrutiny and, in the longer term, the company itself. They should thus be treated with great seriousness and not take place in haste.

Relax the individual you are assessing by talking generally for a short while, before homing in on the specific issues. Prepare yourself thoroughly, with written notes on points on which to praise and which to criticize. If corrective action is needed, have guidance ready and be prepared to meet objections.

Cover strengths, weaknesses and opportunities. Dig deeply into reasons for significant variances from targets set and promise to investigate sensible suggestions for improvements if these come forward. Afterwards, investigate!

Point to where your colleague might have gone wrong, and what alternative lines he might have followed. If others have done a lot better, provide examples of how they have achieved this, although, if it is possible, on an anonymous basis.

Never forget that the purpose of the interview is to motivate. Give definite means of achieving objectives and praise where it is called for.

Allow ample time; some companies suggest these interviews can take up to two hours, with perhaps a further hour of preparation beforehand. They should not, of course, be interrupted in any way and should be set in harmonious and confidential surroundings.

Afterwards, provide your team member with a written statement of his performance to date, suitable comments, suggestions as to how this might further be improved, if necessary, and define clearly any specific targets agreed for the next review period.

Be Tolerant of Others

No-one is perfect and you must not, therefore, expect colleagues for whom you have responsibility to be any different. Everyone has his foibles, peculiarities, mannerisms, and so on, and this is something we all have to learn to live with – especially at work.

Learn to be tolerant of colleagues and never make enemies. You never know when you might have need of them. At worst, you could one day find yourself working for one of them!

Standards will vary according to experience, ability and how well people are motivated. Management styles also differ and can depend as much on the organization as on the individual. You may find your own style criticized, especially during appraisal interviews, and you must make certain that you do not merely defend it; listen to constructive views and balance these against your own. Then decide whether change is justified.

Team effort is very dependent upon each member fully pulling his weight, and there may be instances of an apparently poor performance of one being affected by another. It is important to detect this at an early stage in order to nip it in the bud, for it can be very contagious!

If this appears to be the case, talk to everyone concerned before reaching any decisions. It is surprising how an otherwise obvious answer can come forward from even the most junior member of a team.

Beware of trying to deal with very personal problems yourself; professional counselling may be needed. By all means identify such problems but leave the settling of them to the individual involved after encouraging him to talk about them. Person-to-person interviews can become quite emotional when an employee is under pressure elsewhere involving family or friends; try to guide someone in this position to where you believe the remedy might lie.

Recognize that strengths in one department of an individual's character may be counterbalanced by weaknesses elsewhere. We have all heard of the true artist's inability to cope, for instance, with administration, or the back-room boffin unable to understand human relations. They do exist, although these may be extreme examples. Ideas people can sometimes have their heads in the clouds; shop-floor workers may not always accept changes in technology; and so on.

Accept people for what they are. Concentrate upon their strong side and overlook any minor drawbacks. That way they will be far happier employees – and the company will benefit.

Earning Respect

If you are going to advance in your organization, do not necessarily expect to be popular. The perfect boss is not always the most popular, but he must be respected.

So getting on well with people must be a priority. For some, it comes naturally; for others, it has to be worked at. You will know into which category you fit without a great deal of self-analysis, but let us assume you are in the latter!

Recognizing other's good sides, and overlooking their weaknesses, as suggested above, is a good way to start. Find out what colleagues – and bosses – like to talk about, and encourage them to do so. They may be gardening fanatics, golfers, regular theatre visitors or even avid television watchers, but your job is to find out whatever turns them on – and regularly do so!

A good time is when relaxing, perhaps during a lunch period or when having a quiet drink together. Be positive if you are uncertain what their leisure interests are; ask the question directly. The answer will often surprise you!

After finding out, make a careful mental note of their interest and, from time to time, bring it into the conversation. There is nothing devious in even making a written note of colleagues' hobbies and so on, but either keep these in a personal code or carefully at home, for obvious reasons!

If antagonized, remain cool and calm. Learn to take knocks on the chin, even when they are not fully justified, for to fight back in business is not always the wisest course. You may easily say something which you later regret and which may be remembered for longer than you wish.

The odd disagreement is no bad thing, especially in committee meetings. But to lose your temper because you disagree with someone will only gain you enemies instead of the respect for which you should be aiming. Convincing others of the strength of your argument is more about persuasion than confrontation.

Businesses cannot be run by command only; people today will not accept this management style. Intelligent corporations are successful through persuasion and consent, and this is what you should be aiming at.

Authority must be earned; only in the armed forces is it recognized through stripes on the sleeve. In business it comes through practised management style and is not achieved overnight.

Win it, however, and you will win a place in colleagues' hearts. And that's another step on the promotion ladder.

Effective Management

It is not enough merely to be a manager of other people; you have to be an *effective* manager to get noticed.

We can all quote instances of people we know in managerial positions whom we consider ineffective; any badly run office, shop or factory must have one of these allegedly in charge. On the other side of the coin, however, are the hundreds of effective managers running successful units up and down the country. Why are some effective and not others?

There are, naturally, a thousand reasons, although one which crops up again and again is the fact that a poor manager is often one who 'does' rather than 'manage'. It is easy to say 'It's quicker to do it myself', although, in the longer run, it is not, of course.

Proper training of staff, and subsequent delegation of duties, is thus of prime importance to an effective manager. Time must be found to achieve these ends.

A manager's duty is to shape events, not run them; to determine directions, not chase them himself; and to motivate and stimulate those working under him in order to achieve the team's overall objectives.

All of these qualities have to be learned and are not gained overnight. Management training courses help, but there is nothing like experience. Use not only your own experience but that of your team members; several heads are much better than one.

Allow yourself time to think. Creativity, research and experimentation are all vital parts of an effective manager's armoury, and you should ensure that not all of your working day is consumed with administrative routines and reacting to problems as they arise. Pro-activity is the key.

MANAGING OTHER PEOPLE

One of your most difficult challenges will be adapting to this new style, especially if you were previously carrying out duties now delegated to others. The garage mechanic promoted to workshop manager finds it far from easy to keep his shirt clean and not don overalls as he did earlier. Equally the new factory supervisor must fight against using the lathe again himself, rather than ensuring his successor learns the trade thoroughly.

To summarize, as an effective manager you should:

- Control routine work sufficiently well to ensure that time is made available for thinking;
- Regularly discuss plans and progress with your team;
- Motivate others;
- Accept change readily and beware of sticking to old routines;
- Train people to do their jobs effectively, and keep up this momentum; and
- Delegate where appropriate; do not do it yourself.

Be a Real Leader

Proving you are an effective manager does not necessarily distinguish you as a leader. Your team, operating within your original guidelines, may be perfectly capable of maintaining its momentum without further leadership qualities being called for. Good leadership is thus a little more.

You are looking to establish a winning team that will be noticed throughout the organization. When it is, people will ask 'Who is the leader?'

Ideally, you should have control over the choice of team members but this is rarely the case in most companies. Either the managing director, or a personnel function, will select employees, often from a limited market. Few employees are 'ideal'; as we have seen earlier; strengths in one area are often counterbalanced by weaknesses elsewhere. Unless, however, any member of your team is completely unsuitable, then you will probably have to mould them as best you can.

Highlight the qualities of each and play to those. Either attempt to correct deficiencies or, if this looks impossible after efforts have been made, merely allow for them when allocating duties. Do not give up too easily, however. Bad memories can be helped by introducing reminder systems; poor telephone techniques improved through specialized courses; inefficient time management cured again through courses, coupled with guidance; and so on.

Some leaders are, admittedly, born. Through history we have witnessed Oliver Cromwell, Hitler and Winston Churchill, none of whom (as far as we are aware!) attended evening courses in leadership.

Others – perhaps you – need guidance. Anyone determined enough to become a leader can almost certainly do so. The determination itself is half the battle; the other half can be acquired through self-tuition.

Leaders must develop skills in planning, organizing, setting objectives, communicating, implementing, supervising and monitoring. On top of all these, problems will have to be solved!

This book will hopefully help you along the way but, if this area remains of concern to your ambitions, then look in your library or bookshop for the many specialist tomes on the subject of good leadership. In the meantime, see how you measure up to the following requirements:

- The ability to anticipate problems and to deal with them decisively;
- To set high standards and ensure they are maintained;
- To research thoroughly and respect the advice of others;
- Not to be bowed down with routines;
- To think clearly and be able to get to the root of a problem quickly;
- To motivate others and communicate clearly.

If you believe you possess most, or all, of these attributes, you are well on your way to establishing yourself as a leader.

Keeping in Touch

Management involves knowledge. The way to make sure your own knowledge is accurate and up-to-date is through looking, listening and enquiring.

Looking around you may be something you think you do every working day, but there is a great deal of difference between seeing something regularly and consciously looking at it. You no doubt pass through several doors daily, but how many do you look at? That fire door that is clearly marked 'Must be kept closed'; why is it often propped open? Are you getting complaints about lack of warmth without spotting the two-inch gap at the bottom of the outer door? And why hasn't someone thought of putting a pane of glass in that entrance to the staff canteen where people keep bumping into one another?

When did you last *look* properly at the working environment, the state of the floor, decoration, or the fabric of the building itself?

Why is there such a long trek to the post-room? Why are blouses and skirts on different floors when they are so often purchased together? Is it really necessary to complete a form in triplicate every time a new drill is required?

These, and other observations, will only reveal themselves on a dedicated tour of the workplace with these features in mind. Normal routines must, temporarily, be disregarded and the mind reattuned to looking for improved methods of working, whether they involve minor refurbishment or major relocation of plant or machinery.

Once a quarter, create a diary note to walk round your company, or your section of it, specifically looking for better ways of doing things. You will be surprised at what turns up!

Listening is another method of managing properly. Just as there is a difference between seeing and looking, so there is between hearing and listening.

We hear all manner of sounds throughout the average working day, from people chattering in the train, through music coming from a building site, to sitting at meetings. It is important, though, to differentiate what we should actually be listening to.

So many people, especially in confrontation situations, hear only what they want to hear, often ignoring the other's point of view. Management involves listening to both sides of a discussion, weighing up the pros and cons, and coming to fair decisions.

Listen to what subordinates are telling you; do not merely hear them. There is usually a very good reason for their views; give them an opportunity to air them. Look for hidden messages; criticism is often veiled. Hear them out, but do listen!

Also, of course, enquire of people – why, how, when, where? Dig deeply into reasons for everything and never accept the often-quoted phrase 'We've always done it that way'. Almost certainly there will be a better way!

Probe into methods of administration, distribution, manufacture, design, advertising, and ask fellow workers if they can offer ideas for improvement. There will be plenty!

By keeping in touch this way, you will learn a great deal more about your particular organization. You will also be able to manage more effectively.

Keeping up Morale

The attitude of employees towards their work is probably the largest single influencing factor upon the Balance Sheet. Happy, contented workers are likely to be more effective, producing higher sales and thus greater profits.

Attitude, when applied to the workplace, is generally referred to as 'morale'.

It is, put simply, a measurement of contentment levels among employees. It is not usually applicable to any one individual, but to the group as a whole. If the group, generally, is happy to come to work, satisfied with the working environment, confident in the products or services they are dealing with and rewarded to their satisfaction, then morale is said to be good. An adverse change in any one of these factors can quickly convert this to bad.

It does not take very much to change, and it can happen very rapidly.

A poorly communicated instruction, for instance, affecting the welfare of the staff can be sufficient to prime the pump of demoralisation. Prior consultation is always advised, and it may also be appropriate to seek a Union view.

Good morale can be maintained by praising workers on suitable occasions, thus confirming for them the satisfaction they perceive in their jobs. Keep on the look-out for opportunities and hand out a suitable verbal bouquet. At performance reviews, do not forget to praise where it is due.

A survey carried out by Robert Half and Accountemps, a recruitment agency, revealed that 70% of people coming on to their books had resigned from their earlier job because they were unhappy about the lack of praise they received. Too many employers believed that generous wages and perks were sufficient to keep their workers happy and contented. So, be warned!

Some large concerns refer to this praise as 'positive stroking'. Bosses are encouraged to seek out instances where a good word can be communicated, however minor the cause, to keep up their 'stroke level'.

Strokes can also be negative and these should be avoided. Admonishing someone in front of their peers would fall into this category and is something a good manager would never do.

Tangible rewards for excellence should stand side by side with praise, and could include:

- Weekend breaks;
- Gift vouchers;
- Donation towards a group party;
- Share incentives;
- Catalogue gift scheme; etc.

Whatever the reward, though, remember that staff like to be acknowledged from time to time for their efforts; a few kind words can have as much impact as a few pound notes.

Motivating Others

Though rewards and words of praise are likely to keep a workforce happy, a little more is required to keep them continually motivated and thus more efficient. This is another task of the team leader.

The behavioural scientist, Maslow, defined a series of human needs as one passed through life, culminating in esteem and self-fulfilment.

Once the basic requirements of food, shelter and security at home and work are met, most individuals then seek status, respect from others and the ability to realise their own potential. All three of these can be achieved through their working environment and, if the employer can assist in bringing about their achievement, a well-motivated employee will be the happy result.

Aim, therefore, in helping colleagues to:

- *Achieve.* Provide tasks where you are certain they will be effectively tackled. Let the employee see that he has done a good job and, if practical, allow him to see it through the implementation stage.
- *Advance.* Wherever you have a say in promotion policies, put in a good word for members of your own team who have shone.
- *Be Recognized.* Push names forward, when justified, of team members who have performed well. Make certain that senior management know of their achievements.
- *Take Responsibility.* You will never know how capable people are until you give them full responsibility for something. It may mean taking a risk, but that is all part of good management.

New employees need initial motivation through making it quite clear what is expected of them, and making their task interesting, challenging and demanding. This will not last for ever and continual updating motivation is called for on your part. Job specifications should, therefore, be regularly reviewed to ensure they remain within those categories we have just defined. Discussions with staff over job content, responsibility levels and so on also demand regular attention, as do objective reviews.

Attention to training is imperative, with constant doses of skill sessions in such disciplines as selling, product knowledge, negotiation, administration, manufacturing techniques or any other aspects appropriate to the job. Evaluate these sessions constantly, as well as seeking delegates' views on their worth. Ask about other training needs which should, at all times, be employee-led.

Motivate, also, through sharing of information with colleagues, involving them as far as possible and encouraging them to think of themselves as part of a team as opposed to a lone voice in the wilderness. Guide them where necessary and stand up for them in the company of others if there is a strong case for this.

One interesting sidelight on the art of motivation was brought out by a study conducted by Kari Lilja of Helsinki School of Economics and Margaret Grieco of Oxford University who found that people become highly motivated when they feel they are the centre of outside interest.

Workers respond well when they know they are the focus of attention, such as machine operatives during a factory tour. Clearly their job must be interesting (even if they would not always agree!) if other people want to watch them at work.

Motivating is helped along by a degree of delegation, as we shall now see.

The Art of Delegation

Have you ever spotted a manager sitting at a desk with perhaps only one or two pieces of paper on it, and thought: 'He must have an easy job'? This may well be true, of course, but it is far more likely that he is an effective manager who has successfully delegated much of his routine work to others, leaving himself time to think and plan ahead.

The unsuccessful manager will probably have mountains of paper on his desk, confirming a high work level but indicating also his ineffectiveness in involving others.

But delegation IS an art. It involves far more than merely handing out work to colleagues, believing that to be the end of it.

Delegation is about sharing. Sharing work loads with those with the most appropriate experience, providing them at the same time with a challenge and allowing the team to operate in the most efficient manner. Consider, firstly, your total workload, secondly what proportion of it should be delegated and, finally, to whom it should be passed and with what precise instructions and deadline limits. There may also be times when the work should perhaps be 'delegated' upwards, or at least discussed with a more senior colleague if you believe that it is outside your authority to make appropriate decisions.

Consider carefully your choice of delegatee. An opportunity for in-house training may present itself through passing work to someone less experienced, although make sure that a colleague checks it afterwards. Not only should it be checked, but follow through the training exercise with advice and encouragement.

It is so often quicker to carry out a task yourself, rather than creating additional work in showing someone else how it is done, but adopting this stance can only in the long run lead to self-destruction, when you reach the point that you are attempting to do everything yourself. In a team environment, work has to be shared to maintain motivation and heighten morale.

It also has to be seen to be fairly shared, so make certain you are aware of each individual's workload, as well as their capacity, which may be entirely different! Every six months re-evaluate workloads and redistribute where possible, if only to provide variety. It remains the spice of work as well as of life!

MANAGING OTHER PEOPLE

When delegating, be certain what is required is fully understood. Outline the task, agree what resources are required, and settle on dates by which the work should be completed. Ask, perhaps, how those chosen intend to plan the task; you may disagree with some of the detail but, if at all possible, give people their heads. They must be allowed to learn from their own errors, providing these are acceptable to the organization in the short term.

Longer projects may call for progress reports and monitoring discussions. Encourage frequent dialogue – and remember to praise it the work is completed ahead of time!

Managing Difficulties

Do not expect an easy road. Managers get paid more than those working for them because they are expected to iron out the inevitable difficulties.

Sometimes you will have to criticize, but, like the proverbial cat, there are many different ways to tackle this. Dig deeply to identify the real cause of the problem which could be a variety of things such as:

- Lack of experience;
- Less than perfect training;
- A failure on someone else's part to communicate properly – it could even be you!;
- Inadequate resources;
- Ineffective machinery;
- Personal problems, influenced either by work situations or externally.

So, firstly, cure the cause. Then tackle the individual in a constructive, and not a destructive, way, encouraging him to do better next time.

Staff grievances are common at work and it is always easy to find something to complain about, whether related to pay, conditions, insecurity, promotion prospects or a million other factors. As a manager you will have to deal regularly with such complaints, many quite minor.

Most, however, can be killed at source, providing effective communication exists within the company. Regular meetings will probably bring forward any common causes for disaffection, although make sure that a lone voice is not swaying others, whilst individual contact should elicit any personal problems. The earlier a difficulty is highlighted, the easier it will be to solve. Long festering disharmony is much more difficult to eradicate. Watch for danger signals.

Gather in all the facts, which may require your talking to several other people in the organization; most arguments have several sides. Decide on the best course of action – which must give priority to the company and not the individual – and explain your reasoning fully and fairly.

But do not leave it there. Make a diary note to discuss progress with the person concerned in, say, a month's time. Make certain that the problem really has been resolved.

There will inevitably be occasions when no answer can be found to suit every party and you may have to resort to a set grievance procedure. This can be a highly specialized task and is best left to the experts, often a personnel officer but, in his absence, possibly the company solicitor. Trade unions involved should be suitably advised.

So you are beginning to learn to manage others. Much of the secret lies in effective communication, a subject all of its own . . .

CHAPTER 8

Communicating With Others

A very large part of every manager's time is spent on communicating. So, if you want to get on in your organization, you must learn to communicate well.

Every time you speak to someone, whether face-to-face or on the telephone, you are communicating. Equally, when you are writing a memorandum or report, talking to a group, using a facsimile machine or even reading, communication is being practised, either from or to you. You cannot avoid it!

More and more companies are recognizing the importance of good communication, whether to, or from, their employees, or to, or from, their customers and suppliers. To find out what customers really want, you have to communicate with them. Employees like to be provided with information, as well as having a medium to communicate their messages to the bosses.

Communication in the working environment is very different from everyday communication, where information is generally being transmitted for interest only. If it is uninteresting, it can be ignored, or quickly discarded. At work, however, messages are passed as a means of getting something done and, if they are overlooked, the result can be disastrous in the extreme. If an instruction to check for gas in a coalmine is not followed, you have only to guess at the possible consequences. Proper communication, therefore, is essential.

How Important is it?

As we have seen, communication outside of work can be optional. A signpost to Birmingham does not have to be followed; the longer route can be taken and, providing no deadlines have to be met, the choice is yours.

You do not have to join in at a party. The evening may prove less entertaining, but again you have a choice and the next day will doubtless be just the same whether you participate fully or not.

Ignoring signals at work is an entirely different matter. The next day is likely to be very different indeed if communication is overlooked; you may not even have a job!

Communication is used in both directions, upwards and downwards, to maintain a cohesive whole in any workplace; if it breaks down, so might the organization. It is used, also, to send messages to customers, suppliers and shareholders where there may be a duty to keep them informed of what is going on. A loss of communication could result in lost custom, unwilling suppliers or shareholders transferring their allegiance elsewhere. So keep everyone in the picture.

Communication is as important to the ambitious individual as it is to the company itself. Why should this be so?

Fail to be in touch and you are far more likely to make mistakes. How often have you heard: 'He doesn't seem to know what's going on'? Make sure this cannot apply to you.

Stay in touch with people, especially those who really matter. Read all company circulars, newspapers and notice boards. Read, also, copies of correspondence where appropriate to keep abreast of what colleagues are doing. Talk to them regularly about working topics. Study the trade press, as well as the national press if your company is a large one. You cannot know too much about the organization for which you work.

Channels of Communication

Three basic forms of communication exist for people at work: written, oral and visual. All three are important but a mix is probably desirable.

Written communication may take any of the following forms:

- Reports and memoranda. Probably the most common type of internal communication between employees, providing them with instructions, amendments and a wealth of sundry information.
- Letters. Most businesses experience a steady flow of inward and outward correspondence, not only with regular customers but with other trade associates, similar bodies, advertising media, etc. A company is perhaps best judged by the quality of its outward mail, so pay due attention to this aspect.
- Magazines, newspapers and journals relating to the business. Study any relevant articles and, if you can, contribute yourself.
- Agendas and subsequent minutes of meetings. Many tend to skip the latter; be an exception and study them.
- Instruction manuals. These may cover a wide variety of topics, from the running of the business itself, to specific subjects or the operation of specified machinery or systems. Always make yourself fully familiar with these or at least know where you can look up references.

COMMUNICATING WITH OTHERS

- Programmed learning courses. Seek the availability of these and volunteer for those likely to advance your promotion prospects.
- Financial reports, where available.

Varieties of oral communication include:

- Meetings. These might be formal, such as conferences, seminars, etc., or informal and on a regular basis. These are probably the most effective means of passing topical information around a business.
- Telephone. Widely used as a communication medium and can often cut out the need for lengthy and detailed letter writing.
- Courses, where speakers are used to convey messages and latest information relevant to participants.
- Formal speeches, useful where large audiences are involved.
- Interviews, considered separately from meetings because they are usually on a one-to-one basis and frequently related to personnel matters.
- Television and radio, where advertising is normally the reason for their use.

Visual means of communication are becoming increasingly used with advancing technology and might include:

- Computer screens, probably the most widely used communication process today.
- Television, which is, of course, both oral and visual.
- Films, used for training, relaying information, recording and educational purposes.
- Photographs, widely used in research and, with the development of microfilm, now used for maintaining records in minute form.
- Posters, graphs and charts which can be used for effective demonstrations of trends, system operations, warning signs and so on.
- Display boards, useful for monitoring production schedules where the daily, or hourly, position can be seen at a glance.

Avoiding Bad Communication

Not all communication is good. Numerous instances exist where the intended message bears no resemblance to the one received. More often that not, it is the meaning which changes from sender to receiver, but even the words can change, like the famous war-time example of 'Send reinforcements – we're going to advance' reaching headquarters as 'Send three-and-fourpence – we're going to a dance'! So make sure your message is clearly understood; check it out if necessary.

The art of communication commences before the message is delivered and you should ask yourself a series of questions before embarking on the task.

Firstly, is it really necessary to pass on the message at all? To whom should it be passed and, especially, what form of communication should be used?

The answer to the first of these questions is helped along by determining the purpose behind the passing of the message. Is it merely a piece of information which might be better processed by some other means, or at some other time, or is it vital that people know quickly of a policy change or something of equal importance? Do they need to have all the information or can it be sieved before it reaches them?

Try to put yourself in the position of the recipient, especially someone new to the scene. Does the message paint sufficient background material to provide reasons for any changes. Do not insult people's intelligence by dictating new procedures without explaining why.

Decide what form the communication should take. Look at the list above to see how many choices there are before you. Would it be more effective to gather colleagues together so that questions can be tackled at the same time, or is the command simple enough to be contained in a memorandum?

Many big companies, when communicating with a large number of employees, attach an appendix covering possible questions and answers, especially if the message is likely to create fear or uncertainty amongst the workforce. If the topic is major enough, then it should first be communicated by a senior manager.

Whatever the form used, make sure you give only relevant information and cut out any ambiguities or unnecessary detail. Provide full reasons why any changes are planned and determine beforehand, as far as is possible, what reactions there might be. Cover these, either in the body of the message or in a special supplement, and offer to answer further questions should they arise. Do not duck any issues.

The Magic of Technology

If you are going to communicate effectively in today's modern and fast-moving business world, you must keep fully abreast of modern methods.

Computers will come immediately to mind, but these are just one of a whole armoury of machines ready to carry your messages across the world if necessary. Data processing and telecommunication will help to move your business into the future; make certain you do not get left behind yourself.

Make yourself familiar with Personal Computers and the special languages they use; you do not have to be a technician, but learn as you go along, on a 'need to know' basis, i.e. delve into the manual only when you need to do so. Then remember the sequence for next time.

Facsimile machines are also widely used. These are able to transmit immediate messages to any other machine owner, anywhere in the world. Although 'telex' is still in use, it has been overtaken by 'faxes' where machines are relatively low cost and where identical messages can be sent to several recipients at the same time. Few modern offices now operate without these machines.

Telephones are about to become more than just a quick message transmission system. The latest telecommunications technology will be able to combine pictures, data and voice traffic simultaneously over the public network. Desk-top conferences will be possible, with participants able to send documents, pictures and graphics over computer screens whilst talking to one another. It will also be quite feasible to see the other person if you really want to!

Portable telephones, in the meantime, need to be mastered, as do modern dictating machines. These can even be combined, with tapes produced at the office whilst dictating along the motorway.

Make all of these tools work for you – do not work for them. Employers are looking for people with social communicating skills on top of technical know-how. This follows the realization that many of the expected cost benefits of information technology have been lost due to misunderstanding the real strategy, and bad communication with the users. Senior technical staff are vital facilitators, but the company's strategies will not work if they are poor communicators.

So learn to use the latest technology wisely. Often the old-fashioned will suffice and can result in better communication. Be selective in the medium you choose, but ensure you are fully conversant with everything the market place can offer.

Face-to-Face

The oldest and quickest communication method will never die, and you should use it whenever circumstances allow. That is, simply talking to one other person on a face-to-face basis.

We all do it every day, and it works. Whether it's merely a cheery 'Good Morning' to your partner, or a colleague, or a meaningful one-to-one dialogue lasting a couple of hours with your boss, messages are transferred in an instant and have the advantage of being accompanied by facial and body language.

Providing both of you are listening properly, there is instant feedback, with each party constantly gathering further information. Agreement can be achieved within seconds and there should be little wasted time. Even the preliminary formalities, usually centred on health and the weather, are important posturing periods, especially if the two individuals have not met before. Each needs to obtain a feel for the other and to adopt a negotiating stance likely to put them on top.

Questions can be direct and without formality, such as 'Can we agree on that?' or 'Shall we fix a deadline for next week?' Answers, similarly, may be instantaneous and, providing they are the ones each is seeking, agreement can be confirmed.

There need have been no lengthy formalities, no waiting for responses and, perhaps, no need for written confirmation. A handshake may well suffice and deals can be all over in a few minutes. Such practices are common in certain parts of the world, as well as in some specialized trades such as commodity buying and selling. The advantages are obvious.

Alertness in these conditions is called for to avoid any embarrassment at a later stage should two versions of what happened emerge. If there is any possibility of this happening, then it is best to insist on a written follow-up of mutually agreed points. This is especially so if quantities are involved, be they pounds sterling or by weight!

Using the Telephone

It is virtually impossible to imagine what business life would be like today if the telephone were abolished – although many people might favour this course!

A little over one hundred years ago companies were more reliant upon the post and personal visitors, although there were not then, of course, the myriad of services on offer to us today. Consumers, and other businesses, can now pick up a telephone and order anything from a barge to a bouquet. Industry and commerce might not grind to a complete halt, but they would find the absence of a telephone highly inconvenient.

Orders are also lost or gained on the telephone, and the art of good telecommunication is thus essential. A completely new industry has grown up around teaching people the right techniques, and another on 'telesales', or the art of selling goods and services over the telephone.

The telephone is far more personal than a letter can ever be and queries can be resolved in much less time. Expressions can be readily communicated in a way impossible by post and, in general, it is a medium that can boast many advantages. But learn to use it properly and effectively.

If you are initiating the call, avoid announcing yourself by Christian name only; this can be annoying to the busy recipient of your call who may know a dozen 'Bills'. So add your surname and, if it is necessary, precisely who you are and the name of your company.

After that, much will depend upon how well you know the person you are calling. A few words of welcome, usually enquiring the health of the other party, is quite in order if you know him well. If he is a stranger, then have the courtesy to explain straight away precisely why you are telephoning him. Bear in mind that you are interrupting whatever else he may have been doing, or about to do, and be ready, if necessary, to be told that he will ring you back later.

If it is an important call – one from which you expect to elicit a sale, for instance – prepare it beforehand, attempting to forestall any likely objections. Have alternatives ready and keep the conversation flowing as smoothly as possible. It is up to you to retain the initiative.

Do not be afraid of jotting down the points you wish to raise, in the most likely order; your opposite number need not be aware of this providing you raise them naturally without appearing to refer to a list.

Accepting a call may, of course, catch you on the hop. Be quick enough, if the circumstances allow, to say it is inconvenient to speak at that precise moment and you will ring back. Ensure you do so. By that time you will be properly prepared.

Some businessmen prefer to stand when taking telephone calls; it is said to create assertiveness. Use the manner which suits you best but, at all times, remain calm. If necessary, allow a pause before you respond to give you that fraction of a second extra to formulate the right answer. It is surprising what a difference this makes, but it is something you need to practice before getting it perfect.

Answerphones can be difficult to deal with, but can also be very useful. Take a deep breath, announce yourself clearly and give your reason for calling. Add your own telephone number if the other person will not know it and say when you are likely to be available.

Meetings

However much some business people claim to hate them, meetings remain the major forum for decision making and are unlikely to be abolished until someone finds an acceptable alternative!

Well prepared, and well chaired, meetings can, however, prove a boon to a business, allowing everyone present to have a say in a, usually, restricted timescale. Preparation is vital and should include:

- Who needs to be present?
- Where is the most effective venue?
- What time of day should it be held and for how long?
- Who is to prepare the agenda?
- Who is to chair the meeting and who will take the minutes?
- Should papers be circulated beforehand?
- What logistics should be considered, e.g. drinks (soft only!), refreshments, notepads, car parking, telephone availability, etc?
- What are the objectives?

The most important of these points is the last one – meetings for meetings' sake are a waste of everyone's time. There must be a very valid reason for getting people together and each one attending should know beforehand (except in exceptional circumstances, such as the announcement of sensitive news) what they are doing there.

There may be many reasons for a meeting, but the purpose must be made clear beforehand so that those attending may prepare themselves. The objective is then more likely to be achieved.

It may be necessary to impart information to a number of people upon which their views may be sought, and a meeting is the ideal medium. A problem may have to be solved or ideas canvassed, in which case getting the right employees together in one place at one time may resolve the issue. But do let everyone know what you are trying to achieve.

Meetings may be formal or informal, and both can be right, according to the circumstances.

An annual general meeting, for example, should follow the first format, whilst regular get-togethers of specialized personnel will probably operate better on an informal basis.

Give a lot of thought to the setting. Is the works canteen the right place to air a grievance, or might the meeting be more suitably held away from the workplace? Hired rooms, in a local hotel for instance, can create the right kind of atmosphere, especially if the meeting is of the 'think tank' variety, where 'revolutionary' thoughts are encouraged.

Consider, also, how people should sit. More discussion is likely to emerge from a circle of chairs, without a table, than the traditional square or oblong arrangement of table and chairs. If there are around 20 attending, a horseshoe pattern, with the chairman at the centre, is probably the best arrangement.

If you are in the chair yourself, there are a number of golden rules to remember:

- Listen to *everything* that is said and give everyone an opportunity to contribute.

- If questions are asked, ensure they are answered.

- Stick to the agenda.
- Deal firmly, but politely, with anyone attempting to disrupt the meeting.
- Thank participants for their contributions and give praise where it is earned.
- Your job is to summarize and, where necessary, obtain the majority view – stick to this!
- Make sure decisions are clear and that everyone present knows what has been decided.

Writing Reports

This section applies as much to writing memoranda, minutes or letters as it does to writing reports. Slight differences in style may be called for, but the basic rules still persist, i.e. keep the message clear, short and simple.

Winston Churchill ordered his general staff to use 'short, crisp paragraphs', whilst Mark Twain, who sold most of his writing, said 'I never write "Metropolis" when I can get the same price for "City"'.

Before putting pen to paper, consider whether you have chosen the best medium. Would it be quicker, and possibly more effective, to pick up the telephone? Or is a meeting called for to iron out differences or views which would take far less time than protracted correspondence? If you are angry, always allow at least twenty-four hours to elapse before responding in writing; your anger will almost certainly show through and will be recorded for all time – something you may later regret.

If a record is called for, or if you may later need proof of your action, then there is no alternative to writing. But give careful thought as to whether this should be by letter, memorandum or one of the other forms referred to earlier.

All written communications should be clearly addressed (and this may include several intended readers), with the subject matter in a heading. Come to the point quickly and do not expect the recipient to get to the bottom of the letter or note before understanding the message. If necessary, recapitulate on the subject in the opening paragraph, such as:

This letter refers to the question of responsibility for purchasing which has been discussed for some time now; you may like to have my views so that a decision can be reached.

Sentences must remain simple to understand, as short as possible and preferably positive as opposed to negative. At all costs avoid double negatives; for example:

The decision to branch out is not inconsistent with our overall policy of decentralization.

Always read through thoroughly before you sign letters or memoranda; credibility can so easily be lost if errors have crept in between dictation and production. Such errors can also be very disconcerting to the reader, who has to work out what he thinks you really meant to say before making his own decisions. If he is your boss, anything other than perfection may also alter his views on your promotion prospects!

One of the shortest words in the English language is often mis-typed, the result of which is to reverse entirely the meaning of what the writer is trying to say. Substitute a '*w*' for the '*t*' in the word underlined to see what I mean:

Employees may <u>not</u> officially clock off two minutes before finishing time, as has been the habit in the past.

Keep all your written communications attractive to look at, with short paragraphs and sufficiently wide margins. Ask yourself, from time to time: 'Would *I* like to receive this?' The answer should tally with the quality of your work.

Consultations

Whilst these may take the form of meetings, they are in themselves a specialized form of communication, often used to ease the path towards general agreement of several parties.

Consultation may be with superiors, subordinates or your own peers, those of approximately equal status.

It can be very useful to float an idea during an informal meeting with your boss merely to gain his initial impression of it; you will then know whether or not it is worth pursuing. At the same time, it can be comforting to know that you are likely to gain his support when you expand upon the idea. But do not take this for granted; he may well take an opposite view after further deliberation or hearing opposing views from colleagues.

Consulting with those working for you is probably the most difficult, for you cannot be certain that you are hearing their real feelings. Initial agreement with your ideas may be converted into antagonism when put to a vote. Make sure, therefore, that you encourage them to give you their honest opinion at the outset; from that you can mould your ideas into something more acceptable to both of you. If you have a secretary or assistant, they may be able to gauge the feelings of other subordinates better than you can yourself.

Gaining support from equally placed colleagues can be very important to the successful implementation of new thought. Bounce your ideas off them to obtain their reaction and take careful note of any additional suggestions for improvements. Their support may prove crucial and, if you have liaised with them up front, they are more likely to be co-operative. Make sure, however, that any original ideas which are your own stay that way; it is surprising how some people claim to be originators of suggestions they have heard elsewhere!

There are many benefits to consultation. As well as improving on the original idea, you will have an inkling as to who will give it their support, how it fits in with ideas of others and how feasible it is in an overall context. It is thus worth spending some time on this form of communication.

If your idea is fairly revolutionary, remember to give others plenty of time to digest it. You will no doubt have given it a great deal of prior thought and it would be unfair to seek an instant opinion from colleagues. It may be appropriate to produce a paper outlining the advantages and disadvantages and circulate this a few days before talking to people about it.

Flexibility is important. If you have fully committed yourself to a change, it will soon become obvious to others that, rather than consulting with them, you are merely canvassing agreement. If you do this too often, you may find no-one is very willing to talk to you at all about your new ideas.

External management consultancy firms play an important part in today's industry planning. But use them as advisers only; final decisions should remain with your company.

Presentations

Giving a presentation to a number of people is merely another form of communication, but one where you are centre stage. In essence, what you are trying to get over is a message; in reality, what others will remember is your performance. But give a good performance, and there is a chance that they will also remember the message.

So many factors help in giving that good performance. Some of the most important are:

- Choosing the right venue. Try to pick one where the audience fits neatly into the space provided.
- Be comfortable with the 'fittings', such as a raised platform, seating arrangements or microphones.

- Time what you are going to say and familiarize yourself with any forms of technical assistance.
- Attend a Speakers' Club for a few sessions if you are not used to talking in front of an audience; it will provide you with courage as well as confidence.
- Keep your notes in a tidy form, preferably on small, hand-held cards.
- Allow time for questions at the end. Plant a few if necessary.

Although some speakers prefer to do so, it is not generally advisable to read your speech word for word. Far better to speak from notes, amplifying as you go along and re-emphasizing where appropriate. Stick, however, to your notes and avoid straying too far from them or your timing will be out.

Run through what you are going to say – speaking out loud – about two or three times (more if you are not bored!), timing each run through. The actual time is likely to be a little longer than the longest of the three. If you have exceeded the period allocated to you, cut the presentation until you get it right. It is always preferable to finish a little short than run over, especially if other speakers are to follow you.

Organize the content of what you are going to say into three clear parts: a beginning, a middle and an end. Tell your audience at the outset what you are doing there; cover the main body of your talk; and, finally, wrap it around with your conclusions. Avoid taking one view only. Try to anticipate what people might be thinking and counter their thoughts before they can convert them into questions. That way they will respect you.

Make your impact at the beginning when people are more attentive, but keep something up your sleeve for the end. Talk naturally and aim your voice level at the person furthest from you – formal speeches are for politicians.

If your presentation is in the form of a self-produced video, only true professionalism is likely to succeed. Take advice, therefore, and do not try to make anything on the cheap. Videos are expensive because they involve a whole team in their manufacture. At the same time we all expect a lot from the small screen in our lounge and your viewers will be no different.

This medium can also have drawbacks since, although it uses both picture and voice, it is also 'flat' and may not portray your message as effectively as a personal appearance. In view of cost and limitations, therefore, it should be used only with discretion.

Going to Press

Apart from reports and memoranda, which we covered earlier, there is another powerful media for you to use in getting your message over via the printed word. This is through a brochure or similar publication, which might be used either in-house or aimed at customers or suppliers.

Anything from a hurriedly-produced, photocopied Newsheet to a glossy brochure fits into this category.

Remember that it will reflect your company's own image and, as with all forms of communication, professionalism is the key to success. Give as much thought to it as you would to a personal presentation.

Expert advice is probably necessary unless the company employs people in this line. The best way to discover a specialist suitable for you is to find someone else's brochure which you admire and track down its producer. There is then no need, of course, slavishly to copy the original; use it only to indicate the style you are seeking.

Cost considerations may limit your horizons and it is wise to obtain a likely approximate cost at the outset. If it appears that what you are trying to achieve cannot be contained within the budget, reconsider the whole thing. To expect the same results from half the cost is only wishful thinking.

Do not cram too much into your publication. It should have an appealing air about it and tempt others to want to open it. Once opened, you must keep the reader's attention.

Make sure he knows what to do next. If it is intended to sell goods or services, an order form or contact point should be clearly identifiable. If it is a message to employees, what follow up is there?

The publication should thus have a clear objective and one only. Too many messages will blur the thought process and confuse the reader. You probably only have a few seconds (minutes at best) of his time, so make good use of them.

Better still that the brochure forms part of an overall policy in communication. Its publication may coincide with a meeting, a circular or perhaps advance notice of its availability. And do not leave it at that; monitor its impact and follow up as necessary.

Better Reading

Every budding executive must learn the art of reading. In many corporations there may be a mountain (sometimes daily) of reading material consisting of internal correspondence, circulars, newspaper clippings and magazines. It is often impossible to read all of these and, indeed, not the intention that you do so. What you must do is

sort the wheat from the chaff. The material will probably fall into one of three categories:
- important, and to be read either immediately or within a short period;
- important but less urgent; or
- optional.

Unless the reading matter is so marked, which is highly unlikely, only you can decide which document, magazine, etc., falls into which category. The choice will also be personal – another colleague may choose differently according to his own priorities.

Each of the categories can be tackled differently. By all means skip read the important, urgent matter initially, but make sure you read it more thoroughly the second time around. The less urgent can also be skimmed through at first and you can then decide when to read it properly. The optional can either be discarded or, again, skip read.

Ask yourself why each piece of material has to be read at all. This will help to categorize it and you can then retain a list, possibly mentally, for future reference. Some reading matter coming across your desk can almost certainly be rejected; question whether it should be directed at you at all. You may even find that no-one reads it and that you can thus save your company some money!

Take a fast reading course, or at least study a book on the subject, if you are a notoriously slow reader, as many people are.

Get used to reading magazine or newspaper headlines alone, only delving fully into the story if it appeals. The headline, especially in business magazines, will generally tell you what the item is about and you can save yourself much time by adopting this method of 'reading'.

Use otherwise 'wasted' time to read, such as train or bus journeys. Read at the meal table if family life allows! Good managers will generally read what hits their desks on the same day. To delay for much longer may either result in a build-up which you cannot cope with or, in the case of something really important, possible disaster.

Communicating Abroad

Obviously the easiest way of achieving this is to learn the appropriate language fluently – but there are other ways.

The first is to at least grasp the basics of the language concerned. This will show your talking companion that you do care about communicating properly and, between you, you should cope. But do not automatically take advantage of the fact that many foreigners, especially in Europe, speak our language.

If it is feasible, take a translator along with you. This may be essential if you are operating in technical terms to ensure that nothing is later misunderstood. Where possible, have the translator write out any important agreements and have them signed or initialled at the time. All this, of course, will push up the cost but will 'pay' in terms of professionalism.

Be wary of body language; every country has its own. Simply because he is smiling at you does not necessarily indicate that he is happy with the arrangements – the smile may well be a cynical one!

Learn the habits and customs of the country you are visiting before leaving. Your opposite number will admire you for doing so and it should smooth along the negotiations. Avoid getting cross with someone unable to speak English; a misunderstanding may well have arisen without your fully realizing it. Stay calm and try to take the conversation back a sentence or two to clarify matters.

CHAPTER 9

Marketing Skills

One of the skills you will have to learn to develop on your way to the top is marketing.

Take a look at almost any management position today and you will find in it an element of marketing. In smaller companies, the role will probably be carried out by the Managing Director, thus emphasizing its importance. Larger concerns will have their own Marketing Manager or Director, and probably a team behind him.

But just what is marketing?

It's a word that has crept in in recent years and there remains some mystique about it. Some people believe it means no more than 'selling'; others that it involves advertising and other communications media. It will be as well for you to understand its meaning fully and retain an explanation for you to back up your knowledge. Perhaps the simplest definition is:

Marketing is the identification of customer requirements, and meeting those needs to the satisfaction of the company.

It thus embodies much more than selling and involves, for example, other important aspects such as research, the use of communications and distribution. Amplified, the list might include:

- Market research
- Consumer research
- Promoting the company
- Promoting the product or service
- Selling
- Distributing
- Servicing, including after-sales.

Clearly, to be successful, the price will have to be right, the product/service offered at the right time and in the right place, and any follow-up service efficiently carried through. All this will have to be contained in a simple plan.

Developing a Plan

As we saw in Chapter 4, every company needs to adopt a strategy in order to know where it is going, how it will get there and how long it will take.

This strategy may be as simple as 'Improving market share to 10%' to something far more complex involving, perhaps, relocation, adding extra resources or effecting a completely new shift in emphasis. It will, however, have to include reference to marketing if the plan is to succeed for, without it, all the goods are likely to finish up on the company's own shelves! Getting them into the customers' hands in exchange for real live money must be the ultimate goal.

A well-thought out marketing plan should, therefore, form part of the overall strategy. It will probably contain six vital elements:

(1) *Marketing targets.* Just what are you trying to achieve? Is it related to volume or income? Is there an ideal geographical spread?

(2) *Budgets.* All income and costs must be translated into currency to ensure there is something left over for the business.

(3) *Products and Prices.* What range is to be available and at what prices? How do the products match up to the competition? Consider discount structures along with margins you are trying to achieve.

(4) *Research.* Of the market place and of consumers' needs. Is this to be carried out internally, or will consultants be used?

(5) *Promotion.* What media will be most effective? Are the products or services to be offered directly to consumers?

(6) *Distribution.* Is this to be through a direct sales force, agents or wholesalers? What logistics are involved?

After completing the plan, it should fall under someone's 'ownership', or responsibility, probably the Marketing Director's. He, in turn, will allocate certain parts of it to his subordinates so that, if everyone achieves that part for which they are personally responsible, the overall aim will be met. That way, everyone will be happy!

A Competitive Edge

This is the ideal for which every company strives. A term which is relatively new in the field of business management, it indicates that aspect of your business which measures it apart from your competitors.

Consider McDonald's Hamburger Company. It took a relatively

simple mixture of ingredients, turned it into a shape not previously known and is now copied all over the world. For a long while, it had a competitive edge which earned the company a fortune. It might argue, additionally, that it still has such an edge in the service it provides. Competitive edges do not last for ever and may change in nature over the years.

Your own company's competitive edge may be in any one of a number of fields:

- Price
- Method of production or distribution
- Technical advantage
- Better presentation
- Image
- Service
- Expertise
- Product range

You will see that it is unlikely, in several of these cases, for your edge to be unique. With the company's image, for instance, this is something merely created, and therefore only perceived in the eyes of the customer. And therein lies the secret.

It does not really matter whether or not your competitive advantage stands entirely alone. What matters is whether or not your customers, or likely customers, believe that it does.

Many products sell exceptionally well (although often only for a limited period) through boasting of their uniqueness in achieving a desired end result – perhaps restoring hair, making car bodies glisten or liquidizing every imaginable food on the market. For a while many of us are taken in, and part with our money. What is being sold to us is not so much the product, as its apparent competitive edge in the miraculous results it is said to achieve. These are merely modern examples of the medicine man's bottles of 'cure-alls'.

There are, of course, equally examples of products and services with genuine competitive edges, and it is these that most businesses seek. Medicinal drug-related companies, in particular, aim to be the first in the field with a new cure; immediately announced, that company's share price, if quoted, will rise, for the analysts will assume future improved profitability based solely upon the discovery.

Knowing Your Customers

Recalling that our original definition required us to identify our customers' requirements, it follows that we must, firstly, know our customers. Not only know them, but know them extremely well.

We must find ways of reaching into both their hearts and their minds, for only by doing this will we be certain what they are looking for. Many companies make the mistake of producing goods for which they believe there to be a market, only to find one does not exist. The Sinclair C.5 mini-car was too far ahead of its time, the size of the skateboard market proved to be much smaller than anticipated, and many food manufacturers find that there is insufficient demand for their products. Such is the fate of those who do not know what customers want.

Today's fast-moving consumer market demands that everything must be right. This includes the product, the price, the timing, the presentation and the place. Offering Blackpool rock at Christmas time in Oxford Street would be a supreme example of getting it all wrong, yet miles of it are sold in the right place at the right time.

Consumers are becoming more sophisticated in their buying habits, and rightly so. There is so much to tempt them to part with their hard-earned money that they are increasingly refining their choices. Quality is in demand and, in many cases, outweighing price in their options. Customers today are far more likely to opt for an item of clothing costing, say, £92 than £82 if they can detect they are getting £10's worth of extra value for the dearer product.

Knowing your customers will involve market research (dealt with below) as well as maintaining contact with them after the sale, where appropriate. Industrial and commercial clients, in particular, should be quizzed as to their satisfaction, or otherwise, with your service. They are the ones likely to come back again and again, and not look elsewhere, if you can keep them entirely happy.

Customers must be encouraged to state their dissatisfaction or you will not know about the problems. Dealing with complaints must be handled at a high level within the company and every one taken very seriously.

Caring about customers should be at the heart of every business, as British Airways proved with their very successful promotional campaign which won many new clients for them and a lasting (but not necessarily permanent) impression.

Market Research

Having a plan is fine but it will not last for ever. The key to successful selling is knowing your market place which, as you will find, is constantly changing.

Even basic commodity habits change. Just compare today's supermarket bread shelves with the baker's van of not so long ago to see what extra varieties have become available.

There is only one real method of market research, and that is out in the field, where the consumer is king. Sampling surveys should be undertaken, preferably by people used to this kind of questioning.

How the questions are framed is very important to avoid misleading answers.

Whilst most direct consumer articles are properly researched, market investigations in the industrial and commercial sectors are sadly scant and, quite often, overlooked entirely. Companies who ignore making checks on their product or service acceptability from time to time are courting disaster and surveys of those going to the wall invariably show that no market research at all had been undertaken.

Research needs to be well planned, however, to be effective. Before embarking on a project, consider the following:

- What is the purpose of my research?
- How long will it take and what will it cost?
- What sample size will give me accurate findings?
- Should professionals be used?
- If so, what precise brief should they be provided with?
- Will the product or service bear the costs involved?
- What shall I do with the findings?

Research can be used to discover much more than mere product acceptability. Questions can be posed relating to possible price changes, distribution methods, packaging, after-sales service, and even whether the name influences the purchaser at all. Would you, for instance, buy a chocolate bar called 'Sludge', however good it was?

Research can also be conducted into the market itself, its size, growth and trends; its character and how this is changing, if at all; and how your item compares with those of competitors.

Once completed, it must not finish there. Many larger concerns in the food industry carry out continuing surveys, constantly adapting their products to meet consumers' changing demands.

Public Relations

Often confused with advertising, public relations goes beyond mere media communication. It is, in fact, the job of 'selling' a company to its customers, suppliers and anyone else who it considers may influence its fortunes. This could include, of course, the Government.

The Institute of Public Relations has described it as 'the deliberate, planned and sustained effort to establish and maintain mutual understanding between an organization and its public'. It would be difficult to better this definition.

Not only must the company itself, through its advertising and other means of promotion, project the image it seeks, but its executives must do so also. Hence the increasing demand for media training in forward thinking organizations.

This image is sustained, once achieved (and that is the hardest part), through everything it does, from selling to the way it treats its employees, customers, suppliers, etc., as well as its 'external' activities, which may include sponsorships, donations to charitable bodies and so on. One major bank, believing it was gaining the wrong kind of image through its sponsorship of horse racing, moved to supporting the arts instead.

Larger concerns will have their own public relations department, usually headed and staffed by people related to that field and, initially, often having no knowledge at all of the company's core activities. Others will make use, either on a continuing basis or from time to time, of P.R. consultants. This is not a cheap exercise but one which can make the difference between life and death to a company, especially if it is experiencing difficult times.

The word 'public' in public relations must include its own employees, for if these are ignored, then the battle may be lost at the start. Whatever other communication media is used, a company's most effective advertisement is its own people, as businesses like Hertz and Cathay Pacific have discovered to their benefit.

Externally, all kinds of promotional activities may be suitable to improve or maintain the image being sought and some of these are looked at in the next section. Major concerns have even used public relations campaigns to win them sympathy in the face of hostile takeovers, including nationalization threats, often quite successfully.

Promotional Activities

There is a wide field of communication media available to businesses today and great care is needed to see that every penny is spent wisely. Apart from selling the company's products, these activities can be used to:

- Attract a new raft of customers who would not otherwise have considered buying the article being promoted.
- Promote the company generally.
- Change buying habits, perhaps through the use of direct mail etc.
- Upgrade products and services in the eye of the user.
- Persuade people to use the product in a different way or for a new purpose etc.

Apart from advertising, where a choice of media is available, promotional activities might include any of the following:

- Trade fairs, exhibitions, roadshows, etc
- Closed circuit television
- Meetings, special events, open evenings and the like

- Sponsorships
- Literature in the form of special books, pamphlets, house magazines
- Films, videos

The ingredients of a good marketing campaign need to be very carefully thought out before embarking on what is usually quite hefty expenditure. The consumer will be paying at the end of the day and the monies involved must, therefore, be built into product cost unless it is to be written off elsewhere in the name of research. Wherever it appears, though, it will have to come off the bottom line of the profit and loss account and this should never be overlooked.

Judge how well your company is marketing its products and services and try to put yourself in the shoes of the consumer. Are there better methods available at equal or lower cost? Put suggestions to your superiors; these may well be welcomed and help you along the road to promotion.

Advertising

Advertising is just one means of getting your company's message across to the public, but it is one which is universally accepted as having real impact.

Whilst Cadbury's make a very good chocolate, in their early days they relied heavily on advertising widely, to such an extent that, if asked to name a chocolate manufacturer, most of us would immediately have replied with their name. At a time when consumers were shopping merely for 'chocolate', but being asked which variety they preferred, Cadbury's policy worked extremely well!

Similarly, today, names that can afford to spend the hundreds of thousands, or even millions of pounds, on television and poster advertising are able to become household words almost overnight.

How much advertising does your company do? Does it spread the word through newspapers or other media? Do products receive the most publicity, or is merely the name advertised? There are, of course, so many methods of advertising that hundreds of agencies throughout the world are kept busy by businesses anxious to promote their image to potential customers.

The secret of a good advert is, firstly, to communicate and then to persuade. If it fails to carry out the former, it has little chance of succeeding in the latter.

The different media for using advertising are numerous, but the principal methods are:

- Newspapers and magazines
- Television and radio

- Posters, such as those seen at bus stops
- Cinema screens
- Exterior and interior displays, as used in retailing
- Exhibitions and shows
- Through samples, gift vouchers, and the like

Research into the most likely method to appeal is essential, especially where a major campaign is planned. Presentation must be professional and aimed at the right people at the right time.

Economic conditions need to be favourable – there is little point in advertising luxury goods during a recession, unless you are aiming at a very limited market. The goods themselves, particularly in the direct consumer market, need to follow current trends (unless you are aiming to start a new one!) and seasonal factors must not be overlooked.

Creative advertising is the vogue and we all know of Saatchi and Saatchi's innovative 'creation' of the Conservative party. Equally clever is advertising which intentionally fails to mention the product being advertised – Schweppes is one famous example and The Independent newspaper another.

Distribution Channels

There is little advantage in communicating your message to the consumer, persuading him that he should buy your product, only for him to find that he is unable to do so because you cannot get it to him on time.

Efficiency of distribution is, therefore, essential to the whole process.

Several choices may be available to you. With consumer goods, the normal method of distribution is via a wholesaler and then a retailer to reach your customer. Direct mail, including mail order, has become very fashionable and a great number of consumers now buy their goods this way, as well as through such outlets as Argos which cuts out the middle man.

Services are bought either directly from the supplier, such as the garage trade or banking, or perhaps through a 'wholesaler' in the shape of a financial intermediary in the case of mortgages and similar products.

If your business is exporting, then a further set of choices is available to it to get its goods in the hands of the ultimate purchaser. These may include manufacturers' agents, joint ventures, buying agencies based in the United Kingdom, importing houses or confirming agents. There are, of course, many other technicalities involved in sending items abroad and you are advised to make a separate study of these in order to advance both your knowledge of international trade and your opportunities for promotion.

Several factors will influence your company in its choices of distribution channels, including:
- Fragility, size and lifespan of the goods being carried
- The distances involved
- The number of reception points which have to be serviced
- Profit margins (the mark-up on diamonds, for instance, easily allows their transport by air, normally the most expensive type of freight travel)
- Difficulties with trade barriers, which could result in goods going the long way round to avoid hold-ups
- Competitors' methods of distribution

All of these, and others of specific relevance, will have to be taken into account before deciding upon the most effective route and means of transport, weighing up both cost and the need for speed.

Distribution is closely related to stocking levels and management in both sectors will have to work together to ensure overall efficiency. Transport managers, therefore, should not be working in a vacuum but hand in hand with storekeepers and, indeed, with those involved in the manufacturing process.

Outside carriers, if used, must be reliable and it should be made clear to them where promises have been made to your customers. Each blaming the other will reflect badly on your company.

Monitoring Progress

Marketing, like the painting of the Forth Bridge, is an ongoing process.

A marketing campaign is not over when the advertisements and other communication methods have appeared. What you need to know is whether or not the campaign has been successful.

The way to do this is to go back to the original objectives which were set prior to the campaign launch. These objectives should, generally, be measurable. For instance, you may have wished to increase your market share, sell a set additional volume of certain products or, simply, added to the bottom line of the profit and loss account.

None of these events is going to happen overnight. Timescales should therefore be established beforehand and the monitoring procedures set up in plenty of time. Any additional resources likely to be needed, in the shape of people, machinery, etc. should be calculated and put in place to allow time for training, teething problems and so on.

Statistics will be necessary during the intervening period and careful

MARKETING SKILLS

thought should be given as to how the results are to be calculated and assessed.

Ensure that what you need to know at the end of the exercise is going to be available and, if current systems are inadequate, add to them or improve them as necessary. Make spot checks to ensure the monitoring systems are working.

Two basic questions will have to be answered at the end. 'Did it happen?' and 'Did it pay off?' Alongside these will go inquests into whether or not it was really worth it and if consideration should next time be given to allocating the resources in a different manner. Both advertising and personnel are heavy costs; would it be advantageous to drop the next campaign in favour of taking on additional salesmen? Such decision making is the bread and butter of management.

Never underestimate your competitors when undertaking a major marketing campaign.

If you are aiming to pick up extra sales in a stagnant market, then someone else is going to lose some. They may not immediately become aware of the effect upon their revenue but if they do so part way through your exercise, then the knives may well be out! Gentlemen may run businesses but they do not behave in that manner when the odds are running against them!

Larger organizations, in particular, have the ability to introduce 'loss leaders', if only for a period. That period, however, may be long enough to dry up your own sales. Equally they may introduce a better product or service, by accident or design, and once again you will have to stay on your toes.

Marketing should never be allowed to flag. As was pointed out at the beginning of this Chapter, poor awareness of the need to sell a company's goods often leads to disaster. So treat marketing as an essential management discipline on your way to the top.

CHAPTER 10

Beating Your Targets

People who get on in an organization are, generally, achievers. They are the ones who have been given certain goals – and who beat them.

It is important, therefore, to understand the system in your own company and to learn how to beat your targets. These targets may be clearly set down for all to see, or they may be implied. Nearly all the larger organizations now have clear target setting systems for the majority, if not all, of their staff. You must know how they work.

Whilst smaller companies may not have such refined systems, it is generally made abundantly clear to employees just what they are expected to achieve in any given period.

Some of these objectives may not immediately be seen as 'targets', although if you closely examine the duties involved, you will generally see that 'end results' become clearer.

Take a receptionist in a busy office, for instance. She may not have been provided with precise 'targets' but quite obviously what is expected of her is prompt and close attention to customers' and others' needs, coupled with any ancillary duties being efficiently completed. Similarly, a maintenance manager may not have been given 'targets', but providing all plant, machinery and premises under his care remain in good working order, at acceptable cost, then he will have achieved what is quite naturally expected of him.

You can see, therefore, that it is not merely salesmen who have targets. Try to define your own and, if this has not been done before, afterwards agree them with your employer and set about beating them!

At the core of every well-run business should be a budget (or a series of budgets) from which targets can then be set. If the targets are achieved, then the budget will have been met and there should be smiles (and, perhaps, even a bonus!) all round. It is very important that you understand the budgeting system, both generally and the way in which it operates in your own company.

Understanding Budgets

There is nothing mysterious about the budgeting procedure, despite the fact that a lot of concerns surround it with enough mumbo-jumbo to put most people off!

Often defined as 'budgetary control', it is nothing more than a management accounting technique to control both income and expenditure within a business. There is no set method of producing budgets and hundreds of differing systems remain in operation. All you need to know are the basics, on top of which you must learn to understand how it is done in your company.

By setting out the objectives of an organization in financial terms, you can then:

- Communicate those yardsticks to the appropriate departments in the company
- Define key actions which may be necessary to achieve those objectives
- Delegate responsibility to certain sections and individuals
- Co-ordinate related activities, such as sales and production, to improve efficiency
- Control progress via monitoring techniques
- Spot potential problems before things go too radically wrong
- Identify where improvements to systems may ease the budget along more smoothly
- Reward people who succeed in reaching their targets

As you can see, achieving all of these ends is a most satisfactory conclusion for any company, and that is why budgeting is taken so seriously. It starts with the Board, or whoever is heading up the business, and cascades down through management to every employee on the books.

It is important, therefore, for everyone involved to understand at least how the budget affects them. A detailed knowledge of how it has been constructed is not necessary, but its importance to your own section or department must not be overlooked. You should find out what part you are expected to play and discuss with your superior how this will be achieved.

Budgeting enables management to fix responsibility at all levels of the business and this allows everyone to play a part in ensuring the budget objectives are met. Reward systems become simpler and, by adopting targeting methods, there should be no doubt in anyone's mind what he has to do to gain his reward.

Types of Budgets

Budgets may span varying periods but are, more often than not, for twelve months.

More commonly, strategies are drawn up for, say, three or five year periods (ten at times, but this involves crystal ball gazing!) and a detailed budget will form part of this exercise, lasting for, probably, the first year only. Financial summaries may be added for subsequent years but not usually in any great detail.

There will, depending upon the size of the company, possibly be a master budget from which others are drawn. This master is simply a summary of each of the functional budgets which will be given to individual departmental heads.

These functional budgets will, according to the type and complexity of the the business, normally fall into some or all of the following categories:

- Sales budget
- Distribution budget
- Production budget
- Purchases budget
- Overheads budget
- Personnel budget
- Capital expenditure budget

All of these may form the basis of the projected Balance Sheet, Profit and Loss Account and, probably, a Cash Flow Projection. Each is a vital component of the overall budgeting process.

You will see from the above that the only budget producing actual income – as opposed to the business spending money – is sales. It is thus the most important and the foundation upon which all the other budgets are built.

It will involve whoever heads up the sales function, along with all of his subordinates as well as administrative support. This department must estimate, for say twelve months ahead, just how many of each product (or service) is likely to be sold and at what price. New markets must be taken into account, including developments overseas if appropriate. Competitive forces will have to be weighed alongside possible price adjustments, as well as technical innovations.

All of these variables make the sales budget the most difficult to produce and it will probably take longer than the others. Get it right, however, and all the other budgets can – with some luck – fall into place.

The cash budget – or projection – is a vital lifeline for every business and needs to be properly controlled. Companies that are making profits still go into liquidation because they lack sufficient cash to cope with day-to-day operations. Warning signs must never be ignored, hoping that the problem will go away.

Flexible Budgets

It is important to have some acquaintance with this form of budgeting which is becoming increasingly common, especially in industries which find themselves in volatile situations, calling for strategy reviews and budget changes.

Budgets should never, of course, be set in cement. Because of the inter-relating factors, especially between sales and costs of producing those sales, it would be foolish to restrict additional sales simply because your costs budget would rise. Some flexibility is essential and this is generally recognized in most companies.

Similarly, of course, if sales are not up to expectations, then the cost of those sales should be less than originally anticipated and this needs to be paid close attention.

Flexible budgeting is thus no more than recognizing that forecasting is not always correct, and that reality must not be overlooked.

What is important, though, is to relate carefully the impact of changes in one budget to what should be happening in another. If sales are 10% less than you hoped for, it would be far too simplistic merely to reduce other budgets by the same amount. Administrative overheads, for example, will probably not be affected at all, whilst there may not be a 10% saving in material costs, for wastage may be on the increase.

If you have responsibility for part of a budget, keep an eye on the need for some flexibility, as well as how your budget relates to others.

'Uncontrollable' Factors

Ideally, budgets should be negotiated with those who are going to take responsibility for them. In the real world this is rarely possible and the decisions that are taken 'on high' have to be directed towards the various divisions. Time, and other, constraints make it impossible for everyone to have his say.

For this reason, there can be objections by some people to taking budgets on board over which they believe they do not have entire control. Again, in reality, those responsible for achieving certain budgets are unlikely to have control over all of the figures making them up.

Wage policy, for instance, may be out of their hands, these decisions being taken by a personnel function in negotiation with trade unions, despite the fact that these costs are likely to account for up to 75% of total costs. Depreciation policies are probably decided by the company's auditors, in collaboration with the directors or owners, whilst rental and similar costs may also be 'fixed'.

It is wrong, however, to restrict the amount of information given to a manager to that which he can control. Although a few companies still use this outmoded practice, most now provide full budgets which include 'controllables' and 'uncontrollables'.

What is considered 'uncontrollable' may often prove not to be the case. Take plant and machinery for instance. If no responsibility at all is given to a superintendent, foreman or manager who makes use of these, then he is unlikely to take a great deal of interest in these assets. Put them in his budget, however, and make him responsible and he will probably take a second look at what he has got.

He will want to know what depreciation policy the company has adopted and how long the assets are expected to last. Maintenance costs and replacement parts will probably come under the microscope, and the very existence of the assets may even be questioned. As a result of allocating responsibility to an individual who might otherwise have felt this to be an 'uncontrollable', significant savings may be made.

These savings could include cash receipts from the sale of any unwanted items, valuable floor space freed up for other uses and, possibly, lower labour costs.

If you are given a budget, therefore, which includes factors which you might otherwise have considered outside your personal control, take another look at them. If, subsequently, productivity can be improved, space reallocated or cost reductions put in place, then you will have done no damage at all to your chances of promotion!

Defining Your Accountabilities

Alongside every budget should be a list of those items for which you are accountable – your accountabilities.

This is not the same thing as a job description, which generally tabulates your duties on a day-to-day basis and provides details of reporting lines, etc.

Accountabilities are those areas for which you have responsibility, either solely or shared with others. They are generally described by words such as 'Responsible for. . . .', 'Contribute to. . . .', 'Provide guidance upon. . . .' and so on. It should be made quite plain that that is your function and that you are accountable for it.

A Sales Manager, for example, might have as his main accountabilities the following:

- Responsible to Sales Director for achievement of agreed sales plan
- Contribute to company sales policy
- Recruit and train sales force
- Monitor sales results and report to Sales Director

- Administer processing system to maximize efficiency

There may be other items for which he is accountable but these priorities make it quite clear to him what he is responsible for. How he goes about these tasks may be entirely in his own hands but, as long as he comes up with the goods, he will have achieved his accountabilities.

Every responsible job should have its own accountabilities, in part to ensure that the overall strategies are delegated evenly throughout the business, and also to help define for those employees involved just what is expected of them. There is then no doubt about who is responsible for what, and this should lead to more coherent and positive management.

Accountabilities, once defined and delegated, can then be sub-divided and delegated further to subordinate employees. The ideal is that everyone in an organization should know his full responsibilities and precisely what is expected of him.

If you are in any way uncertain of your own accountabilities, talk these over with your immediate superior and, if necessary, go higher up the ladder until you are satisfied.

Setting Objectives

In the same way that accountabilities differ from a job description, objectives are different again. Whereas accountabilities define fairly wide areas of responsibility, the precise expectations of any one individual should be encapsulated within set objectives.

Objectives need to be tied to a company's budget, so that if all the former are achieved in a given time span, then the budget also will have been met.

To make the distinction clearer, take another look at the list of accountabilities earlier in this Chapter. The Sales Manager thus knows what he is responsible for but not precisely what is expected of him. He should therefore have a list of objectives which, allied to the accountabilities, might be:

- Achieve sales level of £1m, to include 15% market penetration of Product X
- Attend monthly meetings of Board of Management
- Recruit 10 executive salesmen and organize 6-week training courses to include product knowledge, and selling and negotiating skills
- Establish management information systems sufficient to monitor clearly by product range on a weekly basis
- Set up administrative support in new headquarters

Now, as well as knowing his areas of responsibility, he has precise instructions for a given period. The completion of the various objectives may have to be fulfilled within set periods or by certain dates. Recruitment, for instance, will probably have to be completed within the first two months of the year; training by, say, the fourth month; whilst the sales achievement of £1m will be a twelve-month objective.

Objectives, like accountabilities, can be delegated further, so that everyone in the organization has something positive to aim for. Motivation is thus provided, whilst the employer has something against which it can measure performance of individuals. Systems of measurement are dealt with below.

Information Systems

Setting objectives, and thus targets, is only half the story; the other half is being in a position to know what progress is being made. This is where management information systems come in.

Data (in the form of facts or figures) is collected from various sources and, every so often, summarized to give a running picture of that particular facet of the business. Comparisons can then be made with budgeted expectations and any changes made as necessary.

The information collected must meet certain criteria. Firstly, it must be credible. So much wrong information has been put together across a wide sphere of industry and commerce by the use of computers that an acronym has been invented to describe it: GIGO, i.e. garbage in, garbage out. It's no use blaming the computers; they rarely, if ever, make mistakes. It is the human hand which feeds them which provides false information or gives erroneous instructions as to how to interpret stored data.

Secondly, the information needs to be topical. There is little point in finding out in April that sales for the month of January were down on budget by 20%. By then, too much time has elapsed to put things right, for February's and March's figures were probably also disastrous.

As a third requirement, the information needs to be easily understood and, in computer language, 'user friendly'. Many computer spreadsheets (i.e. tables of figures printed from details showing on the screen) are thrown into waste bins in disgust simply because employees are unable to make head nor tail of them or are unprepared to spend time making sense of them.

Clarity of information is thus essential. Easy to digest statistics will naturally be made more of and enable the reader to make clear comparisons between budgeted and actual results.

Figures may be collected manually in some cases as well as by computer but whichever method is used make certain that the source of the material is the appropriate one and that information is transferred from one medium to another correctly. This is often carried out, for instance, by junior personnel unfamiliar with the figures themselves, or indeed the reasons behind collecting them, leading inevitably to misjudgements being made. For this reason, involve everyone in the importance of the collecting exercise, taking time to explain to all involved, at whatever level they might be, what happens to the results of their efforts.

Assessing Performance

Most of the big companies now assess their employees on a regular basis, and it is at these assessment reviews that you can move forward your chances of promotion.

It is your objectives, and how you are progressing with them, that will generally be reviewed. This will probably be carried out with your immediate superior, possibly quarterly or, sometimes, more informally, from time to time. These interviews can take up to a couple of hours and provide an excellent opportunity for both sides to get to know the other more intimately. Problems can be discussed and hopefully resolved.

The better companies make use of some kind of format for these interviews to encourage uniformity throughout the organization, at the same time recording the conversations in a standard form. By providing the employee with a copy, this enables both parties to refer to what has gone before prior to subsequent interviews, thus making them more effective.

These review, or merit assessment, forms are likely to contain standard markings or comments ranging from 'Unsatisfactory' through 'Good' or 'Average' to 'Excellent' and even 'Outstanding'.

Each aspect under review will then be discussed and marked accordingly with, possibly, a total mark being awarded to give an overall picture of what progress is being made. Any aspect of the work considered by the assessor as below average should be discussed in greater detail and guidance provided as to how it might be improved. It is essential to listen to and follow such guidance to ensure that a better picture is communicated on the next occasion.

If strong disagreement is encountered, there should be in operation a referral system to someone higher up in the organization, although this should only be used where opinions differ widely on a major issue. Some criticism may have to be accepted, bearing in mind that the assessor may have different criteria and, in turn, is seeking to maximize his own objectives.

Assessing progress of objectives by employees is becoming more and more popular as employers realize the important part each one can play in bringing about an achievement of the whole. If your company has not yet caught up with the twentieth century, see what you can do to encourage it!

Assessing Yourself

Whether you have been given set objectives or not, make an effort to assess your own performance regularly. Ideally, in the absence of targets to meet, try to get your employers to agree these with you so that you have something to aim for. Make the point that you are ambitious – never attempt to hide this – and seek guidance as to what is expected of you in a set period.

At best, therefore, you will have a clear table of targets and, at worst, perhaps some verbal indication of your own part in the organization for which you work. In either event, sit down quietly every three months and make a critical appraisal of how you are doing.

If your boss will be conducting this appraisal with you, sit down nevertheless a week or so beforehand (try to set a date when he will see you in the absence of a formal interview) as a practice session ready for the real thing.

Be as objective as you can in the circumstances and aim to look at your own work and achievements through the eyes of the employer. If you can, set a standard slightly higher than you otherwise would and this may help to cancel out the fact that you are trying to be two people at once!

Where objectives are intangible, assess whether you might have done any better with improved resources, in the shape of additional assistance, extra machinery, better technological back-up, more time, improved conditions and so on. If any of these appear to be lacking, and you are confident that results could be bettered with their addition, this will help prepare you for the real interview. Get your case ready beforehand, taking costs and extra benefits into account. Consider pros and cons and look at both sides of the argument.

Do not be afraid of talking these 'private' sessions through with work colleagues or good friends; many heads are better than one in these circumstances and someone may well provide you with pointers as to how you can better even a good performance.

Where clear targets have been set, it should not prove too difficult to ascertain your rate of progress, although it might be a good idea to seek to achieve something a little higher than expected of you!

Making Sure of Success

Grab every opportunity you can to show your bosses how keen you are to move up the ladder in your organization.

Assessment reviews are an ideal time to do this, but do not overlook other opportunities of projecting your personality and desire to succeed.

BEATING YOUR TARGETS

For beating targets is only part of the story of success; you must make certain that your face fits as well.

Some people are puzzled, when restructuring and fresh rounds of promotion take place in a company, why they have been left behind whilst others, to them less capable, are chosen. Often, especially in larger organizations, it is because those given higher duties fit neatly into the culture of the company, discussed in an earlier Chapter. Do not overlook the importance of this aspect.

Getting on is about charisma, style and flair, as well as more straightforward things like reaching your targets.

It is also about managing change, a relatively new management technique gaining in importance as businesses recognize that to stand still is to die. Fixed ideas will stunt innovation and have been the cause of demise of many a family run concern where the 'Adam and Eve' principle of grandfather and father always having done things that way can spell disaster in a rapidly changing environment.

Be ready to recognize that change will form a natural part of most managerial jobs today; policies are no longer set in cement, as we saw above. Study the changes that are taking place in your own industry by reading the appropriate Press and talking to the people who matter. Set aside periods free of routine work to enable you to concentrate upon innovation.

Do not be afraid of experimenting, and look upon 'mistakes' as experience gained. Hold regular sessions with colleagues specifically to look forward, rather then dealing with the day's crises. Be pro-active in your thinking.

Flexibility is the key, and if you are the one to produce new ideas and new thinking, this will obviously help along your chances of success.

People who are rapidly promoted, according to Professor Fred Luthans of Nebraska University, are the ones who pay a lot of attention to social and political skills within their own company. He goes on to say, however, that they are not necessarily always the most effective managers, so if you are able to balance other skills – like inter-personal communications and human resource issues – with these, you should double your chances of climbing a few rungs!

CHAPTER 11

Fit for the Job

No matter how keen you are to gain promotion, your chances are likely to be much better if you are fit in both mind and body.

Take your body first. If you are overweight, smoke too much (or perhaps, even at all), or not eating healthily, then you may find yourself feeling tired at work and this will clearly show. Your work is likely to be affected and, if you are studying for further qualifications in the evenings, this in turn may suffer.

The way you live will affect the way you work and lack of proper attention to the former will result in a less than satisfactory application to the latter.

Your mind demands just as much attention as your body and, if it is ignored, will let you down in much the same way that a tired body will.

Give it equal attention. Do not let it fester but keep it honed to provide you with a mobile mini-computer, ready to respond instantly to a million and one commands. Our brains are wonderful instruments, but do require regular polishing to keep them in tip-top order.

Keep both – body and mind – well trained through regular exercise and neither will let you down.

A Healthy Body

There is a world of difference between being fit and being healthy, although the two can – if you wish – be combined.

Maintaining fitness for a particular sport or pastime involves specialized training, often under supervision. Certain muscles may have to be built up as in the case, say, of javelin throwing, or the entire body may require to be kept at a positive response rate to whatever is demanded of it. Competitive sport will merely heighten these demands.

Staying healthy is another matter. This is merely a question of adjusting your style of living towards ensuring a longer life, and this will involve more than mere exercise. It will certainly include what you eat and drink, your general lifestyle, as well as your attitude towards most things. It is this, rather than fitness, which we will look at here.

Before you go any further though, you should ensure that you are at least fit enough to indulge in extra exercise and you might prefer to have this confirmed by your doctor. With the advent of preventative medicine, most general practitioners will be glad to give you a check over to keep everyone's mind at rest.

If, of course, you already have problems with such things as high blood pressure, asthma, limited movement or are overweight or pregnant, then medical advice becomes essential.

On the basis that you are both fit and ready to dive into a health regime, what should you do?

The first priority is to do something which you enjoy. Slavish obedience to a particular routine merely because you believe it may be doing you some good will do just the reverse. Although, possibly, some physical benefit may be felt, this is likely to be counter productive if you are continually concerned about keeping up the momentum. So make sure the exercise, sport or pastime is one that will fit into other schedules and not become a bore.

Swimming, for instance, takes some beating, but if it means a regular half-hour journey to the baths, your nerves may have to take the extra strain! If there is a pool, especially as part of a leisure centre, around the corner, this may be the ideal solution. Cycling is another hobby high on the health list, but try and get away from city fumes if you can!

Sports such as squash, badminton and tennis can be good for you, although regular fanatics do seem to suffer from an uncanny number of broken wrists, black eyes and assorted bruises!

That leaves us, amongst the more common sports, with such activities as walking, running and playing golf. Any 'walking sport' probably benefits you as much by being in the fresh air as anything else, and although running is good exercise for the heart, hard surfaces can bring about other ailments. Keep-fit classes have their uses but once-a-week activity adds little to basic health and there is always the danger of pulling a muscle.

Most healthy activities, therefore, tend to have their drawbacks and it is for this reason, if none other, that you choose one which is both enjoyable and where regular participation will not upset other routines.

Health Clubs

These have sprung up over recent years all around the country and are proving an ideal way for the busy executive (or potential executive!) to maintain peak levels of both health and fitness.

They are also, of course, more than a mere method of partaking in some healthy activity or other; most have a social element and this, alone, may help you in other, communicating skills towards achieving your goal.

Regular, structured exercise is the ideal and if this can be selected to suit your own individual needs, you need look no further than a local health club providing it is properly run and will not eat into your pocket beyond what you can afford.

These clubs are very keen to attract corporate members, making individual costs very much less, and if you can persuade your masters to join en masse, so much the better.

Most are very professionally organized and boast a variety of ancillary benefits including sauna, Turkish baths, pools and beauty therapy clinics. A social atmosphere is encouraged through the provision of bars and perhaps a tennis or squash club adjoining the major building. Equipment is often state of the art with a highly trained professional staff ready to cater for bespoke needs coupled with regular monitoring to measure success rates.

Members are offered, normally, an initial assessment of just how healthy – or otherwise – they are, after which a detailed programme is drawn up on an individual basis for periods of between three and twelve months. Regular checks are introduced and benefits can often be seen quite quickly.

Opening hours are generally set to allow you to spend up to an hour before work, at lunch-times or immediately after the end of the working day; some flexibility is accepted and there may also be separate male and female sessions.

Pleasant surroundings, companionship and the knowledge that you are surrounded by like-minded human beings all add to the pleasure of knowing that you are doing your body some good and it is little surprise that these health clubs are proving so popular.

Check your Body

Whether you elect for a regular sporting activity or joining a health club, it is important to know where you are starting from.

A thorough health check is thus recommended; consider the cost as part of a longer-term investment in your own career and this should take some of the sting out of it. A full B.U.P.A.-style 'M.o.T.' may cost a few hundred pounds but, after it, you will have the satisfaction either of knowing you have a healthy body or, at worst, having identified something of which you were unaware at an early stage, when something can be done about it.

Do not be frightened about going; it cannot possibly make things worse and the chances are that you will feel elated afterwards.

Heart problems, in particular, benefit from being identified at an early stage and, the younger you are, the more likely that rectification is possible. If you have been a heavy smoker in the past – or are still on the weed – be brave and go along; even discussing it with someone on an expert level helps.

If you really cannot summon up either courage or cash, then try a few do-it-yourself tests. Smoking or heavy indulgence in drink are considered later but no-one needs to tell you the likely long-term effect of either of these. Checking your ideal weight is fairly easy, with guides regularly published.

If you really know how, check your pulse rate. But, if you are unfamiliar with the method, it is probably better left alone; you might otherwise send it up unnecessarily after a wrong reading!

How well do you climb up and down stairs? Do you start panting heavily on the twentieth stair – or the third? Be honest with yourself; there's no-one looking.

Can you get through a game of table-tennis without feeling faint or unwell? And does running for a bus or train cause strain?

Most sensible people will know by their reaction to these kinds of tests, coupled with their general well-being, whether or not they are healthy in the accepted sense of that word. If you have any doubt at all, obtain a medical opinion.

You Are What You Eat

Only a fool would be unaware in today's world what is likely to be good or bad for him on the food table. Newspapers, magazines, the radio and television all scream at us what we should and should not be eating. The difficulty, of course, is that the messages are often conflicting.

One day, cholesterol may be harmful in high doses; the next, it is pardoned. Junk food is said to be anything from suicidal to 'quite good in measured amounts'. Salt, sugar, fat and most basic food constituents are claimed to be harmful to our health, whilst less common items such as tomato ketchup have also from time to time appeared on the danger lists. What are we to believe?

Just as a fool would ignore all the warnings, so a sensible man would treat them with caution. Clearly, the answer – as so many are discovering – is a balanced diet, leaving out as much as possible of the most guilty items but allowing the occasional 'naughty but nice' lapse.

Variety is probably the best answer we will find but cutting down on sugar, salt and fat will do you no harm, nor will eating plenty of fresh fruit, vegetables and fibre-rich foods.

Fibre – at least so far – has found no enemies. It is found in certain foods grown from the ground and therefore includes all fruit and vegetables, but also such items as beans, peas, wheat, corn and rice. Obviously bread, most cereals, rice and pasta are also included and you can see that there is not the limitation to good foods that some suggest.

Fibre is retained during cooking and fibre-rich foods do not contain too many calories, so can form part of a weight-watching diet. Thirty grams of fibre a day are recommended and tables exist to enable you to keep count.

Sugar and salt, in particular, should be avoided, for although some salt in the diet is necessary, sufficient can be found without adding it to the meal. Look out for 'no added salt' foods and avoid particularly salty things like crisps and salted nuts and the like. Sugar adds nothing but calories but is found in so many snacks, cakes, sweets and drinks that it is difficult to avoid entirely.

Most meats and dairy products contain the fat that we should avoid, but – rather than cutting all these items out – the answer is again sensible eating. Skimmed milk is clearly preferable to full-cream whilst polyunsaturated fat is less harmful and appears in certain vegetable oils, margarines and fish like mackerel, trout and herring.

Fish, in particular, is good for you but so is the oil found in them which can be bought in capsule or liquid form. Eskimos, who obviously eat a lot of fish, seem to avoid many modern ills, including heart attacks, bronchial asthma, diabetes, and even fare better with their teeth than their European mainland counterparts.

If you are still thoroughly confused, send for details to the Health Education Authority, 78 New Oxford Street, London, WC1A 1AH, who provide first-class literature on the subject.

. . . and Drink

Medical opinion upon alcohol has shifted quite considerably in recent years from a point when all drinks of this nature were considered harmful to man. Now, drinking in moderation is generally believed to be better for you than not drinking at all, which has given cheer to many.

Alcohol does, of course, cause (sometimes in part) damage to your liver, cancer, road accidents and hooliganism. But this is only when it is taken in excess and this has been made official by a report, *Drinking To Your Health*, published by the Social Affairs Unit.

The Health Education Authority has also issued guidelines laying down maximum consumption rates at levels of 21 units of alcohol a week for men and 14 for women. One unit is equal to half a pint of beer or lager, a single glass of wine or a single measure of spirits. Clearly these must not be taken all at once!

Doctors have thus returned to the physicians of a century and more ago who prescribed reasonable quantities of alcohol for their patients, both to improve their quality of life and to help them sleep at night.

In the modern, stress-related world similar conditions apply and the remedy is unchanged. Social pressures can be relieved by the use – but only in moderation – of alcohol-based drinks, although *never* when driving. A tot of whisky to aid sleep remains valid and is considered quite unharmful.

Pregnant women, and anyone otherwise advised by their doctor to avoid alcohol, should, of course, do so. When on company business, make sure you drink no more than you can reasonably consume or it is likely to be noted.

Drinks do, of course, contain a lot of calories so beware if you are also watching your weight.

Avoiding the Weed

If you do not smoke at all, you can save yourself a few moments by skipping this section.

If you do smoke, however, no matter how little, resolve NOW to give it up if you are really determined to reach your goal of promotion. Whilst medical opinion has softened towards drinking of alcohol, albeit in moderation, it is quite unanimous in its condemnation of smoking. The habit *does* adversely affect the chest and lung, and the fact that your great uncle smoked thirty a day until he died at ninety is far from sufficient evidence that it will not do you any harm.

Admittedly, everyone who smokes does not die young from cancer, or a related disease, but the chances are statistically much higher.

As more and more companies are screening their employees through health tests, they become more demanding in what they seek from potential executives. In some businesses smokers are secretly segregated in personnel records; in others they are advised quite openly that, if they wish to succeed, they will firstly have to show a clean bill of health.

Smoking is also becoming more anti-social, especially amongst businessmen. Whereas ten years ago the majority might be seen to be smoking following a business lunch, today the reverse is the case and it is quite common for there to be no smokers at all in, say, a company of a dozen.

Many offices have been designated 'non-smoking', again making quite clear that it is a minority habit. The public at large is becoming increasingly sensitive to passive smoking, that is the inhaling of smoke created by others.

Pipe and cigar smokers claim that their pastime is less harmful than smoking cigarettes; this has yet to be clearly proven. The tobacco industry itself puts out misleading statistics. Reference to the UK's '17 million smokers' would suggest that 1 in 2 adults do so regularly; you have only to look around you to know that this is not the case.

How do you give up? Willpower is, of course, the obvious answer, but we are all human and need something a little more positive to encourage us.

If you have a friend or relative who also smokes, try to give up together. If cutting from thirty a day to none at all proves too dramatic, cut initially to ten and then to five before dropping the habit entirely. Avoid having a cigarette at set times but try instead to adopt an alternative, such as sucking a mint.

If you really cannot do it alone, experiment with one of the aids on the market. Or try a hypnotist, which has worked wonders for some smokers.

Dealing with Stress

If you are – or going to be – someone important in your organization, the first thing to learn is that you will have to deal with stress. It is not something to learn to avoid, for you will not be able to do so; the task is to know how to cope with it.

What is stress? It is simply the result of a large number of demands, normally mental as opposed to physical, placed upon an individual. Some of these individuals will learn to live with that stress; others will not, and in those it can lead to anxiety, depression and even mental illness.

If you have the sort of job (or are looking to move into one) where demands will almost certainly lead to stress, then recognize it and take appropriate action. This may involve such diverse activities as organization of your working day, the way you breathe, how you sit, exercise, eating and drinking and so on.

Take organization first. Learn to recognize priorities and keep them top of your list. Cut out wasted time (searching for files because of system shortfalls, doing things yourself when they should be delegated to others, writing out letters instead of dictating them, etc.) and improve your rate of productivity. If you find all of this difficult, seek out a course on time management and treat yourself.

Practise good breathing habits; the slower you breathe, the more relaxed you will feel. Spend a few minutes every day doing nothing other than breathing. Take in as much fresh air as you can and avoid working in stuffy surroundings.

Sensible posture is important to relaxation and the money spent on a comfortable chair, if yours is a sitting job, will pay handsome dividends. Your head weighs about ten pounds and can only be carried properly when directly over the spine; as soon as it droops forward you are demanding extra effort from your muscles. If you are having to push your neck forward to read, get your eyes tested. Do not put off bifocal lenses if you really need them.

If your job involves long periods at a desk, get up every so often if only to walk around it. Ignore colleagues' stares; you are an individual and know where you are going.

Exercise, and what you fill your body with, have already been dealt with, but all are important features of coping with stress and must not be overlooked.

Stress is a wide subject and has already filled hundreds of other books. If it is something you are still struggling with, make a more detailed study of it.

On the Road

Driving to work is bad for you and if an alternative can be found, then take it. Even rush-hour commuting by public transport is less stressful if you handle it properly.

But what if you have to drive? You can make the journey slightly more bearable by remembering a few basic tips.

Problems are caused by the abnormal rises in your heart beat, up to as many as 180 beats a minute as potentially dangerous hazards arise as you drive along. A pedestrian unexpectedly stepping out, traffic lights changing abruptly, or the motorist in front braking suddenly are all stressful due to the rise they cause in blood pressure without any corresponding physical exercise.

Tension increases, especially if a deadline has to be met, and so does your possibility of an early heart attack.

You must relax, although this will come only with self-training; work at it to keep yourself alive! It isn't easy but can be eased along if you remember a handful of rules:

- Eat and drink sufficiently before you start your journey because you may not know when your next break will come
- Do not drive if you are over-tired
- Always allow sufficient time to complete your journey with a few minutes, at least, to spare
- Adjust the driving seat to its most comfortable position and use a lumbar support if it helps
- On long journeys remove heavy jackets and coats and keep the air in the car as fresh as possible
- Practise deep breathing exercises as you drive
- Listen to a relaxing programme or tape

There are also tapes available which demonstrate and help you try relaxation techniques. Never get yourself worked up over traffic volumes or another driver; count to ten and remind yourself that you will be taking a few minutes off your life if you do.

A Good Night's Sleep

Approaching a third of your life will be spent in slumber and this should not be wasted.

Sleeping is not just a matter of going to bed for a spell. It should be taken every bit as seriously as your waking hours and, if wisely used, will keep you more alert and help you achieve promotion.

Firstly, the bed. Cheap mattresses are a poor investment in your overall health, whilst a relatively firm version will aid healthy slumber. Bones will be allowed to lie more naturally and muscles relaxed.

The air in the room is important and, ideally, should be supplemented by keeping a window or door open. Avoid draughts, of course, but never sleep in a stuffy atmosphere or your lungs and head will only feel that way the following morning.

Have no more clothes on than you feel necessary and do not pile blankets on top of you until they nearly suffocate. Equally, keep warm and work on the balance until you get it right. Partner's needs may be different and a compromise should always be reached, even to the extent of folding blankets in half.

Avoid eating for at least three or four hours before retiring, and preferably longer. Polishing off a steak an hour before climbing into your bed will almost certainly keep you awake for longer than you should be and you will pay for it in the morning. A little alcohol will aid good sleep; a lot may keep you unconscious but you are unlikely to be your normal self the next day!

The number of hours sleep you need can only be decided by you; there is no norm. Several famous Prime Ministers have claimed they require only five but once you know your own requirements, stick to them as far as possible. Occasional lapses will be inevitable but take account of these the next day whenever you can. Prior to important conferences and meetings, a good night's sleep should play an equal part in the planning process.

If any difficulties are encountered in sleeping, seek medical advice. There are all sort of cures on the market and you must make sure you get the right one, but follow the simple rules above and a visit to the doctor may prove unnecessary.

A Rounded Life

'All work and no play makes Jack a dull boy', as we all know. Your priority goal of seeking promotion at work, therefore, needs to be supplemented by other, perhaps less demanding, objectives.

To maintain variety, these should be in other fields such as sport or a hobby. It is important that your mind has other interests to fill it and that it is not endlessly concentrating on one subject only.

Ancillary objectives will depend upon what else interests you and need not be particularly testing at all. If you are a fisherman, to catch a fish may be entirely satisfying, as may be attending a certain opera for a musical fan.

Some people will prefer something more demanding and, providing the effort that goes into achieving this does not seriously conflict with the major priority, no problem exists. The golfer, therefore, seeking to play a round which would be the envy of a professional may, as long as time and effort allow, aim at this alongside his promotional goal. But as soon as the two conflict, the first priority must be remembered and favoured.

You will become a bore – both at work and outside – if all you talk about is that one subject. A specific knowledge of something else, as well as a general knowledge of major topics, is necessary for a rounded life.

If work is your over-riding passion, force yourself to take an interest in another subject if only to provide some counter-balance. The list of possibilities is endless, as a visit to your local library will confirm. Clubs and societies abound, although choose one which has some relevance to the rest of your life if you can.

Are you a collector, or do films or operas appeal? Does writing take your fancy, or perhaps rambling? Something more adventurous such as hill climbing, scrambling or gliding are ideal pursuits to take you away from everyday life – and add spice at the same time.

Positive Thinking

Whatever else you do to achieve your goal of promotion, think positively!

By now you should have taken stock of your present situation, begun to gain further qualifications if necessary, adopted a structured approach to your career, learned a lot about your own company, experimented with managing others and practised dealing with superiors, learned the arts of communication and marketing, and how to beat your targets. You should certainly be ready!

On top of all this, though, success may elude you if you fail to adopt a positive attitude towards reaching your goal.

Write down all the things you know you must do to get there. Number each one in order of priority and set dates by which they will be achieved. Pin your list where it will be seen every day and, once a week or so, review how far you have reached and whether any revision is needed.

Think constantly about the subject and work on ways and means which will ease you along your desired route. Talk it over regularly with whoever you can trust and get him to play devil's advocate to test how well you are progressing.

Question everything. In particular, review regularly why colleagues around you are promoted – or not promoted. See who gets on, and why.

Is it purely luck? It may appear so on the surface, but this is highly unlikely in practice. What factors do you think came into their being promoted; was it:

- Length of service
- Level of qualifications
- Personal qualities
- Keeping close to their boss
- Excellence of work
- Being in the right place at the right time

Probably an element of two or three (or more) of these qualities came into play, plus that little bit of luck portrayed in the final item. Luck plays its part in everyone's lives at some stage or other, even if it is bad luck!

But one thing you can be certain of. If you work hard at achieving your desire, and couple this with a constantly positive attitude towards getting there, your chances of success will be raised several-fold.

Good luck!

Further Reading

Arthur Young (Accountants). 1986. *The Manager's Handbook*. Sphere Books Ltd., London.
Brady, C. 1986. *Flying High*. Columbus Books, London.
Donald, V. 1986. *How To Choose a Career*. Kogan Page, London.
Gilbert, R. 1989. *Employment in the 1990s*. Macmillan Press, Basingstoke.
Hall, L. 1979. *Business Administration*. Macdonald and Evans Ltd., Plymouth.
Knasel, E. 1986. *Your Work in Your Hands*. National Extension College, Cambridge.
Lancashire, R. and Holdsworth, R. 1976. *Career Change*. Hobson's Press (Cambridge) Ltd.
Lock, D. and Farrow, N. (Eds.). 1986. *The Complete Manager*. Wildwood House Ltd., Aldershot.
Luthans, F. 1988. *Real Managers*. Ballinger Publishing Company.
Markel, R. and Faulkner, C. 1987. *Moving Up*. Fontana, London.
Maude, B. 1974. *Practical Communication for Managers*. Longman, London.
Morse, S. 1982. *Management Skills in Marketing*. McGraw Hill Book Co. (UK) Ltd., London.
Nolan, V. 1987. *Communication*. Sphere Books, London.